MELVILLE'S THEMATICS
OF FORM

The Great Art of Telling the Truth

MELVILLE'S THEMATICS OF FORM

The Great Art of Telling the Truth

Edgar A. Dryden

The Johns Hopkins Press, Baltimore

For Bobba

PREFACE

IN RECENT YEARS a number of important studies of Melville
have appeared. Although these have approached his fiction
from radically divergent points of view, there has been, for
the most part, an implicit agreement with Charles Feidelson's
belief that Melville "from first to last . . . presents himself as
an artist, and a conscious artist. It is in this character that he
seizes our attention."[1] Valuable studies of Melville's artistry
and the formal aspects of his work have been contributed by
Constance Rourke, F. O. Matthiessen, Charles Olson, Newton
Arvin, and most recently, Warner Berthoff; a wide interest in
his literary reactions to religions and mythologies has culmi-
nated in H. Bruce Franklin's *The Wake of the Gods*; and a
general concern with the themes and meanings of his books
has produced, among others, the illuminating studies of Merlin
Bowen and Milton R. Stern, as well as countless articles in
scholarly journals.

Closer to my own approach, however, is the work of those
critics whose interests center on the predilections of form in
Melville's fiction. Deserving special recognition here are Charles
Feidelson's seminal discussion of Melville in *Symbolism and
American Literature*; R. W. B. Lewis' account of Melville in
The American Adam; Daniel Hoffman's analysis of *Moby Dick*
and *The Confidence-Man* in *Form and Fable in American Fic-
tion*; Leo Marx's comments on Melville in *The Machine in the
Garden*; and Paul Brodtkorb's recent study of *Moby-Dick,
Ishmael's White World*.

All of these investigations are taken for granted here, and
without them and the source materials provided by such schol-
ars as Jay Leyda, Howard Vincent, Charles Anderson, and
Merton Sealts, this study could not have been undertaken.
Therefore I am anxious to acknowledge here my great debt to

---

[1] Charles Feidelson, *Symbolism and American Literature* (Chicago,
1953), p. 163.

the many students of Melville's life and work and especially to those critics who have helped shape my own view of his work. However, my focus has been slightly different from theirs: I have attempted to describe the internal morphology of Melville's fictional world and to trace the implications of the form of his vision of things as it gradually develops throughout the span of his career as a writer. My special perspective is provided by "Hawthorne and His Mosses" in which Melville defines fiction as the "great Art of Telling the Truth" and implies that an essential part of the career of any writer is his search for a form which will allow him safely to explore and reveal a destructive and maddening Truth. This focus is necessarily restrictive, but Melville's fictional world, like that of any great writer, is composed of an unlimited number of horizons, and an unlimited number of critical perspectives are possible. I have chosen one which seems to me to reveal an interesting and important portion of Melville's fictional landscape.

ACKNOWLEDGMENTS

I N PREPARING THIS STUDY I have incurred a number of debts which I am glad to acknowledge here. I wish to express my gratitude to Charles R. Anderson and to J. Hillis Miller, who read several versions of the entire manuscript, and to Jackson I. Cope and Earl R. Wasserman, who graciously read and commented on portions of it. Without them the book could not have been written, and to them must go much of the credit for such virtues as it may have. I wish too to record my thanks to the following friends and colleagues for their important contributions: Royal Roussel, Alistair Duckworth, Joseph Riddel, and Stefan Fleischer. To Homer Brown I owe a special debt, which I can begin to repay only if our many discussions were half as illuminating to him as they were to me.

I must also thank the Samuel S. Fels fund, for financial support during the academic year 1964–1965, and Martha Hubbard of The Johns Hopkins University library, for her kindness and attention. Needless to say, the greatest debt of all is recorded in the dedication.

CONTENTS

Preface vii

Acknowledgments ix

A Note on Texts.. xiii

I. Metaphysics and the Art of the Novel 1

II. Portraits of the Artist as a Young Man: Narrative Form
in Melville's Early Novels 31

III. Ishmael as Teller: Self-Conscious Form in *Moby-Dick* .. 81

IV. The Failure of the Author-Hero: Narrative Form in
Pierre and *Israel Potter* 115

V. The Novelist as Impostor: Subversive Form in *The Confidence-Man* 150

Epilogue 197

Index 217

A NOTE ON TEXTS

Because the standard edition of Melville's writings (*The Works of Herman Melville* [London: Constable, 1922–1924]) is unavailable to the general reader, I have used readily accessible paperback editions of *Typee, Mardi, Redburn, White Jacket,* and *Israel Potter.* Although the incomplete Hendricks House edition of the *Works* is also scarce, its valuable annotations and introductions have forced me to use this edition wherever possible. For this reason I have provided for each quotation the chapter in Roman numerals and the page in Arabic numerals. The editions of Melville's works cited and the abbreviations used for them are given below.

BB   *Billy Budd, Sailor (An Inside Narrative)*, ed. Harrison Hayford and Merton M. Sealts, Jr. (Chicago: University of Chicago Press, 1962)

"BC"   "Benito Cereno," *Piazza Tales*, ed. Egbert S. Oliver (New York: Hendricks House, 1948)

C-M   *The Confidence-Man: His Masquerade*, ed. Elizabeth S. Foster (New York: Hendricks House, 1954)

"HHM"   "Hawthorne and His Mosses," *Moby-Dick*, Norton Critical ed., ed. Harrison Hayford and Hershel Parker (New York: Norton, 1967)

IP   *His Fifty Years of Exile (Israel Potter)*, introd. Lewis Leary (New York: Sagamore Press, 1957)

JUS   *Journal Up the Straits: October 11, 1856–May 5, 1857*, ed. and introd. Raymond Weaver (New York: The Colophon, 1935)

L   *The Letters of Herman Melville*, ed. Merrell R. Davis and William H. Gilman (New Haven, Conn.: Yale University Press, 1960)

M   *Mardi*, introd. H. Bruce Franklin (New York: Capricorn Books, 1964)

M-D   *Moby-Dick*, ed. Luther S. Mansfield and Howard P. Vincent (New York: Hendricks House, 1952)

P   *Pierre: Or, the Ambiguities*, ed. Henry A. Murray (New York: Hendricks House, 1949)

R   *Redburn: His First Voyage* (New York: Doubleday Anchor Books, 1957)

T   *Typee*, ed. and introd. Milton R. Stern (New York: E. P. Dutton, 1958)

WJ   *White Jacket: Or the World in a Man-of-War*, introd. William Plomer (New York: Grove Press, 1956)

METAPHYSICS AND THE ART
OF THE NOVEL

The novel is a subjective epopee in which the author avails himself of the privilege of treating the world in his own manner. Thus the question is only whether he has a manner; the rest will take care of itself.

JOHANN WOLFGANG GOETHE, *Proverbs in Prose*

A fictional technique always relates back to the novelist's metaphysics. The critic's task is to define the latter before evaluating the former.

JEAN-PAUL SARTRE, "On The Sound and the Fury"

THERE HAS DEVELOPED in recent years a remarkable interest in the aesthetics of the novel, an interest which at once expresses a disenchantment with the state of contempory novel criticism and seeks to establish a broad poetics for the genre which will permit a more coherent and precise description of individual works. That much of the discussion has centered on the question of the relation of fiction to reality is not surprising, for realism has been the perennial problem of the novel. The novel was born of a tension between the realm of romance and that of reality, and its history may be seen as an attempt to resolve the paradox that this tension implies.[1] The problems which such a struggle involves are nowhere more obvious than in the nineteenth-century American novel and especially in the fiction of Herman Melville. This study suggests that the recent interest in the poetics of the novel reveals another dimension of the modernity of Melville's fiction and also that Melville's battle with this problematical genre illuminates and clarifies much of the commentary on its nature and origins.

Until recently twentieth-century criticism of the English and American novel has been controlled to a large degree by the aesthetics of Henry James or, perhaps better, by Percy Lubbock's interpretation of James's aesthetics.[2] One of the most important effects of this domination has been the recognition of narrative point of view as fiction's basic structural principle. Few modern critics of the novel would question the importance of point of view. However, some might deplore the direction the discussion has taken. Both James and Lubbock are prescriptive, the latter more so than the former. This may be a necessary and expected approach for James because, as a novelist, he is primarily concerned with defining his own approach to art and life. It is, however, less admirable for the practical critic. Lubbock's tendency to present James as the model for all aspiring novelists to follow involves some rather

[1] See José Ortega y Gasset, *Meditations on Quixote* (New York, 1961), pp. 112–65; and Paul de Man, "Georg Lukács's Theory of the Novel," *MLN*, 81 (1966):527–34.
[2] *The Craft of Fiction* (New York, 1945).

questionable assumptions. Behind his analysis is a belief that the novel has a "progressive history" (272)—that it is moving from a direct and pictorial method toward an indirect and dramatic one. He assumes the existence of an ideal form so dramatic and "true" (67) that the old problem of the discrepancy between it and life is put to rest forever. This rather confusing blend of conceptual and empirical assumptions resulted in the development of an almost purely technical approach to the novel and its concern with point of view.[3]

More recently Wayne Booth has attempted to repair the damage done to the reputations of important eighteenth- and nineteenth-century writers by the advocates of the disappearing author.[4] And, as Ronald Paulson pointed out in a review of four recent studies of the novel, most critics "have accepted gratefully and confidently the tone set for them by Wayne Booth's *The Rhetoric of Fiction* and his reviewers."[5] Certainly no one can deny that Booth performs a much-needed service by exposing many of the assumptions hidden beneath the "general rules" which critics have gradually established for the practice of the art of fiction. But although he calls for a repudiation of "false restrictions imposed by various forms of objectivity" (397), he too finds some techniques more advantageous than others. As the title of his book implies, Booth regards fiction as "the art of communicating with the reader." Point of view, therefore, is defined as "the form an author's

[3] See, for example, Mark Schorer's seminal essay, "Technique as Discovery," in *Critiques and Essays on Modern Fiction, 1920–1951*, ed. John W. Aldridge (New York, 1952); and Norman Friedman, "Point of View in Fiction: The Development of a Critical Concept," *PMLA*, 70 (1955): 1160–84. A summary of the key discussions of point of view in fiction may be found in Jacques Souvage, *An Introduction to the Study of the Novel* (Ghent, 1965), pp. 50–60.

[4] *The Rhetoric of Fiction* (Chicago, 1961).

[5] *JEGP*, 66 (April, 1967):44. The books under consideration were *Nature of Narrative*, by Robert Scholes and Robert Kellogg (New York, 1966); *Man's Changing Mask: Modes and Methods of Characterization in Fiction*, by Charles Child Walcutt (Minneapolis, 1966); *Character and the Novel*, by W. J. Harvey (Ithaca, N.Y., 1965); and *Language of Fiction*, by David Lodge (London, 1966).

voice can take." For Booth, those forms which tend to hinder communication by keeping the author's "second self" locked up within the world of the novel and obscure his ethical judgments are not only inartistic but immoral. He disapproves of impersonal narration because its use has led to moral confusion, has indeed at times actually "seduced" the reader. As his final chapter reveals, in his view the rhetoric of fiction, like more traditional kinds of rhetoric, finally aims not only at communication but at conversion as well.

The nature and extent of Booth's disapproval of impersonal narration is revealed by the pattern of satanic imagery which runs through his discussion of the modern novel. The twentieth-century novelist is ego-ridden, swollen with false pride, and bent on confusing, seducing, and ultimately corrupting or destroying his reader. Armed with his greatest weapon, impersonal narration, he is made to seem as formidable as Satan himself.

Booth's suggested solution to the rhetorical problems raised by the techniques of the modern novel is in line with his Christian analysis. The novelist must find a way to break out of the "subjectivism" on which his difficulties are based. He must humble himself, learn how to "transform his private vision, made up as it often is of ego-ridden private symbols, into something that is essentially public" (395).

Needless to say, in the end such an attitude is as prescriptive and limiting as that of the objective critics. The one denies us Fielding because he is unrealistic, the other Joyce because he is impersonal and ambiguous. In both cases, however, what is unconsciously being objected to is not the technique but the metaphysics which it implies. Interestingly enough, the technical preferences of both Booth and his antagonists reflect the desire to rid the novel of subjectivism, which seems, on the one hand, to subvert the rhetorical function of fiction and, on the other, to destroy its validity as an actual transcription of reality.

Such prescriptive approaches lead away from rather than

toward the central issues raised by the novel's form. The problem of subjectivity in fiction cannot be solved by the writer's making the correct technical choice, since both objective and intrusive narrators are equally subversive. It is no accident that the century in which the novel became the most popular form of literature was also the one in which a subjective theory of artistic creation was developed. The novel, like romanticism, is the product of a post-Cartesian world. Defined by Lukács as *"l'épopée d'un monde sans Dieux"*[6] and by Ortega as the product of Renaissance man's discovery of the subjective,[7] it may be seen as the art form which best expresses the "modern theme."

If the novel is viewed from this perspective, its preoccupation with questions of realism becomes an indication that the form is not so much an imitation of a unified reality as it is a search for one. Indeed, the novel might be said to be an expression of modern man's longing for the synoptic vision of the Christian God. Unfortunately, however, man's great expectations and his actual experience fail to coincide. Only the most naïve novelist can be so self-forgetful as to offer his work as though it had made itself, and then we do not see it as he does but rather view it as an expression of his own individuality. The self-conscious novelist is painfully aware of his fiction as fiction. He recognizes the subversive implications of his demiurgical acts and understands that his own presumptuous world is ultimately unified by personal and largely arbitrary choices, with the result that the novel becomes self-reflexive and develops a bad conscience. As Jean Rousset points out,[8] the anti-novel is as old as the novel, since *Don Quixote* is the ancestor of both, and J. Hillis Miller[9] finds a "secret

[6] Georg Lukács, *La Théorie du Roman*, trans. Jean Clairevoye (Geneva, 1962), p. 84.

[7] *Meditations*, pp. 138–39.

[8] "*Madame Bovary* or the Book about Nothing," in *Flaubert: A Collection of Critical Essays*, ed. Raymond Giraud (Englewood Cliffs, N.J., 1964), p. 113; translated by Raymond Giraud from *Forme et signification* (Paris: José Corti, 1962).

[9] "Some Implications of Form in Victorian Fiction," *CL*, 3 (1966):109.

nihilism" at the core of the apparently realistic Victorian novel, which results, finally, in the "metaphysical" fiction of Joseph Conrad.

The novel, then, may be seen as a metaphysical rather than as a descriptive or rhetorical form: it is not primarily concerned with explaining or reflecting a pre-existing reality without disturbing its fabric but rather with formulating an experience which is both particular and unified. Therefore the fact that a novel is organized by virtue of its being written from a particular point of view becomes a thematic rather than a technical consideration. Implied in every novel is the operation of a special organizing principle, of which the method of narration is the most obvious sign. This special perspective or point of view is neither a technique of discovery nor a rhetorical device, although it may both show and tell. It is not merely a means of access to the fictional world but is one of its component parts. The world is as it is seen.[10] Point of view is at once a literary technique and a metaphysical principle. It is a *process* which determines the controlling pattern and movement of the fictional world; to identify and describe it is to reveal the theory of the fiction, its internal cause. Hence the critic who asks a writer to tell his story in a different way is requiring of him a total renunciation of his experience. Criticism of technique is tacitly a criticism of vision.

Such a perspectivistic approach seems justified by the fact that elements of self-conscious form are found even in those novels which try to deny the implications of subjectivism. Consider, for example, the authorial intrusions in *Tom Jones*. While Fielding insists, on the one hand, that he follows the traditional literary forms, he is, on the other, well aware that he is the creator of a new kind of writing. Although his book is a reworking of the universal myth of the Fortunate Fall,

---

[10] For a full discussion of the epistemological implications of perspectivism, see Ortega y Gasset, "The Doctrine of the Point of View," in *The Modern Theme*, trans. James Clough (New York, 1961), pp. 86–96.

he finds it necessary to intrude into the action of the novel to discuss his own and his reader's relationship to that traditional world:

> Though we have properly enough entitled this our work, a history, and not a life, nor an apology for a life, as is more in fashion; yet we intend in it rather to pursue the method of those writers who profess to disclose the revolutions of countries, than to imitate the painful and voluminous historian, who, to preserve the regularity of his series, thinks himself obliged to fill up as much paper with the detail of months and years in which nothing remarkable happened, as he employs upon those notable eras when the greatest scenes have been transacted on the human stage.
>
> .   .   .   .   .
>
> Now it is our purpose, in the ensuing pages, to pursue a contrary method. When any extraordinary scene presents itself (as we trust will often be the case), we shall spare no pains nor paper to open it at large to our readers; but if whole years should pass without producing anything worthy his notice, we shall not be afraid of a chasm in our history, but shall hasten on to matters of consequence, and leave such periods of time totally unobserved.[11]

Although the neoclassical assumption that the artist creates for the pleasure of his audience is certainly present in the above quotation, several important complications are also introduced. This and other similar passages in *Tom Jones* ask the reader to consider more than his own relationship to the story. He is asked—indeed forced—to take into account the artist's relationship to the fiction and to the reader. By intruding into the world of his creation to discuss with the reader the problems of the art of fiction, Fielding effectively destroys the reader's illusion of participating in a real world by reading the novel.

His fictional world, the narrator tells us, is a grand meal prepared from the vulgar foodstuffs of nature by the skillful "cookery of the author" (2). As this metaphor makes clear, the real and fictional worlds are two different realms, and

[11] Ed. George Sherburn (New York, 1950), pp. 40–41.

the uniqueness of the fictional one derives from the contribution of the writer. The writing of fiction apparently involves more than reflecting, representing, or counterfeiting nature. Like Henry James, who was to speak in similar terms one hundred and fifty years later,[12] Fielding understands the importance of the process which the novelist applies to the materials he plucks from the "garden of life."

It is the nature of this process which is the narrator's main concern in the authorial intrusions in *Tom Jones*. By interrupting his story to discuss the problems implicit in its creation, the narrator forces the reader to view the fiction as fiction and asks him to recognize and appreciate the skill of the creator. He insists, in other words, that its value lies in the unique flavor which his special culinary skill has given to it.

The narrator's concern with the special qualities of his own originality is also present in his description of his book as a "new province" founded by himself. As founder and divine ruler he makes his own special laws, which the reader is "bound to believe in and to obey" (41). As with the culinary metaphor, the political one serves to stress the origin and uniqueness of the book's world. Unlike ordinary historians, the narrator of *Tom Jones* is no "amanuensis" (40) of time; he is the creator of a special world and as creator is able to make time serve him. In this world time and space do not rule the writer but are carefully and symbolically manipulated by him. He is careful, moreover, to make sure that his "great creation" (446) remains perfect. By trying to anticipate and defend himself against attack by critics, he hopes to keep these satanic reptiles excluded from his carefully constructed world. He even warns them that an attack on the creation will be taken as an attack on the creator (489). The political metaphor expands into a cosmic one as the narrator makes his greatest assertion of originality. Although concerned with the imperfections of a fallen world, his creation, new and unique, is as

---

[12] Henry James, Preface to *The Ambassadors*, in *The Art of the Novel*, ed. R. P. Blackmur (New York, 1934), p. 312.

yet unfallen. While *Tom Jones,* like *Paradise Lost,* is partially concerned with man's tie to a traditional past, it also contains elements which seem destined to destroy the controlling myth from the past. Not only is the Fortunate Fall myth secularized in *Tom Jones,* but the novelist's powers of invention seem to imply a world where it functions—if at all—only as metaphor.

As is clear to any student of the nineteenth-century English novel, the intrusive narrator, so important in Fielding's fiction, does not disappear. This should not, however, be taken as evidence of a retarded development, but as an indication of the subjective nature of the form itself. The apparently realistic fiction of George Eliot, for example, illustrates the continuity of the tradition in a striking way. The narrator of *Adam Bede,* while emphasizing her devotion to the commonplace or the real, interrupts her "faithful representing of commonplace things" to discuss the implications of that representation. Although the narrator's intrusion sharply divides the worlds of life and art by introducing another level of reality, there is an even more revealing distinction drawn between the two realms. It is significant that the narrator does not insist that her fiction is a pure transcription of reality: "My strongest effort is to . . . give a faithful account of men and things as they have mirrored themselves in my mind. The mirror is doubtless defective; the outlines will sometimes be disturbed, the reflection faint or confused; but I feel as bound to tell you as precisely as I can what that reflection is, as if I were in a witness-box narrating my experience on oath."[13]

It is important to recognize the subjective origin of the narrator's vision. As she implies in the above passage, a totally mimetic art is impossible. The world of the novel is a product of a very special mirror, one which reflects but which also transforms. The experience of the narrator is a unique one which is colored, shaped, and flavored by her own special way of seeing. The reflected world is, in fact, so special that it requires a detailed commentary. Before it can be understood, the

[13] Ed. Gordon S. Haight (New York, 1956), p. 178.

motives and acts which underlie its creation must be examined and explained. The narrator's central purpose in the chapter "In Which the Story Pauses a Little" is to explain the genesis of her book. The tone of the chapter is appropriately personal. Personal habits and preferences are described in detail; and there is even a mention of the "ill shapen nostrils" of the British. As this personal tone, along with the extensive use of the "I" form, implies, the narrator is well aware that her fictional world is the product of her own special vision.

As with the authorial intrusions in *Tom Jones*, the narrator's presence in *Adam Bede* calls the reader's attention to the subjective center of the fictional world. It matters little that the narrator may wish to put the reader into direct contact with the real world; the important point is the implication of the impossibility of the task. The narrator of *Adam Bede* is "the centre of [her] own world," as the narrator of *Middlemarch*[14] recognizes that we all are. For this reason the novelist is never merely an observer, but a creator as well. Hence the fictional world, if it is to be adequately understood, must be viewed from the inside as well as the outside.

But at present this caution against a too hasty judgment interests me more in relation to Mr. Casaubon than to his young cousin. If to Dorothea Mr. Casaubon had been the mere occasion which had set alight the fine inflammable material of her youthful illusions, does it follow that he was fairly represented in the minds of those less impassioned personages who have hitherto delivered their judgments concerning him . . . ? Suppose we turn from outside estimates of a man, to wonder, with keener interest, what is the report of his own consciousness about his doings or capacity: with what hindrances he is carrying on his daily labours; what fading of hopes, or what deeper fixity of self-delusion the years are marking off within him; and with what spirit he wrestles against universal pressure, which will one day be too heavy for him, and bring his heart to his final pause. Doubtless his lot is important in his own eyes; and the chief reason we think he asks too large a place in our consideration must be our want of room for him, since we refer him

[14] Ed. Gordon S. Haight (New York, 1956), p. 62.

to the Divine regard with perfect confidence. . . . Mr. Cassaubon, too, was the centre of his own world. . . . this trait is not quite alien to us, and, like the other mendicant hopes of mortals, claims some of our pity. (62)

The narrator's fluctuation in this passage—from an objective position, seeing Casaubon as his associates see him, to a position of complete identification with him, seeing the world as it exists in his consciousness—is characteristic of the narrative strategy of the entire novel. Because she believes that it is necessary to see both objectively and subjectively, her fluctuating movement provides the moral and artistic foundations of the novel. The narrative mode is at once the fiction's organizing principle and the manifestation of its theme. It is, moreover, the narrator's self-conscious discussion of her method of procedure which forces the reader to view her fictional world as she does. It reminds him that she too is "the centre of [her] own world" and asks him to consider the implications of its subjective origins as well as its objective operations.

An even more revealing example of the dangers implicit in the failure to recognize and explore the metaphysical basis of a fictional technique is found in current evaluations of the theories and fiction of Henry James. More than any other writer or critic, James is invoked by those who view fiction as a totally objective art. To suggest, however, as many have done, that James's major contribution to our understanding of the art of the novel is the distinction which he makes between direct and indirect presentation is to miss the point of much of his argument. No novelist has made a clearer or more definitive statement of the subjective nature of the art of fiction than Henry James:

The house of fiction has in short not one window, but a million—a number of possible windows not to be reckoned, rather; every one of which has been pierced, or is still pierceable, in its vast front, by the need of the individual vision and by the pressure of the individual will. These apertures, of dissimilar shape and size, hang so, all together, over the human scene that we might have expected of them a greater sameness of report than we find. They are but windows at the best, mere holes in a dead wall, disconnected, perched aloft; they are not hinged doors opening straight upon life. But they have this mark of their own that at each of them stands a figure with a pair of eyes, or at least with a field-glass, which forms, again and again, for observation, a unique instrument, insuring to the person making use of it an impression distinct from every other. He and his neighbors are watching the same show, but one seeing more where the other sees less, one seeing black where the other sees white, one seeing big where the other sees small, one seeing coarse where the other sees fine. . . . The spreading field, the human scene, is the "choice of subject"; the pierced aperture, either broad or balconied or slit-like and low-browed, is the "literary form"; but they are, singly or together, as nothing without the posted presence of the watcher—without, in other words, the consciousness of the artist. Tell me what the artist is, and I will tell you of what he has *been* conscious.[15]

James's insistence here and in other places on the importance of the special nature of the writer's consciousness should not be dismissed or ignored. He is always sensitive to the importance of perceiving and describing the unique quality of a writer's world; he recognizes the importance of defining the quality of vision behind the "dead wall." For this reason, to note that James confines himself to the consciousness of a central intelligence in his fiction is only to begin a discussion of his use of narrative point of view. While it is true that the central intelligence is used as "the impersonal author's concrete deputy or delegate, a convenient substitute or apologist for the creative power otherwise so veiled and disembodied,"[16] it is equally clear that the crucial relationship in fiction is the one between the narrator and the central consciousness chosen. In the Preface to *The American* James writes of Christopher Newman:

If Newman was attaching enough, I must have argued, his tangle would be sensible enough; for the interest of everything is all that

[15] Preface to *The Portrait of a Lady*, in *The Art of the Novel*, p. 46.
[16] Preface to *The Golden Bowl, ibid.*, p. 327.

it is *his* vision, *his* conception, *his* interpretation: at the window of his wide, quite sufficiently wide, consciousness we are seated, from that admirable position we "assist." . . . A beautiful infatuation this, always, I think, the intensity of the creative effort to get into the skin of the creature; the act of personal possession of one being by another at its completest—and with the high enhancement, ever, that it is, by the same stroke, the effort of the artist to preserve for his subject that unity, and for his use of it (in other words for the interest he desires to excite) that effect of a *centre*, which most economise its value.[17]

The "assistance" given is of the utmost importance in a James novel. An awareness of a creative consciousness surrounding and possessing the consciousness of the central character is a necessity if James is to accomplish his artistic purpose—the complete possession of one being by another. The house of fiction has within it smaller houses with smaller windows, narrowed and humanized versions of the creative power. This does not, however, minimize the importance of that "majesty of authorship" which has created the smaller house and smaller window and which stands behind and assists. James tells the reader in the Preface to *The Ambassadors* that Strether arrives at Chester "for the dreadful purpose of giving his creator 'no end' to tell about him";[18] and the reader is acutely aware of the narrative voice in *The Ambassadors*. He finds the narrator referring to himself as "I" on the first page of the novel, and he always senses a consciousness faced with the problem of discovery and revelation through the use of artistic selection: "All sorts of other pleasant small things— small things that were yet large for him—flowered in the air of the occasion [Strether's walk around Chester with Miss Gostry]; but the bearing of the occasion itself on matters still remote concerns us too closely to permit us to multiply our illustrations. Two or three, however, in truth, we should perhaps regret to lose."[19]

[17] In *ibid.*, pp. 37–38.
[18] In *ibid.*, p. 320.
[19] Ed. Leon Edel (New York, 1960), p. 24.

Not only is the reader told that this occasion marks Strether's first step toward understanding Europe and hence his first step toward self-understanding, but he is also made aware that all which is to happen already exists within the mind of the narrator. Strether's mind is, to be sure, the focal point of the novel, but his mind, in turn, is inside a larger one. As James implies in the Preface to *The Ambassadors*, his discovery of Strether, "the happiest of accidents" (311), was the first and easiest step in his creative task:

Art deals with what we see, it must first contribute full-handed that ingredient; it plucks its material, otherwise expressed, in the garden of life—which material elsewhere grown is stale and uneatable. But it has no sooner done this than it has to take account of a *process*. . . . The process, that of the expression, the literal squeezing-out, of value is another affair—with which the happy luck of mere finding has little to do. . . . There is the story of one's hero, and then, thanks to the intimate connection of things, the story of one's story itself. (312–13)

Like Fielding and Eliot, James finds "the story of one's story itself" at the center of the novelist's creative task. The writer of fiction does not tarry long in the garden of life; his primary interest is not in the raw materials but in the imaginative process they undergo. Germs from the real world provide the novelist with the "virus of suggestion," but the novel is the story of the history of the inoculated imagination. It is for this reason that James devoted so much attention to the writing of the Prefaces for the New York edition of his works:

The private history of any sincere work, however modest its pretensions, looms with its own completeness in the rich, ambiguous aesthetic air, and seems at once to borrow a dignity and to mark, so to say, a station. . . . These notes represent, over a considerable course, the continuity of an artist's endeavour, the growth of his whole operative consciousness and, best of all, perhaps, their own tendency to multiply, with the implication, thereby, of a memory much enriched.[20]

[20] Preface to *Roderick Hudson*, in *The Art of the Novel*, p. 4.

The prefaces are valuable not because they set up artificial rules for the practice of the art of fiction, but because they attempt to clarify, in each case, the relationship between the "operative consciousness" of the artist and the world of the novel.[21] Concerned with private history, each preface attempts to re-create the attitudes with which the artist approached his materials. For this reason the prefaces do not exist—as is usually assumed—apart from the fictional world to which they are appended. In fact, they function in much the same way as do the authorial intrusions in *Tom Jones* and *Adam Bede*. In the Preface to *The Ambassadors*, for example, James, in attempting to tell the story of his story, defines the laws which govern his world and recalls "old intentions" (319). As implied by his discussion of the "memory of the thrilling ups and downs, the intricate ins and outs of the compositional problem" (319) he had solved, he is attempting to identify and elucidate the "operative consciousness" of the artist as it is manifested in *The Ambassadors*. That he is successful is suggested by the way in which the metaphors of the Preface extend and partially explicate the metaphors within the novel itself.

In an attempt to define the nature of Strether's change in the novel, James writes in the Preface: "He had come [to Paris] with a view that might have been figured by a clear green liquid, say, in a neat glass phial; and the liquid, once poured into the open cup of *application*, once exposed to the action of another air, had begun to turn from green to red, or whatever, and might, for all he knew, be on its way to purple, to black, to yellow" (314). When Lambert Strether arrives in Europe, he is dependent, both literally and figuratively, on Mrs. Newsome, the wealthy widow to whom he is engaged and the main representative of the world he has left behind. The nature of Strether's tie to the Woollett world is

---

[21] See Laurence Holland's discussion of the prefaces as the "celebration of a process . . . rather than a statement of a theory," in *The Expense of Vision* (Princeton, N.J., 1964), pp. 155–82.

figured for him in the green cover of a review which he edits with the funds supplied by Mrs. Newsome: "His name on the green cover, where he had put it for Mrs. Newsome, expressed him doubtless just enough to make the world—the world as distinguished, both for more and for less, from Woollett—ask who he was. . . . He was Lambert Strether because he was on the cover, whereas it should have been, for anything like glory, that he was on the cover because he was Lambert Strether" (63).

The nature of Strether's identity, then, is defined at the beginning of his journey by the green covers of the review. As he becomes more and more influenced by the atmosphere of Europe, however, he begins to change, and that change is expressed through a series of color metaphors. He is introduced to Europe by Maria Gostry, a woman who dresses "in a manner quite other than Mrs. Newsome's, and who [wears] round her throat a broad red velvet band" (43). Strether is impressed by this band, which "somehow added, in her appearance to the value of every other item" (43). Although he wonders at this point what "had a man conscious of a man's work in the world to do with red velvet bands" (43), he is unable to escape its influence. The red band does not, however, remain the primary object in Strether's experience. When he and Miss Gostry attend a play, his attention is directed toward an actress "in a yellow frock who made a pleasant weak good-looking young man . . . do the most dreadful things" (45). As with his discovery that Madame de Vionnet owns the books with the "lemon-coloured covers with which his eye had begun to dally from the hour of his arrival" (153), Strether's encounter with the yellow dress marks an important step in his movement toward the development of a "Paris" vision.

The important point for the present discussion is, of course, the nature of the connection between the figurative language of the Preface and the metaphoric development of the novel. As the example of the color metaphor implies, the relationship is a continuous one; and the continuity of metaphor implies a continuity of consciousness. Because the Preface to *The Ambassadors* is a "private history" of the novel, it attempts to define the motives of the creative consciousness which organize and control the development of the novel. The Preface explores the goals and methods of the "chronicler" of the hero (43), not those of Strether himself. "Compositional problems" become for James "the question at issue" and "keep the author's heart in his mouth" (319) precisely because they are the sign of the artist's relationship to his fiction, his point of view.

i

But if I go further and seek among these characteristics the principal one, which includes almost all the rest, I discover that in most of the operations of the mind each American appeals only to the individual effort of his own understanding.

America is therefore one of the countries where the precepts of Descartes are least studied and are best applied.

.   .   .   .   .

Everyone shuts himself up tightly within himself and insists upon judging the world from there.[22]

The nineteenth-century American novelist justifies in a striking way Alexis de Tocqueville's brilliant insight into the nature of the American mind. He differs from his English counterpart in his willingness to accept—indeed, to affirm—the subjective origins of his art. In contrast to novelists like Dickens, Eliot, and Trollope, he finds no pre-established institutional, moral, or rational order on which to ground himself, but, as R. W. B. Lewis has noted,[23] finds himself alone in a neutral universe and goes forth to invent his own character and personal history. For this reason a central concern of his art becomes the nature of the creative task itself.

Thoreau rejects established order as represented by Concord

[22] Alexis de Tocqueville, *Democracy in America* (New York, 1945), 2:3–4.

[23] *The American Adam* (Chicago, 1955), pp. 110–11.

and retreats to the woods in order to reduce life "to its lowest terms"[24]—the naked self and the natural world. In his case, the reductive process leads to affirmation. The inner and outer worlds are discovered to be products of a divine order. "The Maker of this earth but patented a leaf" (275). This insight, however, comes only to the man who is willing to reject all previous grounds for order and create his own. It is important that *Walden* derives its structure from the seasonal cycle; for Thoreau, like the sun, "this first spring morning" is "re-creating the world" (280). *Walden* is directly concerned with this creative process: "In most books, the I, or first person, is omitted; in this it will be retained; that in respect to egotism is the main difference. We commonly do not remember that it is, after all, always the first person that is speaking. I should not talk so much about myself if there were anybody else whom I know as well" (3).

It is significant that the "I" is retained in so many American books. The American writer continually sings a "Song of Myself." He may appear in his own person, as Hawthorne does in "The Custom House," his introduction to *The Scarlet Letter*, or he may be figured in the form of a fictitious first-person narrator who tells his story as he writes his book. From Washington Irving's *Sketch Book* to John Barth's *The Floating Opera*, the first-person point of view has been used to dramatize the American writer's concern with the nature of the relationship between art and life. The artist's presence in his own work—either as a dramatized version of himself or as a fictitious narrator—serves to imply a radical distinction between the two realms. This is especially true of the fiction of America's two great nineteenth-century novelists. For Hawthorne and Melville the novelist is not an observer but the creator of fictitious life.

The decision of Hawthorne and Melville to refer to their fiction as "romance" reflects their concern with the act of creation itself, as well as their desire to call attention to the

[24] *Walden*, ed. Brooks Atkinson (New York, 1937), p. 82.

vital perspective which is responsible for their art. Hawthorne prefers the romance to the novel because while the latter "is presumed to aim at a very minute fidelity, not merely to the possible, but to the probable and ordinary course of man's experience," the former "has fairly a right to present [the truth of the human heart] under circumstances, to a great extent, of the writer's own choosing or creation."[25] The writer's creative act is crucial, for the fictional world is a "neutral territory, somewhere between the real world and fairy-land, where the Actual and the Imaginary may meet, and each imbue itself with the nature of the other" (V,55). It is in this neutral territory, and only here, that inner and outer, subject and object, are joined in meaningful intercourse.

As "The Custom House" suggests, the real world is one of fragments. Hawthorne is forced to live either at the old manse within the magical circle of imaginative isolation or in the decaying public world of the customhouse. Within the world of *The Scarlet Letter*, however, the faded scarlet "A" which is discovered in the attic of the customhouse takes on a new beauty and meaning because it now exists harmoniously within an atmosphere created by the author's return to the private world. Although Hawthorne the man must live in either one realm or the other, Hawthorne the author is able to create a world where public and private may not only coexist but interact. In "The Custom House" the private author, seized by an "autobiographical impulse" (17), attempts to "complete the circle of his existence" through public utterance, "since thoughts are frozen and utterance benumbed, unless the speaker stand in some true relation with his audience" (18). It is important to realize, however, that the speaker here is Hawthorne the artist, not Hawthorne the man. The "inmost me" is kept "behind the veil" (18). It is only the voice of the author speaking from a neutral realm which is able to bridge the gap between self and world.

[25] Preface to *The House of the Seven Gables, Complete Works of N. H.*, Riverside ed. (New York, 1883), 3:13. All subsequent references to Hawthorne's works will be to this edition.

It is in the fiction of Herman Melville, however, that the acutely self-conscious artist is given his most radical and important role. If Hawthorne's experience of the world, as divided into subject and object, private and public, looks backward toward romanticism, Melville's vision of a white universe looks forward to the nihilism of a Conrad. Melville's theory of fiction is based on a vision of life as an empty masquerade. The human and natural worlds are lies. The mind of man and the material of nature are "nothing but surface stratified on surface" (*P*, XXI, 335) and both are hollow at the core. To penetrate beneath these surfaces, however, is no easy task. As with Conrad's darkness, direct confrontation with Melville's whiteness brings madness and death. Man seems destined to be either a naïve innocent, a raving madman, or a dying misanthrope. Characters like Jackson, Pip, Bulkington, Pierre, Billy Budd, and Claggart—among a host of others—dramatize the scope of the problem. Nevertheless there is always someone else present in Melville's fiction, someone who loses his innocence and also retains his sanity. There is the narrator, who in his role of fictive author seeks to approach the truth indirectly by viewing it through the experiences of created characters in a fictional world. It is this quest which provides the generative formal principle in Melville's early fiction and results, finally, in *Moby-Dick*, a book which demonstrates the writer's ability to forget life by creating another world. But it was the destiny of Herman Melville to expose the subversive implications of this subjective aesthetic by uncovering an internal blankness which renders it absurd. This exploration generates *Pierre, Israel Potter,* and *The Confidence-Man.*

The assumptions which form the foundation of Melville's theory of the novel receive their most concise statement in his famous essay, "Hawthorne and His Mosses." One of five surviving book reviews which Melville wrote for *The Literary World,* the Hawthorne essay is by far the most important in that only there does Melville deal with matters other than plot. The other reviews, however, furnish an important clue to the central meaning of "Hawthorne and His Mosses." It is by noting an important difference between them and the longer Hawthorne piece that the reader becomes aware of the literary device by which the meaning of the essay is rendered. The only one of the five reviews which has any kind of authorial signature (the other four were published anonymously in *The Literary World*), "Hawthorne and His Mosses," the reader is told, is written "By a Virginian Spending July in Vermont." As the existence of the other reviews suggests, this pseudonym serves a more important purpose than the concealment of the writer's identity. The symbolic development of the essay depends upon the narrator's dramatization of himself as a Virginian spending the summer in Vermont:

A papered chamber in a fine old farm-house—a mile from any other dwelling, and dipped to the eaves in foliage—surrounded by mountains, old woods, and Indian ponds,—this, surely, is the place to write of Hawthorne. Some charm is in this northern air, for love and duty seem both impelling to the task. A man of a deep and noble nature has seized me in this seclusion. His wild, witch voice rings through me; or, in softer cadences, I seem to hear it in the songs of the hill-side birds, that sing in the larch trees at my window. (535–36)

From the very beginning of the essay the reader is asked to consider the special nature of the Virginian's experience of New England. As the literary character of the essay's introductory paragraph (quoted above) suggests, the narrator's introduction to the area is a bookish one. The farmhouse covered with foliage, the mountains, woods, and Indian pools, have reference to the poetic New England landscape described by Hawthorne in his Preface to the *Mosses*. Because of the special nature of his introduction to his new environment, the narrator does not remain an ordinary tourist. Although his "sightseeing" is at first limited to the usual and commonplace

—people, places, and food—he soon enters a more meaningful realm:

> At breakfast the other day, a mountain girl, a cousin of mine, who for the last two weeks has every morning helped me to strawberries and raspberries,—which, like the roses and pearls in the fairy-tale, seemed to fall into the saucer from those strawberry-beds her cheeks,—this delightful creature, this charming Cherry says to me—"I see you spend your mornings in the hay-mow; and yesterday I found there 'Dwight's Travels in New England.' Now I have something far better than that,—something more congenial to our summer on these hills. Take these raspberries, and then I will give you some moss."—"Moss!" said I.—"Yes, and you must take it to the barn with you, and goodbye to 'Dwight.'" (536–37)

The narrator's farewell to Dwight and his acceptance of Hawthorne's *Mosses* marks his entrance into another world and the essay's movement into metaphor. A glance at the index of the first volume of Dwight's *Travels* reveals a complete if somewhat dull guide book to New England. The book, which includes everything from a description of the climate to a discussion of the morals of Indian tribes, attempts, in Dwight's words, "to describe New England in a manner resembling that in which a painter would depict a cloud."[26] The Virginia tourist, visiting in New England, loses interest in Dwight's factual description of the actual landscape, accepts Hawthorne as his guide, and is magically transported into the "enchanting landscape" of Hawthorne's fictional world. As his actions imply, the narrator finds Hawthorne's landscape more appealing and meaningful than Dwight's descriptions of the actual one.

Because the narrator's movement from the *Travels* to the *Mosses* controls the metaphoric development of the essay, it is important to recognize the implications of the shift. That the Virginia tourist faced with the problem of understanding a new environment apparently finds fiction more helpful than

[26] Timothy Dwight, *Travels in New England and New York* (London, 1823), 1:iv.

the factual guide book is not surprising to the student of Melville. As the reader of *Redburn* knows, guide books are "the least reliable books in all literature" (*R*, 151). In the "world of lies" ("HHM," 542) the "sands are forever shifting" (*R*, 151). Nature, who "absolutely paints like a harlot" (*M-D*, XLII, 193), is always changing her face. She never lures the unsuspecting traveler with the same temptation. Hence the tourist who depends on a guide book is destined to become hopelessly lost.

Implicit in the narrator's contrast of Dwight and Hawthorne is a superficial similarity between the *Travels* and the Preface to the *Mosses,* in which Hawthorne takes the reader "sight-showing" (II, 14) around the New England countryside. Hawthorne, however, recognizes that it is "difficult to view the world precisely as it exists" (41). For this reason he adjusts "his inward eye to a proper focus with the outward organ" (33) and introduces the reader to a "fairy-land," midway between dream and reality. Like Dwight, Hawthorne discusses New England history, climate, flowers, rivers, apples, and vegetables, but, as Melville sees, these descriptions are intended to introduce the reader to a fictional world, not to provide him with a guide to the actual one. Hawthorne's Preface is a "stream of thought . . . flowing from my pen" which attempts to describe the "broad tide of dim emotions . . . which swell around me from that portion of my existence" (43). The Preface takes the reader "just within the cavern's mouth" of Hawthorne's fictional world (44) and leaves him there free to explore at will.

It is this fictional landscape which the Virginia tourist prefers to Dwight's descriptions of the actual one, and so he feeds on Hawthorne's fictional apples, finds mountains and valleys in his humor and love, and enjoys his Indian-summer melancholy:

For spite of all the Indian-summer sunlight on the hither side of Hawthorne's soul, the other side—like the dark half of the physical sphere—is shrouded in a blackness, ten times black. But this darkness but gives more effect to the evermoving dawn, that forever advances through it, and circumnavigates his world. . . . Certain it is, however, that this great power of blackness in him derives its force from its appeals to that Calvinistic sense of Innate Depravity and Original Sin, from whose visitations, in some shape or other, no deeply thinking mind is always and wholly free. . . . Still more: this black conceit pervades him, through and through. You may be witched by his sunlight,—transported by the bright gildings in the skies he builds over you;—but there is the blackness of darkness beyond; and even his bright gildings but fringe, and play upon the edges of thunder-clouds. . . . He is immeasurably deeper than the plummet of the mere critic. . . . You cannot come to know greatness by inspecting it; there is no glimpse to be caught of it, except by intuition; you need not ring it, you but touch it, and you find it is gold. (540–41)

It is important that the narrator of the review uses aspects of the New England climate which Dwight regards as characteristic of the area as a basis for his metaphoric description of Hawthorne's fictional world. As his comments make clear, however, the symbolic landscape reveals a truth which remains hidden in Dwight's purely factual account. In the fictional landscape the Virginian discovers the "Calvinistic sense of Innate Depravity," an aspect of the New England tradition which is not visible in the natural landscape. It is only in the fictional world that the "background" leads to a "mystical depth of meaning."

Having indicated the limits and nature of his tour, the narrator moves on, through a discussion of Shakespeare's fictional world, to define more precisely the ways in which the fictional world differs from the actual one. After suggesting that Shakespeare's popularity is due to his use of a sort of rant which "brings down the house," he goes on to discuss what he considers to be at the heart of Shakespeare's genius:

But it is those deep far-away things in him; those occasional flashings-forth of the intuitive Truth in him; those short, quick probings at the very axis of reality:—these are the things that make Shakespeare, Shakespeare. Through the mouths of the dark char-

acters of Hamlet, Timon, Lear, and Iago, he craftily says, or sometimes insinuates the things, which we feel to be so terrifically true,
that it were all but madness for any good man, in his own proper
character, to utter, or even hint of them. Tormented into despera-
tion, Lear the frantic King tears off the mask, and speaks the sane
madness of vital truth. . . .[27] For in this world of lies, Truth is
forced to fly like a sacred white doe in the woodlands; and only
by cunning glimpses will she reveal herself, as in Shakespeare and
other masters of the great Art of Telling the Truth,—even though
it be covertly, and by snatches. (541–42)

Shakespeare, like Hawthorne, "plays his grandest conceits"
against a symbolic "background." By creating a fictional
surrogate for himself and placing him within a fictional world,
Shakespeare is able to penetrate to the very "axis of reality."
This indirection is necessary not only because the actual
world is a "world of lies" but because of the destructive
nature of Truth itself. As with Conrad's darkness, Melville's
Truth is a positive threat to sanity and life. To face it directly,
in one's "own proper character," is to be driven mad. Only
when it is articulated by a fictional character in a realm whose
landscape is designed to reveal rather than hide can Truth be
experienced as "sane madness." By turning his back on life
and entering a world which does not exist, the writer is able
to approach the "axis of reality" without being destroyed or
driven mad. Fiction, paradoxically, puts man in touch with
Truth while protecting him from it.

As the narrator of the "Mosses" is well aware, his theory
implies a radical distinction between the actual and fictional
worlds. "Would that all excellent books were foundlings,

---

[27] *The Literary World* read "same," a mistake which was not corrected
until the publication of Eleanor Melville Metcalf's *Herman Melville:
Cycle and Epicycle* (Cambridge, Mass., 1953). Here was printed for the
first time a letter from Sophia Hawthorne to her mother in which she
reports Melville's reaction to the publication of the "Mosses" essay: "He
told me that the Review was too carelessly written—that he dashed it off
in great haste & did not see the proof sheets, & that there was one provok-
ing mistake in it. Instead of 'the same madness of truth' it should be
'the *sane* madness of truth' " (p. 92).

without father or mother," he writes, "that so it might be, we could glorify them, without including their ostensible authors" (536). This radical separation of the man from the artist points directly to the difference between the natural and literary landscapes:

I know not what would be the right name to put on the title-page of an excellent book, but this I feel, that the names of all fine authors are fictitious ones, far more so than that of Junius,—simply standing, as they do, for the mystical, ever-eluding Spirit of all Beauty, which ubiquitously possesses men of genius. Purely imaginative as this fancy may appear, it nevertheless seems to receive some warranty from the fact, that on a personal interview no great author has ever come up to the idea of his reader. (536)

It is of crucial importance to distinguish between Hawthorne the man and "Hawthorne in his writings" (547). In his "own proper character" a great writer is, as we all are, merely a part of this "world of lies." In his role of fictive author, however, he inhabits another world. He possesses the power of a "wizard" who "magically" constructs and inhabits an "enchanting landscape" (536). The value of fiction is, then, dependent upon the reader's recognizing and approaching it as fiction. Art which imitates life is merely meaningless gesture.

But if this view [the Virginian's] of the all-popular Shakespeare be seldom taken by his readers, and if very few who extol him, have ever read him deeply, or, perhaps, only have seen him on the tricky stage (which alone made, and is still making him his mere mob renown)—if few men have time, or patience, or palate, for the spiritual truth as it is in that great genius;—it is, then, no matter of surprise that in a contemporaneous age, Nathaniel Hawthorne is a man, as yet, almost utterly mistaken among men. (542)

To put Shakespeare on the "tricky stage" is to bring fiction too close to the lies of the actual world. The stage is "tricky" precisely because it drives the white doe of truth into "the infinite obscure of [the] background" (541). The words of

Lear are meaningful only as long as they are spoken within the symbolic landscape of the fictional world. Removed from this context and spoken by a real man on the stage, they are no longer the "sane madness of vital truth," but are instead mere "popularizing noise and show of broad farce, and blood-be-smeared tragedy" (542).

The only connection which exists between the realms of life and art is that materials from one are used in the construction of the other. As the metaphoric development of Melville's essay implies, Hawthorne the man, a resident of New England, is related to the inhabitor of the symbolic landscape of the *Mosses.* So it is that Hawthorne the artist does not appear in "the costume of Queen Elizabeth's day," and is not "a writer of dramas founded upon old English history, or the tales of Boccaccio" (543). Because "great geniuses are parts of the times," indeed "themselves are the times; and possess a correspondent coloring" (543), Hawthorne the artist employs raw materials taken from the world of Hawthorne the man in constructing his symbolic landscape. He takes, as it were, a "skeleton of actual reality," and builds about it "with fulness & veins & beauty."[28] Referring by implication to Melville's own fiction as an example, the narrator insists that the nineteenth-century American writer must have "plenty of sea-room to tell the Truth in" (544).

Because the writer of fiction attempts to reveal the truth which lies hidden beneath the surfaces of nature and entangled in the labyrinth of the multiple avenues of experience, he must begin with the facts of his own experience. "Clear Truth," however, "is a thing for salamander giants only to encounter," and hence the writer must see these facts as the basis for the creation of another realm where the "dread goddess's veil" (*M-D*, 336) may be lifted with impunity.

The theory of fiction implied in the Hawthorne essay has a special relevance to Melville's practice of his craft. When

[28] *L*, p. 157.

these two attitudes—that "all fine authors are fictitious ones" and that the art of fiction is the "Great Art of Telling the Truth"—are combined, the critic is provided with the important suggestion that all of Melville's narrators are, in some way, portraits of the artist at work.

II

PORTRAITS OF THE ARTIST AS A YOUNG MAN: NARRATIVE FORM IN MELVILLE'S EARLY NOVELS

Like Kierkegaard, he is the Job of temporality.
GEORGES POULET on Melville, *Studies in Human Time*

THE FACT THAT MELVILLE'S first five novels were first-person narratives assumes a special significance when viewed in the context of his insistence that the names of all fine authors are fictitious ones. The striking autobiographical elements in his fiction have long been of interest to his critics. Indeed, many find his use of personal experience important enough to make unnecessary, if not misleading, any critical distinction between writer and narrator. Nevertheless, the unusual names of Melville's author-heroes certainly suggest their fictive nature. Tommo, Taji, Wellingborough Redburn, White Jacket, and Ishmael seem unlike characters one meets "in the same old way every day in the same old street" (C-M, XXXIII, 206) That Melville's decision to combine personal experience and an obviously fictitious narrator is an attempt to deal with the problem of the discrepancy between man and the artist is suggested by Montaigne's discussion of this same issue. He too recognizes the fact that often "the work and the artificer contradict one another." For him, as for Melville, the world "eternally turns around, all things therein are incessantly moving; the earth, the rocks of Caucasus, and the pyramids of Egypt, both by public motion and their own." Because Montaigne is content to describe the world "as it is the instant I consider it," to "paint its passage," not "its being," he presents himself to the reader as "Michael de Montaigne, not as a grammarian, a poet or a lawyer."[1] Melville, however, is interested in discovering the truth which lies hidden beneath the shifting and turning surfaces of things, in describing the world's "being" rather than its "passage." For this reason he finds it necessary to distinguish between the private and the literary consciousness. This he accomplishes by the creation of a fictive first-person narrator who stands as a portrait of the artist *par excellence*.

All first-person narrators are, of course, artists. As one critic has remarked, "this is at once true and tautological."[2] None-

---

[1] *Works*, trans. W. Hazlitt (New York, 1861), 3:64–65. Melville bought his copy of Montaigne in January, 1848 (see Merton M. Sealts, Jr., *Melville's Reading* [Madison, Wis., 1966], entry 366, p. 80).

[2] Joseph Riddel, "F. Scott Fitzgerald, the Jamesian Inheritance, and the Morality of Fiction," *Modern Fiction Studies* (Winter, 1965–66), 11:335.

theless, when Melville's preference for the first-person point of view is placed in the context of his discussion of the art-life relationship in the Hawthorne essay, an obvious function of technique is charged with a special suggestiveness. His fictive narrators are embodiments of the magical creative power which "ubiquitously possesses men of genius." Although related through their experiences to their "ostensible author," they are in an important sense "foundlings," Ishmael-like creatures with no familial connections to the world of lies.

Parallel to the problem of the author's relationship to his hero is the more complex question of the narrator's tie to his own earlier experience. Like the later eighteenth-century and romantic poets, Melville was interested in the activities of memory. All of his first-person narrators are engaged in a conscious act of remembering: in their narratives there are always two landscapes present, an experienced one and a recollected one. The Melvilleian hero, however, endows the operation of memory with a complexity which distinguishes it from the faculty which was so widely discussed at the end of the eighteenth century. Like Hartly most of the poets and philosophers regarded memory as "that faculty by which traces of sensations and ideas recur, or are recalled, in the same order and proportion, accurately or nearly, as they were once presented."[3] At a time when associationism insisted on the successive character of experience, memory became the faculty which not only allowed man to organize his world, but provided him with his strongest argument for the existence of a personal identity. Thomas Reid writes in 1786:

What evidence have you that there is such a permanent self which has a claim to all the thoughts, actions, and feelings which you call yours?

To this I answer that the proper evidence I have of all this is re-memberance. . . . My memory testifies not only that this [a conversation in the past] was done, but that it was done by me who now

---

[3] David Hartly, *Observations on Man* (London, 1801), 1:iii.

remember it. If it was done by me, I must have existed at that time, and continued to exist from that time to the present. . . .[4]

The pleasures of memory, then, derive largely from the power that that faculty has to constitute an orderly picture of a self and a world, which otherwise threaten to disintegrate into a series of disconnected and fragmented sensations and ideas. The tendency of the turn-of-the-century poet to invoke the memory of a past experience in order to lend vitality to a present one illustrates a literary implication of Reid's idea. In the prefatory argument to Part II of "The Pleasures of Memory" Samuel Rodgers writes that "even in madness itself, when the soul is resigned over to the tyranny of a distempered imagination, she [memory] revives past perceptions, and awakens that train of thought that was formerly most familiar."[5]

It is, however, just this emphasis on memory's ability to authenticate present experience which distinguishes Melville's use of the faculty from many of the earlier discussions of it. For the Melvilleian narrator memory is an imaginative act which makes the present a moment of creative understanding of a past adventure that was experienced initially as an unintelligible and frightening chaos of sensations. At time of writing—often years after the original experience—the mature writer fictionalizes his earlier experience in an attempt to define its truth or meaning to himself and to his reader. It is the creative remembering in the present which gives meaning to the past. The emphasis, in other words, is on the act of remembering rather than on the content of memory. The past self is distinguished from rather than substituted for the present self, and a literary landscape replaces the natural one in which the experience initially occurred. Melville would regard Cowper's attempt to

---

[4] *Essays on the Intellectual Powers of Man*, ed. A. D. Woozley (London, 1941), p. 203.
[5] *The British Poets* (Philadelphia, 1844), p. 238.

retrace
(As in a map the voyager his course)
The windings of my way through many years[6]

as a futile exercise because it merely repeats the confusing
fluctuations of the experience itself. The "white doe of truth,"
object of all the narrators' memorial quests, can be glimpsed
only within the verbal landscape created at the time of writing
from the materials of the past. For these men the only meaningful way of recapturing the past is to invent it, to turn it
into a fiction.

Although this idea is best illustrated in Ishmael's vision of
his whaling voyage as a symbolic drama, it is present in less
obvious ways in the earlier books. Like the narrator of "Hawthorne and His Mosses" Ishmael and his progenitors understand the necessity of turning experience into a *story* if they
are to face and survive the horrible truth implicit in it. Because
of his double role of author-hero the Melvillean narrator is
both creature and creator, man and artist. The story that he
tells is both experienced and invented. The young man, who
begins his quest by throwing himself into the destructive sea
of experience, is caught up in all of the confused sensations
of the moment. Although he is unable to recognize any order
in the chaos to which he is exposed, his very involvement demands that he assume that one exists. To imagine that the
apparent confusion is a real one would render his experience
absurd. The quest would end before it began.

It is, of course, the realization that experience is indeed
meaningless which lies at the center of the mature narrator's
vision—a truth which makes ordinary human life impossible.
But since he is telling a story rather than living an experience,
he is able to see the truth and survive. As storyteller he is able
to approach the events from an opposite direction, starting
at the end of the experience rather than at the beginning.
Hence he is able to give a spatial dimension to a series of
successive temporal events. By the act of turning his experience

[6] "The Task," bk. 4, *English Poets* (London, 1810), 18:698.

into a story, he places himself outside of that experience—in effect, treats it as though it belonged to someone else.

The narrator's relation to his earlier experience, then, may be seen as a dramatization of the writer's relationship to his fiction. Just as Melville maintains the important distinction between art and life by the use of fictive first-person narrators, so these author-heroes affirm the importance of this distinction as they tell their stories. Both the author and the narrator (the author's portrait of himself) maintain their sanity and discover truth by the creation of a rational lie, a fiction.

i

I am like one of those seeds taken out of the Egyptian Pyramids, which, after being three thousand years a seed and nothing but a seed, being planted in English soil, it developed itself, grew to greenness, and then fell to mould. So I. Until I was twenty-five, I had no development at all. From my twenty-fifth year I date my life. Three weeks have scarcely passed, at any time between then and now, that I have not unfolded within myself. But I feel that I am now come to the inmost leaf of the bulb, and that shortly the flower must fall to the mould. (*L*, 130)

Writing to Hawthorne in the throes of the labor which preceded the birth of *Moby-Dick,* his first great novel, Melville not only reveals his despair at approaching what he thought was the peak of his creative career, but he also establishes an important connection between artistic and inward growth. That he chooses the year in which he wrote *Typee* to date the beginning of his development is suggestive, for it implies that his fiction is an expression of the progressive unfolding of the self. To read Melville's fiction, then, is to encounter, in James's words, "the growth of his whole operative consciousness." *Typee,* along with *Mardi, Redburn,* and *White Jacket,* dramatizes the initial stages in the blooming of his creative vision.

Moby-Dick and the later fictions not only ensure that their author will not "go down to posterity . . . as a 'man who lived among the cannibals' " (*L*, 130), but they also help to identify

37

the ways in which *Typee* is more than a "Peep at Polynesian Life." Tommo's assertions that "appearances all the world over are deceptive" (XXIV, 172) and that "I saw everything, but could comprehend nothing" (175), when they are seen in the light of the later fiction, assume a special significance which is only vaguely suggested by the context of the novel itself. Similarly, Moa Artua, the deaf and dumb baby god of the Typees with the "time-serving disposition" (174), becomes more than an interesting part of Polynesian culture when placed in the company of such figures as Plotinus Plinlimmon, the lamb-like man, and Billy Budd. *Typee* is the first expression of a vision which was to continue to grow and develop.

As with Melville's later more complex first-person narratives, the structure and meaning of his first book depend on an important distinction between the real and literary worlds. Juxtaposed in *Typee* are the vision of the young Tommo, who, immersed in the chaos of successive temporal moments, "saw everything, but could comprehend nothing," with that of the mature narrator, whose later experiences of "the pent-up wickedness" of civilized savages while "one of the crew of a man-of-war" (XXVII, 200) have allowed him to construct a place to stand in his effort to find the meaning of his earlier experiences. By taking the view of the detached anthropologist, the narrator is able to bridge both the smaller gap between the successive sensations of his Typee experience and the larger one between the primitive and civilized worlds.[7] In experience the past is partially lost because it is pushed aside by the demanding details of the present moment. Forced always to remain "distressingly alive to all the fearful circumstances of our present situation," the mind of the young

[7] Claude Lévi-Strauss advocates a similar procedure in *Tristes Tropiques* (trans. John Russell [New York, 1964]): "The study of these savages does not reveal a Utopian state of nature; nor does it make us aware of a perfect society hidden deep in the forests. It helps us to construct a theoretical model of a society which corresponds to none that can be observed in reality, but will help us to disentangle 'what in the present state of man is original, and what is artificial'" (p. 391).

Tommo is "oppressed" by "various and conflicting" thoughts (XI, 73). "In the midst of this tumult" the past exists for him only in the two English words which he teaches Marheyo, "Home" and "Mother" (XXXIV, 243). Within the spatial imagination of the narrator, however, the events of the Typee adventure as well as those of his western experience form a wide and symbolic panorama.

To the young hero, immersed in the sea of experience, life seems interminable and monotonous. Aboard the "Dolly," each day is an absurd repetition of its predecessor: each meal consists of "salt-horse and sea-biscuit"; each object is painted the same "vile and sickly hue" (I, 1); even the movement of the ship itself, "rolling and pitching about, never for one moment at rest" (3), adds to the overwhelming sense of dullness. It is the unrelieved tediousness of his life which drives Tommo out to seek new experiences. Tired of merely existing, he hopes by jumping ship to turn his dull, repetitive life into a meaningful and exciting adventure. Because he is familiar with the glowing accounts of "olden voyagers," the Marquesas seem rich with exciting possibilities. He sees himself as one of those "adventurous rover[s]" who "once in the course of a half century . . . would break in upon their peaceful repose, and, astonished at the unusual scene, would be almost tempted to claim the merit of a new discovery" (3).

Experience, however, fails to live up to Tommo's adventurous expectations. After leaving the ship, he and Toby find themselves imprisoned in an "interminable" thicket of canes (VI, 37). Lost in a world which "seemed one unbroken solitude," the young man is "almost unmanned" by the "dismal sense of our forlorn condition" (VII, 44). Although this sensation is momentarily relieved by the exciting discovery of Typee Valley, the sense of adventure is not sustained. As with his experience aboard the "Dolly," life among the Typees is "uniform and undiversified" (XX, 147). Here, as one day follows another without rhyme or reason, Tommo "gradually . . . lost all knowledge of the regular occurrence of the days of the week" (XVII, 120).

In the mind of the narrator, however, meaningless experience is transformed into suggestive adventure because he, like God, knows the story's end before its beginning. For him the characters and events have an inner consistency which makes them intelligible. Sensations and events do not pile up chaotically; each one is caught up and drawn on by the end of the story. In this selective account no detail is inconsequential, for everything exists as a part of a complete adventure and carries with it a promise that its meaning finally will be revealed. For Melville the meaning of a thing is the form of its coexistence with other things; it is the light which everything else casts over it. But because things in experience exist in isolation, discovering meaning involves a process of creating a structure for experience, an ideal landscape of interlocking parts.

In addition to giving his experience meaning by placing it within the traditional structure of the story of the Fall of man, the narrator isolates one sensation and uses it as the symbolic center of his structure.[8] Immediately after his initial glimpse of the Eden-like valley, Tommo experiences for the first time a malady which is to trouble him at several important times during his stay in Typee: "During the hour or two spent under the shelter of these bushes, I began to feel symptoms which I at once attributed to the exposure of the preceding night. Cold shiverings and a burning fever succeeded one another at intervals, while one of my legs was swelled to such a degree, and pained me so acutely, that I half suspected I had been bitten by some venomous reptile" (VII, 46–47). Since the Eden-like Typee is "free from the presence of any vipers" (47) the ailment—which inexplicably vanishes and returns—forms an important part of Tommo's irrational experi-

---

[8] For an account of Melville's use of the Fall myth in *Typee*, see Milton R. Stern, *The Fine Hammered Steel of Herman Melville* (Urbana, Ill., 1957), pp. 29–65.

ence. The narrator, although still without a factual or medical explanation of the illness, understands its relation to his total experience. The symbolic leg is reintroduced whenever he discusses Tommo's plans for escaping from Typee. Not only does it prevent him from making an active effort to flee, but it becomes inflamed whenever escape is thought of or discussed:

> But, notwithstanding the kind treatment we received, I was too familiar with the fickle disposition of savages not to feel anxious to withdraw from the valley, and put myself beyond the reach of that fearful death which, under all these smiling appearances, might yet menace us. But here there was an obstacle in the way of doing so. It was idle for me to think of moving from the place until I should have recovered from the severe lameness that afflicted me; indeed my malady began seriously to alarm me; for, despite the herbal remedies of the natives, it continued to grow worse and worse. Their mild applications, though they soothed the pain, did not remove the disorder. . . . (XIII, 95)

Although the "rich profusion" of Typee Valley seems to imply that Tommo has escaped the "vile and sickly" world of the "Dolly," he has not been able to discard the prejudices of that world. His dissatisfaction with the fertile primitive environment, tied as it is to his horror of the "fearful death," is a reminder of the Captain's early warning to the sailors to "keep out of the way of the bloody cannibals altogether" (VI, 32). The frightening yarns of that "lying old son of a sea-cook" (33) now seem more valid than the "smiling appearances" of the Typee world. It is true that aboard the "Dolly" "the sick had been inhumanly neglected" and the healthy subjected to "the butt end of a handspike" (IV, 18). But in Typee, although the sick are cared for, the primitive herbal remedies are ineffective. The swollen leg can be cured only by the higher knowledge of the "surgeons of the French fleet" (XIII, 95). Moreover, it is impossible to escape the suspicion that the kind treatment may be part of a plan to fatten up the victim.

Tommo's problem is clearly tied to his desire both to possess and to escape from the past, to have the advantages of both the primitive and civilized worlds. Once he decides that escape from Typee is impossible and surrenders himself to the sensations of the moment, there is an important change in the condition of the injured leg:

> Day after day wore on, and still there was no perceptible change in the conduct of the islanders towards me. Gradually I lost all knowledge of the regular occurrence of the days of the week, and sunk insensibly into that kind of apathy which ensues after some violent outbreak of despair. My limb suddenly healed, the swelling went down, the pain subsided, and I had every reason to suppose I should soon completely recover from the affliction that had so long tormented me.
>
> As soon as I was enabled to ramble about the valley in company with the natives, troops of whom followed me whenever I sallied out of the house, I began to experience an elasticity of mind which placed me beyond the reach of those dismal forebodings to which I had so lately been a prey. (XVII, 120)

As long as Tommo sees the present moment in terms of the past and future—the world he has left behind and to which he will eventually return—the leg remains swollen. Like the swollen foot of Oedipus, it is a symbol of his inability to possess the past entirely or escape it completely. It is a measure of the distance between the present moment and the lost past, between the primitive and civilized worlds.

When Tommo gives himself up to the "perpetual hilarity reigning through the whole extent of the vale" (XVII, 123), his wound suddenly disappears. Because the present moment is no longer seen as either coming from the past or moving toward the future, time imposes no burden. He is now a new Adam with no dependence on the past and without responsibility for the future. "The hours tripped along as gaily as the laughing couples down a country dance" (123).

But Tommo's physical and mental health does not last. When Karky, a professor of the fine art of tattooing, develops an insatiable desire to decorate the hero's attractive skin, his awareness of time returns and with it his mysterious malady;

From the time of my casual encounter with Karky the artist, my life was one of absolute wretchedness. Not a day passed but I was persecuted by the solicitations of some of the natives to subject myself to the odious operation of tattooing. . . .

It was during the period I was in this unhappy frame of mind that the painful malady under which I had been labouring—after having almost completely subsided—began again to show itself, and with symptoms as violent as ever. (XXXII, 226–27)

Because "the whole system of tattooing was . . . connected with their religion," Tommo is convinced that "they were resolved to make a convert of me" (XXX, 217). Conversion is a double act, implying both a rejection of the old self and an acceptance of the new. For this reason the tattooing is a threat to his identity which results in the revival of his sense of temporal duration. Faced with the possibility that he will be "disfigured in such a manner as never more to have the *face* to return to my countrymen, even should an opportunity offer" (215), Tommo is driven to define his identity by the life lived before and after the present moment. Paralleling this rebirth of self-consciousness is the return of his Oedipal-like symptoms, for to be aware of the past is to experience the pain of the distance between it and the present moment. Since Tommo is unwilling to have his old *face* destroyed, he must live with the burden which it entails.

It is significant that just after his crucial decision to preserve his old face Tommo discovers evidence that cannibalism is practiced by the natives, and this accident completes his alienation from the primitive society. From this point until he hobbles to the beach to be rescued, he is painfully aware of the passage of time. Ten days separate his horrible discovery from the second visit of Marnoo, the wandering native, and three weeks after his arrival Tommo finally escapes. The career of the young hero, then, moves from a total rejection of the civilized world as represented by the "Dolly" through a search for an adventurous life of sensation in the primitive world of Typee to a total rejection of that world and a return to civilization. This traditional circular pattern of the symbolic death and rebirth of the hero, however, is called into question by the narrator. Although he is writing "amidst all the bustle and stir of the proud and busy city" (XXXIII, 239), he is, in an important sense, removed from both the primitive and Western cultures. Just as he has been able to bridge the gaps between the successive moments of his earlier experience by taking one sensation (the painful leg) and making it the center of a symbolic structure, so he is able to join two cultures meaningfully by seeing them as related parts of a single world:

But it will be urged that these shocking unprincipled wretches are cannibals. Very true; and a rather bad trait in their character it must be allowed. But they are such only when they seek to gratify the passion of revenge upon their enemies; and I ask whether the mere eating of human flesh so very far exceeds in barbarity that custom which only a few years since was practised in enlightened England:—a convicted traitor, perhaps a man found guilty of honesty, patriotism, and such like heinous crimes, had his head lopped off with a huge axe, his bowels dragged out and thrown into a fire; while his body, carved into four quarters, was with his head exposed upon pikes, and permitted to rot and fester among the public haunts of men!

.   .   .   .   .

The term "Savage" is, I conceive, often misapplied, and indeed when I consider the vices, cruelties, and enormities of every kind that spring up in the tainted atmosphere of a feverish civilization, I am inclined to think that so far as the relative wickedness of the parties is concerned, four or five Marquesan Islanders sent to the United States as Missionaries might be quite as useful as an equal number of Americans dispatched to the Islands in a similar capacity. (XVII, 122–23)

As this passage implies, the recurrent "burning fever" to which the young Tommo is susceptible identifies a disease which he brings from the "feverish civilization" he is trying to escape. Like the syphilitic sailors who infect whole islands of healthy primitives, Tommo, too, ends by partially destroying the primitive society he has sought. He demonstrates the universal trait of savagery which the narrator finds in both cultures when, during his escape, he strikes a pursuing native in the throat with a boathook.

By creating a world in which the primitive and civilized, past and present, exist side by side and illuminate one another, the narrator is able to identify the truth which lies hidden beneath the discontinuous sensations of his earlier experience. Looking back from his time of writing in this perspective he can "scarcely understand how it was that, in the midst of so many consolatory circumstances, my mind should still have been consumed by the most dismal forebodings, and have remained a prey to the profoundest melancholy" (XVI, 115). Now from his position as detached social critic he is able to see and understand things that were, at the time of action, "a little curious to my unaccustomed sight" (XI, 81).

The extent to which the narrator sees beyond the limits of his earlier vision is revealed in his comparative treatment of the Polynesian culture. Every effort is made to associate apparently unique primitive practices with accepted civilized modes of behavior. Some of the more obvious examples include his discussion of the participants in primitive religious ceremonies, who seem "much like . . . a parcel of 'Freemasons' making secret signs to each other" (XXIV, 175); his description of arva, the native beverage, which is said to possess "medicinal qualities" (XXIII, 162); and that of Ti, gathering place of the Typee warriors, which seems a "sort of Bachelor's Hall," a "savage Exchange, where the rise and fall of Polynesian Stock was discussed" (XXII, 155).

It is, then, the narrator's detached spatial imagination which allows him to see the implications which underlie the confusion of his earlier experiences. The world is seen as inherently "wolfish" and man as essentially a savage. Civilization has succeeded only in magnifying and developing a basic savagery which is found in a less appalling form in a primitive culture. It is this basic truth about himself and his world which the narrator of *Typee* confronts and reveals through his account of his earlier "Peep at Polynesian Life. . . ."

ii

After the completion of *Omoo,* a sequel to *Typee* and an obvious attempt to capitalize on the success of the earlier book, Melville decided to branch out in a new direction. Motivated by both his own need to resolve important metaphysical and aesthetic problems and by critics who had accused him of writing romance disguised as factual narrative, he resolved to write a full-scale romance. One year before the publication of *Mardi,* Melville, in a letter to John Murray, his English publisher, discusses the intent and nature of his next book:

To be blunt: the work I shall next publish will [be] in downright earnest a "Romance of Polynisian Adventure"—But why this? The truth is, Sir, that the reiterated imputation of being a romancer in disguise has at last pricked me into a resolution to show those who may take any interest in the matter, that a *real* romance of mine is no Typee or Omoo, & is made of different stuff altogether. This I confess has been the main inducement in altering my plans—but others have operated. I have long thought that Polyniesia furnished a great deal of rich poetical material that has never been employed hitherto in works of fancy. . . . However, I thought, that I would postpone trying my hand at anything fanciful of this sort, till some future day: tho' at times when in the mood I threw off occasional sketches applicable to such a work.—Well: proceeding in my narrative of *facts* I began to feel an incurible distaste for the same; & a longing to plume my pinions for a flight, & felt irked, cramped & fettered by plodding along with dull common places,—So suddenly standing [abandoning?] the thing alltogether, I went to work heart & soul at a romance which is now in fair progress, since I had worked at it under an earnest ardor. . . . It opens like a true narrative—like Omoo for example, on ship board—& the romance & poetry of the thing thence grow continually, till it becomes a story wild enough I assure you & with a meaning too. (*L,* 70–71)

The most striking aspect of this passage is the implied assertion of narrative continuity, since it is the almost unanimous opinion of critics that *Mardi* breaks into several discontinuous parts. Melville, however, stresses the point that although the book begins as a factual narrative, the "romance & poetry of the thing thence grow *continually*" (italics mine), thus implying that he intended *Mardi* to move gradually and logically from fact to fancy. There is an abundance of evidence in the book to indicate that he accomplished his purpose.

As is clear from the letter to Murray, *Mardi* was written at least partially in response to the critics of *Typee* and *Omoo* and is a deliberate voyage away from the world of these earlier books. Nevertheless it is also an attempt to examine the implications of these earlier efforts. In fact, *Mardi* in many ways forms the axis of Melville's vision. In addition to furnishing an interpretive commentary on the earlier books, it introduces and partially explores problems which are central in the later fiction. This inclusive quality derives in part from the fact that *Mardi* is directly concerned with the nature of fiction itself. Although this is a central problem in all of Melville's major novels, in no other book is it confronted as directly. *Mardi* is both structurally and thematically a voyage from fact to fiction, from object to subject, a voyage to the very center of the writer's creative imagination. It is with the process and implications of inhabiting this mental world that the book is centrally concerned.[9]

Mardi begins as Melville had said that it would in a realistic world which is reminiscent of that of *Typee*. The tone is set by a narrator who, while engaged in the acts of remembering and writing, provides assurance that he has survived the dangers which he now begins to describe:

Ay, ay, Arcturion! I say it in no malice, but thou wast exceedingly dull. . . . The days went slowly round and round, endless and

[9] I am indebted here to Charles Feidelson's *Symbolism and American Literature* (Chicago, 1953), p. 166.

uneventful as cycles in space. Time and time pieces! How many
centuries did my hammock tell, as pendulum-like it swung to the
ship's dull roll, and ticked the hours and ages. Sacred forever be
the Arcturion's fore-hatch—alas! sea-moss is over it now—and rusty
forever the bolts that held together that old sea hearth-stone, about
which we so often lounged. Nevertheless, ye lost and leaden hours,
I will rail at ye while life lasts. (I, 3)

Having survived the ship which now lies at the bottom of the
sea, the narrator, as his predecessor in *Typee* had done, begins
to re-create the atmosphere which initially drove him to
begin his quest. In this case, however, the motivation is not
physical but metaphysical. The world of the "Arcturion" is
at once monotonous and imprisoning. As the young man lies
in his "pendulum-like" hammock his existence seems reduced
to pure measurement. In a world where "backward or forward, eternity is the same" (LXXVIII, 208), the self is a prisoner
of time. It is "The Center of Many Circumferences" (LXXIX,
209) which join together to form an "endless tunnel" (LXXV,
202) from which escape seems impossible. Here isolation is
complete. There is "no soul a magnet to mine; none with
whom to mingle sympathies" (I, 3). The presence of other
conscious selves merely adds another imprisoning circle: "Bill
Marvel's stories were told over and over again, till the beginning and end dovetailed into each other, and were united for
aye. Ned Ballad's songs were sung till the echoes lurked in the
very tops, and nested in the bunts of the sails" (4).

Within this circular world "no place, nor any thing possessed of a local angularity, is to be lighted upon." With the
destruction of the sense of time as a linear progression comes
the loss of the experience of a defined, limited space. "Parallels
and meridians become emphatically what they are merely
designated as being: imaginary lines drawn round the earth's
surface." One seems in "the region of the everlasting lull,
introductory to a positive vacuity" (II, 8).

In view of his experience of time and space aboard the
"Arcturion" it is fitting that the young hero should envision

adventure as the discovery of new lands. To search for unknown worlds is to attempt to escape from "Time's endless tunnel" by breaking through the circles which form it. Once the young man conceives of the existence of another world composed of "low and fertile" (III, 9) islands, the previously threatening "watery waste" (II, 8) seems merely "so much blankness to be sailed over" (III, 9). Similarly, the endless cycles of time apparently have been broken, for each day need not be seen as simply a dull repetition of past ones but may be envisioned as leading toward an unknown and exciting future.

Typee, however, had demonstrated that there is "No need to travel! The world's one Lima" (*M-D,* LIV, 250), and *Mardi* is not a repetition of the earlier book. The young hero's encounter with the "Parki" and with Somoa and Annatoo, the two natives who pilot the ship, is an indication that the world he seeks cannot be another Typee Valley. Although members of a primitive culture, Somoa and Annatoo have been associated with the white man. The effect of this cultural intercourse is made painfully clear by the brutal history of the "Parki" and the marital discord of the two natives. Questing within the actual world is doomed to failure. All lands are the same. It is significant, then, that immediately following the "Parki" episode the narrative slowly begins to shift from a factual account to a dream-like allegory as the hero prepares to continue his search within the "world of mind" (CLXIX, 488).

Although it is not until the advent of Aleema and Yillah that the reader becomes positive that the narrator's recollections are composed of dreams and fantasies from his past, this suggestion has been present from the beginning. The tendency to indulge himself in "seraphic imaginings" (XLIV, 123) is one of the young man's most characteristic traits. While still aboard the "Arcturion" as a lookout on the masthead, he is drawn toward the world of dreams:

I cast my eyes downward to the brown planks of the dull, plodding ship, silent from stem to stern; then abroad.

In the distance what visions were spread! The entire western horizon high piled with gold and crimson clouds. . . . Vistas seemed leading to worlds beyond. To and fro, and all over the towers of this Nineveh in the sky, flew troops of birds. Watching them long, one crossed my sight, flew through a low arch, and was lost to view. My spirit must have sailed in with it; for directly, as in a trance, came upon me the cadence of mild billows laving a beach of shells, the waving of boughs, and the voices of maidens, and the lulled beatings of my own dissolved heart, all blended together.

Now, all this, to be plain, was but one of the many visions one has up aloft. But coming upon me at this time, it wrought upon me so, that thenceforth my desire to quit the Arcturion became little short of a frenzy. (I, 6–7)

The exciting realm of visionary dreams is set against the dull, drab actual world as represented by the "Arcturion" and makes life there intolerable. The hero's decision to leave the ship is more than a simple act of desertion; it is a rejection of actuality and the standards and rules which govern it. He ignores Jarl's advice "to stick to the ship, and go home in her like a man" (IV, 15) because he prefers the freedom and fulfillment which the dream world seems to promise. This decision at first seems a wise one. Not only does his escape "unconsciously" save him from a "sailor's grave" (VII, 22), but it seems to have brought him to the end of his quest. Yillah, who declares herself "more than mortal, a maiden from Oroolia, the Island of Delights, somewhere in the paradisiacal archipelago of the Polynesians" (XLIII, 122), is an embodiment of his masthead vision. She becomes "my meadow, my mead, my soft shady vine, and my arbor . . . all things desirable and delightful" (XLVI, 128).

His association with Yillah, however, raises a number of problems for the hero. From the beginning their relationship is based on a fiction, a "gracious pretense" (XLIV, 124). "I asked myself, whether the death-deed I had done was sprung of a virtuous motive, the rescuing a captive from thrall; or whether beneath that pretense, I had engaged in this fatal affray for some other, and selfish purpose; the companionship of a beautiful maid" (XLII, 119–20). This initial self-deception is followed by other more conscious feignings. Although the young man recognizes that Yillah's "mystical account" of her origins is the result of the crafty delusions of native priests, whose pupils "almost lose their humanity in the constant indulgence of seraphic imaginings" (XLIV, 123), he continues the deceptions of Aleema. In order "to lead her thoughts toward me, as her friend and preserver; and a better and wiser than Aleema the priest" (XLV, 126), he induces her "to fancy me some gentle demigod, that had come over the sea from her own fabulous Oroolia" (124).

> Yet as our intimacy grew closer and closer, these fancies seemed to be losing their hold. And often she questioned me concerning my own reminiscences of her shadowy isle. And cautiously I sought to produce the impression, that whatever I had said of that clime, had been revealed to me in dreams; but that in these dreams, her own lineaments had smiled upon me; and hence the impulse which had sent me roving after the substance of this spiritual image.
>
> And true it was to say so; and right it was to swear it, upon her white arms crossed. For oh, Yillah; were you not the earthly semblance of that sweet vision, that haunted my earliest thoughts? (LI, 140)

Recognizing that Yillah's "mystical" origin is incompatible with his material one, at first Taji is driven to assume a fictitious identity. As Yillah draws him deeper and deeper into the world of dreams, however, the role of demi-god seems less and less a fiction, until finally he reaches a point where "her dreams seemed mine" (141). This apparently authentic movement by Taji toward the world of dreams is matched by a counter-motion on the part of Yillah. At first she too sees herself as a prisoner of time. Her destiny as well as her magical origins have been revealed to her by the prophetic Aleema. Having miraculously sprung from the sea, she is doomed to descend in a whirlpool, an offering to the gods of Redaidee. Because she views her life as predestined, the circumstances of her history are not "narrated as past events; she merely recounted them as impressions of her childhood, and of her destiny yet unaccomplished" (XLIV, 123). "Her fabulous past was her present" (140).

Taji's discovery and rescue of Yillah, then, seems to have accomplished a double purpose. By finding the "substance of this spiritual image" that had "haunted my earliest thoughts," he has broken out of a life of circular monotony and also has saved Yillah from a similar slavery to the tyranny of time. His escape from the material world is matched by her rescue from a wholly mystical one, and an important balance seems maintained as they live together in the allegorical Mardi, an imaginative world existing midway between the two realms and continuing elements of both. "We lived and we loved; life and love were united; in gladness glided our days" (141).

The experience of Paradise on earth, however, is a momentary illusion. Yillah's angelic qualities are unable to survive her contact with the all too human Taji. With the "extinguishment in her heart of the notion of her own spirituality" (141) comes her capture and destruction by Hautia, dark goddess of the sensual and material. With her loss comes Taji's decision to "rove throughout all Mardi" (LXIV, 172) in search of her. "The dawn of day is passed, and Mardi lies all before us: all her isles, and all her lakes; all her stores of good and evil" (LXVI, 176).

True to Hawthorne's description of the realm of Romance, Mardi, "the world of mind," is a meeting place of the "Actual and Imaginary," a place where each may "imbue itself with the nature of the other." As Taji's experiences suggest, however, Melville regards this union as momentary and destructive. After being touched by the Actual Yillah is inextricably bound to the sensual Hautia, who is herself a fallen angel. Taji, kissed by the dream, is paradoxically doomed to the endless circularity he had initially sought to escape. His commitment to the lost Yillah makes him as "fixed as fate." He is destined to an endless circular pursuit of Yillah, himself pursued by Hautia: "Yillah I sought; Hautia sought me" (CXCI, 569).

The extent to which Taji's quest is the exploration of an aesthetic problem does not become completely clear until the narrator's relationship to the action is understood. Since the narrative method of *Mardi* is based on the recollecting of past fantasies, Taji is presented to the reader as a portrait of the dreamer as a young man. Superimposed on the account at the time of action (Taji's voyage into the world of dreams) is the drama of the narrator's self-conscious creation of it. Consequently, the reader is asked to consider simultaneously two levels of aesthetic action. The relationship between these two planes is at once confusing and of crucial importance. Much of the confusion derives from the fact that once the voyage through Mardi begins, Taji's quest—which until this point has been the center of interest—becomes of secondary importance. The reader is reminded that the search continues in a series of widely scattered chapters describing the maidens of Hautia and the pursuing avengers. Primary attention, however, is given the characters of Yoomy, Babbalanza, Media, and Mohi and the land through which they voyage in their quest of earthly perfection.

With this decrease in young Taji's importance comes an apparent shift in narrative point of view. At times the reader loses all sense of a self-conscious narrator engaged in the act of recollecting. The "I" form shift to the less personal "we." The voice takes on a tone of detached disinterestedness. Even Taji is sometimes referred to in the third person. At several points, however, the self-conscious narrator inexplicably returns to make subjective comments on the drama both at the time of action and at the time of writing.

There is, however, a method in this narrative madness. Much of the confusion can be dissipated if we realize that the narrator's description of Taji's journey into the world of dreams triggers a corresponding movement at the time of writing. As the book moves further and further away from its factual beginnings, the distinctions which the narrator has made between past and present gradually dissolve until *Mardi* becomes not only an account of past dreaming but an account of present dreaming as well. While feasting in Willamilla with Donjalolo, the young Taji is overcome by the "sedative fumes" of incense. "Steeped in languor, I strove against it long; essayed to struggle out of the enchanted mist. But a syren hand seemed ever upon me, pressing me back" (LXXXIV, 228).

The reader, well aware of the young man's susceptibility to dreaming, pays little attention to this passage until the same action is repeated by the narrator at time of writing: "As in dreams I behold thee again, Willamilla! as in dreams, once again I stroll through thy cool shady groves, oh fairest of the valleys of Mardi! the thought of that mad merry feasting steals over my soul till I faint" (LXXXV, 229). The narrator's situation here seems similar to that of Bill Marvel and Ned Ballad aboard the "Arcturion." The beginning and end of his story dovetail into each other, and he is deafened by the echoes of his own song. The occurrence of passages in the present tense along with the occasional third-person references to Taji imply that the narrator, like Yillah, must tell his story as "impressions of [his] childhood, and of [his] destiny as yet unaccomplished" (XLIV, 123). "All, all recur" (LXXXIV, 225) as he engages in the act of recollecting until it seems that his "past was [his] present." His dreams, initially written down in the form of recollections, tend to feed back into the present, interfuse it with further dreams, and stimulate him to act out everything all over again. His "last limit" is his "everlasting beginning" (LXXV, 202).

Some of the implications of this narrative circularity are explored in the important chapter "Dreams," which is placed almost in the center of the book. It is here that the narrator attempts to define the precise relationship between himself and the book that he writes:

> Dreams! dreams! golden dreams: endless, and golden, as the flowery prairies, that stretch away from the Rio Sacramento, in whose waters Danae's shower was woven;—prairies like rounded eternities: jonquil leaves beaten out; and my dreams herd like buffaloes, browsing on to the horizon, and browsing on round the world; and among them, I dash with my lance, to spear one, ere they all flee. (CXIX, 316)

This portrait of the artist as dreamer provides the enclosing frame into which the rest of the dream motifs in the book fit. Mardi and its inhabitants, Taji, the image of the narrator's past dreaming, and Yillah, the ultimate goal of all dreams, have their being within the pregnant imagination of the narrator. The precise nature of this center of creativity is the subject not only of this chapter but of the novel as well.

> And far in the background, hazy and blue, their steeps let down from the sky, loom Andes on Andes, rooted on Alps; and all round me, long rushing oceans. . . .
> But far to the South, past my Sicily suns and my vineyards, stretches the Antarctic barrier of ice: a China wall, built up from the sea. . . . Deathful, desolate dominions those. . . .
> But beneath me, at the Equator, the earth pulses and beats like a warrior's heart; till I know not, whether it be not myself.
>
> .   .   .   .   .
>
> In me, many worthies recline, and converse. I list to St. Paul who argues the doubts of Montaigne; Julian the Apostate cross-questions Augustine. . . . My memory is a life beyond birth; my memory, my library of the Vatican, its alcoves all endless perspectives, eve-tinted by cross-lights from Middle-Age oriels. (316–18)

Within the mind is a universe of intense activity and energy. Time is not experienced as a monotonous succession of moments. Like mighty rivers, past and present flow together, making one rushing ocean. Here there is freedom from both time and space. One can move in an instant from the Amazon to the Mississippi and listen simultaneously to both Homer and Ossian. It is, of course, the memory which makes this radical freedom possible by creating an inner panoramic landscape. Like a library it allows access to all times and places.

As was the case with Taji's experience with Yillah, however, close association with this ideal world brings enslavement rather than freedom:

> My cheek blanches white while I write; I start at the scratch of my pen; my own mad brood of eagles devours me; fain would I unsay this audacity; but an iron-mailed hand clenches mine in a vice, and prints down every letter in my spite. Fain would I hurl off this Dionysius that rides me; my thoughts crush me down till I groan; in far fields I hear the song of the reaper, while I slave and faint in this cell. The fever runs through me like lava; my hot brain burns like a coal; and like many a monarch, I am less to be envied, than the veriest hind in the land. (CXIX, 318–19)

As Babbalanja reveals in his discussion of the great artist Lombardo, the writer is driven to activity by two important forces, "a full heart:—brimful, bubbling, sparkling," and the necessity of bestirring himself "to procure his yams" (CLXXX, 521). The "iron-mailed hand" of inspiration is necessity. This is the force which plunges "spur and rowel" into the writer and "churn[s] him into consciousness," (522). At the very center of the creative act is an almost unbearable tension between the freedom of the inner world and the restrictions of the outer.

This conflict has an unavoidable effect on the work of art. What the writer experiences as a rich and meaningful totality must be articulated as episode and fragment. The Koztanza, the great work of Lombardo, "lacks cohesion; it is wild, unconnected, all episode" because the world itself is "nothing but episodes; valleys and hills; rivers, digressing from plains; vines, roving all over" (CLXXX, 526–27). The literary work can never be more than "a poor scrawled copy of something within" (531). As Media, one of the "imaginary beings" (527) in the narrator's own Koztanza, remarks, "though in your dreams you may hie to the uttermost Orient, yet all the while you abide where you are . . . you mortals dwell in Mardi, and it is impossible to get elsewhere" (CXX, 320). If it is "vanity . . . to seek in nature for positive warranty to these aspirations of ours" (LXIX, 184), it is equally illusory to expect to find justification in the work of art. "Things visible are but conceits of the eye: things imaginative, conceits of the fancy. If duped by one, we are equally duped by the other" (XCIII, 248).

The inner world of dreams turns out to be as deceptive as the external "world of lies." Time reigns supreme in both: "duration is not of the future, but of the past . . . whence, the vanity of the cry for any thing alike durable and new; and the folly of the reproach—Your granite hath come from the old-fashioned hills" (LXXV, 200-1). Because the whole material universe is the product of an "Ineffable Silence" (202), time is motion from nothing to nothing. Each man is "death alive," for he carries his skeleton around with him, although it is hidden by "nature's screen." "Backward or forward, eternity is the same; already we have been the nothing we dread to be" (LXXVIII, 208). For this reason man is most himself when he "sleep[s] and dream[s] not" (CXLIII, 398). Like the God of creation, "truth is voiceless" (XCIII, 248). Hence the "great Art of Telling the Truth" is finally self-defeating. "The whole story is told in a title-page. An exclamation point is entire Mardi's autobiography" (CLXXVI, 510).

Both Taji, inhabitor of the world of romance, and the narrator, creator of that world, illustrate the truth of man's subjection to the tyranny of time. The youthful pursuer of dreams becomes the "unreturning wanderer" (CXCV, 579) and the mature writer a "seeker, not a finder yet," ("HHM," 547). The narrator's statement of method ("Oh, reader, list! I've chartless voyaged" [MCLXIX, 487]), like his inability to maintain a distinction between past and present, dramatizes the extent of his failure as an artist: "But fiery yearnings their own phantom-future make, and deem it present. So, if after all these fearful, fainting trances, the verdict be, the golden haven was not gained;—yet, in bold quest thereof, better to sink in boundless deeps, than float on vulgar shoals; and give me, ye gods, an utter wreck, if wreck I do" (488). Taji's decision, at the end of the book, to continue his useless search for Yillah—"Now, I am my own soul's emperor; and my first act is abdication" (CXCV, 580)—is clearly parallel to the narrator's courting of literary chaos in the above passage. As the narrative method of the book illustrates, the narrator is bound to his past and doomed to repeat it. The future produced by man's "fiery yearnings" is indeed a phantom one, a ghostly apparition leading back to a past that is never really dead. It is no accident that the narrator seems finally to be destined for that "sailor's grave" that he had thought he had eluded by "quitting the Arcturion" (VII, 22).

iii

With its suggestions of the writer's defeat by the world of lies, *Mardi* looks beyond the deep but good-natured cynicism of the verbose Ishmael toward the darker, more appalling visions of the narrators of *Pierre* and *The Confidence-Man*. Melville, faced with the problem of providing for himself and family, is denied the chance of pursuing immediately the implications of *Mardi*. The iron hand of necessity drives him in another direction.

But I hope I shall never write such a book [*Redburn*] again—Tho' when a poor devil writes with duns all round him, & looking over the back of his chair—& perching on his pen & diving in his inkstand—like the devils about St: Anthony—what can you expect of that poor devil?—What but a beggarly "Redburn"! And when he attempts anything higher—God help him & save him! for it is not with a hollow purse as with a hollow balloon—for a hollow purse makes the poet *sink* —witness "Mardi." But we that write & print have all our books predestinated—& for me, I shall write such things as the Great Publisher of Mankind ordained ages before he published "The World"—this planet, I mean—not the Literary Globe.— What a madness & anguish it is, that an author can never—under no conceivable circumstances—be at all frank with his readers.— Could I, for one, be frank with them—how would they cease their railing—those at least who have railed. (L, 95–96)

Both *Redburn* and *White Jacket* are regarded as "two jobs, which I have done for money—being forced to it, as other men are to sawing wood" (*L*, 91). Nevertheless, as Ishmael understands, "chance, free will, and necessity—no wise incompatible —all interweavingly [work] together" (*M-D*, XLVII, 213). Although Melville is prevented from "writing the kind of book I would wish to; yet, in writing these two books, I have not repressed myself much—so far as *they* are concerned; but have spoken pretty much as I feel" (*L*, 92). Although deterred by necessity from being totally frank with his readers, he finds a way to leave "free will still free to ply her shuttle between given threads" (*M-D*, XLVII, 213). He develops the double-edged irony which we associate with his later and greater fiction, an irony which was finally to lead him to regard the artist as a confidence man, a dealer in double meanings. After *Mardi* his books became less direct and less frank, more obviously works of art.

Redburn is a deceptively simple book. On the surface it seems a traditional story of innocence and experience. A sudden reversal in family fortune forces a naïve young man to earn his way in the world. He goes to sea as a "boy" on a merchant ship, makes a predictable discovery of injustice and evil, and returns home knowing a great deal about himself and the world. This familiar picaresque theme and structure, however, is complicated in at least one important way. The distance between the young man who leaves home at the beginning of the novel and the one who returns at the end is paralleled by the distance between the latter and the mature narrator. The time-of-action voice never merges with the time-of-writing voice as it does in *Great Expectations* and most other picaresque first-person narratives. As the title of the book makes clear and as the reader is reminded several times during the story, *Redburn* is an account of a "first voyage." The narrator, "having passed through far more perilous scenes than any narrated in this, *My First Voyage*" (LXII, 301), sees from a distance not only the beginning but also the end of his voyage.

For this reason the self-directed irony so obvious early in the novel does not disappear but merely shifts its emphasis.

Redburn, it is important to remember, is the *"Confessions* and *Reminiscences* of the Son-of-a-Gentleman in the Merchant Service" (italics mine). The act of reminiscing implies a continuity of self. The "I" which is remembering is ineluctably linked to the "I" which is the object of the memory. Confession, on the other hand, has traditionally required a point outside of the stream of time from which the self can be contemplated and analyzed. To confess and accept a past guilt is to imply the assumption of a new level of awareness, if not a new self. The necessary gap between past and present, the old and the new selves, is insisted upon by the narrator when he writes that "many years have elapsed, ere I have thought of bringing in my report" (XLI, 193). His ironic vision is to be distinguished from that of his younger self, which was "blind to the real sights of this world; deaf to its voice; and dead to its death" (LVIII, 282).

Like Melville's other youthful heroes, Redburn confuses experience and adventure. He views the world rationalistically as a place where exploration and discovery lead inevitably to educational adventure. Foreign lands possess "a strange, romantic charm" (I, 1) because they promise answers to all the mysterious problems of the present. Travel will enable him "to read straight along without stopping, out of that book [a copy of d'Alembert in French], which now was a riddle to every one in the house" (5). He is, indeed, so certain of the import of his journey that he is able at the beginning to anticipate his triumphant return home: "As years passed on, this continual dwelling upon foreign associations, bred in me a vague prophetic thought, that I was fated, one day or other, to be a great voyager; and that just as my father used to entertain strange gentlemen over their wine after dinner, I would hereafter be telling my own adventures to an eager auditory" (6).

Redburn plans to live his life as a story he is telling. Like a hero from an eighteenth-century novel, his journey into the world is to result in the discovery of his selfhood and lead him back to his rightful place in a stable society. He lives from the beginning not in experience but within the pages of books in his father's library and behind the paintings which hang on the walls. Most effective in formulating the impression of the world of adventure which awaits him, however, is an old-fashioned glass ship:

> But that which perhaps more than anything else, converted my vague dreamings and longings into a definite purpose of seeking my fortune on the sea, was an old-fashioned glass ship. . . .
>
>   ·   ·   ·   ·   ·
>
> In the first place, every bit of it was glass, and that was a great wonder of itself; because the masts, yards, and ropes were made to resemble exactly the corresponding parts of a real vessel that could go to sea. She carried two tiers of black guns all along her two decks; and often I used to try to peep in at the portholes, to see what else was inside; but the holes were so small, and it looked so very dark indoors, that I could discover little or nothing; though, when I was very little, I made no doubt, that if I could but once pry open the hull, and break the glass all to pieces, I would infallibly light upon something wonderful. . . . And often I used to feel a sort of insane desire to be the death of the glass ship, case, and all, in order to come at the plunder. . . . (6–7)

The glass ship is a perfect symbol both for Redburn's great expectations and for his eventual disillusionment. This "curious ship" which is the "undisputed mistress of a green glassy sea" (7, 8) suggests permanence and stability. With its pure and rigid lines it is a falsification of a world where things are heaped up and confused. To the child its careful design seems to hide and protect some wonderful treasure, the cause and essence of its attractive form. "Indoors," however, is no plunder but the same darkness which is found behind all of society's empty forms. Like Captain Riga's fine clothes and civilized manners which are discarded the moment the "Highlander" sails, the glass ship will not bear the test of experience.

We have her yet in the house, but many of her glass spars and ropes are now sadly shattered and broken,—but I will not have her mended; and her figure-head, a gallant warrior in a cocked-hat, lies pitching headforemost down into the trough of a calamitous sea under the bows—but I will not have him put on his legs again, till I get on my own; for between him and me there is a secret sympathy; and my sisters tell me, even yet, that he fell from his perch the very day I left home to go to sea on this *my first voyage*. (8)

The young Redburn's introduction to experience reveals the lie implicit in the construction of the glass ship. Like all other human creations, including social and religious institutions, it does not impose a structure on the world outside of man but forms an illusory veneer which is inevitably destroyed by the chaos it attempts to hide. The mature narrator's refusal to repair the ship until he finds some order in his own experience is a measure of his grasp of its symbolic implications. Indeed, his entire account of his youthful journey to Liverpool may be seen as a commentary on the symbolic object which instigates it.

Although the young Redburn begins his journey as a social outcast, with the "scent and savor of poverty" (II, 10) upon him, he retains a belief in the stability and predictability of experience. As the nephew of a senator and the son of a wealthy merchant, he feels that his present condition is merely temporary. By the use of ingenuity and effort he hopes to regain his rightful place near the top of the social hierarchy. Education furnishes the means for conquering experience.

Soon after beginning his voyage he puts his plan into effect by reading Adam Smith's *The Wealth of Nations*, hoping that it will teach him "the true way to retrieve the poverty of my family, and again make them all well-to-do in the world" (XVIII, 83). Repeating his childish mistake with the glass ship, he assumes that within the body of the book "lay something like the philosopher's stone, a secret talisman, which would transmute even pitch and tar to silver and gold" (83). However, instead of discovering some "grand secret," he is made "dull and stupid" (84) by a collection of meaningless facts. The book apparently has no relevance to experience, and, with the aid of some padding, it is turned into a convenient pillow.

As useless as *The Wealth of Nations* is another book which the narrator discusses in connection with its more practical counterpart. The *Bonaparte Dream Book*, owned by a sailor named Jack Blunt, represents another attempt to explain and control experience:

The magic of it lay in the interpretation of dreams, and their application to the foreseeing of future events; so that all preparatory measures might be taken beforehand; which would be exceedingly convenient, and satisfactory every way, if true. The problems were to be cast by means of figures, in some perplexed and difficult way, which, however, was facilitated by a set of tables in the end of the pamphlet, something like the Logarithm Tables at the end of Bowditch's Navigator. (87–88)

Unfortunately, the *Dream Book* is also a failure. One night while Blunt is trying to interpret a wonderful dream, the "Highlander" almost collides with another ship. The possibility that two ships could accidentally meet on the "broad boundless sea" and the men "suddenly encounter a shock unforeseen, and go down, foundering, into death" (XIX, 91) points to the uselessness of human measurements and calculations and makes Blunt and his *Dream Book* absurd.

Although young Redburn discards Adam Smith and sees through Blunt's pamphlet, he retains his faith in another kind of dream book. At the center of the novel is a chapter entitled "Redburn Grows Intolerably Flat and Stupid Over Some Outlandish Old Guide Books." Here the narrator reveals that much of his youth had been spent in reading European and English guide books. Although he mentions several, the one with the most suggestive title is *Voyage Descriptif et Philosophique de l'Ancien et du Nouveau Paris: Miroir Fidèle. All* guide books profess to be faithful mirrors of reality and hence reliable guides to experience. Like Blunt's dream book, they apparently allow one to prepare for anticipated encounters with the world. Experience, the guide books suggest, can cause few problems if one has a map to follow.

It is by the use of another guide book, *The Picture of Liverpool*, that Redburn hopes to experience in an orderly and meaningful way the world of Liverpool which (rather than Paris) is his destination. Complete with a short history, population tables, and pictures of all important buildings and monuments, the book professes to be a "Stranger's Guide and Gentleman's Pocket Companion" (XXX, 139). After carefully studying its pages, the young hero—stranger and gentleman—feels confident of his ability to conquer the city:

> In imagination, as I lay in my berth on ship-board, I used to take pleasant afternoon rambles through the town. . . . I began to think I had been born in Liverpool, so familiar seemed all the features of the map. And though some of the streets there depicted were thickly involved, endlessly angular and crooked, like the map of Boston, in Massachusetts, yet, I made no doubt, that I could march through them in the darkest night, and even run for the most distant dock upon a pressing emergency. (XXXI, 145)

Because Redburn's copy of *The Picture of Liverpool* is a special annotated edition, it enables him not only to anticipate and prepare for future events but also to relate them to a meaningful past. The book belonged to his dead father and thus contains a complete itinerary of an earlier visit to Liverpool; in addition, the flyleaves are filled with childish scrawls (*"drawn at the age of three years," "executed at the age of eight"* [XXX, 137]) which mark the young man's own growth and development. Hence as he prepares to explore Liverpool with his guide book in hand, he hopes that by following in his father's footsteps he will at once complete his own maturation and successfully recapture the past.

Redburn's dreams and illusions are quickly and systematically destroyed. Experience shows *The Picture of Liverpool* to be another version of the *Bonaparte Dream Book*. Not only does it fail to prepare him for the poverty, vice, and inhumanity that he encounters, but it also proves to be an ineffective guide. The "endlessly angular and crooked" streets of the city are shown to be metaphors for experience itself, as the young man becomes hopelessly lost and confused. "The thing that had guided the father, could not guide the son" (XXXI, 150).

Here, now, . . . thought I, learn a lesson, and never forget it. This world, my boy, is a moving world; its Riddough's Hotels are forever being pulled down; it never stands still; and its sands are forever shifting. This very harbor of Liverpool is gradually filling up. . . . And, Wellingborough, as your father's guide-book is no guide for you, neither would yours . . . be a true guide to those who come after you. Guide-books, Wellingborough, are the least reliable books in all literature; and nearly all literature, in one sense, is made up of guide-books. . . . Every age makes its own guide-books, and the old ones are used for waste paper. But there is one Holy Guide-Book, Wellingborough, that will never lead you astray, if you but follow it aright. . . . (150–51)

Although Redburn has gained an important insight into the nature of experience, he fails, at this point, to grasp the full implications of his knowledge. Like Blunt, he believes that "they have plenty of squalls here below, but fair weather aloft." As Jackson cynically observes, this is an idea which might have come from the "silly Dream Book" (XXII, 99). The Bible, like all other guide books, assumes the necessity and validity of the quest. Man's end is knowledge and his means the journey of education. But within a shifting, turning world where everything is discontinuous, any sense of spatial and temporal progression is an illusion. So it is that the mature narrator, remembering the earlier failure of the guide book, is "filled with a comical sadness at the vanity of all human exaltation" (XXX, 142–43). He knows that "he who lives in a nut-shell, lives in an epitome of the universe, and has but little need to see beyond him" (XLI, 195).

As the novel's heavily ironic tone makes clear, Redburn's experiences aboard the "Highlander" and in Liverpool call into question all of his middle-class Protestant assumptions. His loss of membership in the "Juvenile Total Abstinence Association" (VIII, 40) and the "Anti-Smoking Society" (IX, 44) is followed by a more serious confusion when he is confronted with Jackson's atheistic misanthropy. Like Bland, Ahab, and Claggart, Jackson is a man who has faced the truth in his "own proper character" and has been driven mad. There is "more woe than wickedness about the man; and his wickedness seemed to spring from his woe" (XXII, 100).

The inhumanity, poverty, and evil which have driven Jackson mad pose a positive threat to Redburn: "at last I found myself a sort of Ishmael in the ship, without a single friend or companion; and I began to feel a hatred growing up in me against the whole crew—so much so, that I prayed against it, that it might not master my heart completely, and so make a fiend of me, something like Jackson" (XII, 60). It is Redburn's faith in the "Holy Guide-Book" which protects him from the truth implicit in Jackson's madness. His Ishmaelism is momentary and inauthentic, and he anticipates his return home apparently wiser but basically unchanged.

The narrator, however, separated from his younger self by many years and several voyages, is engaged in the creation of a special guide book designed to reveal the illusory nature of all dream books. The precise nature of this "report," which is brought in after "so many years have elapsed" (XLI, 193), is best described by the narrator in connection with his reminiscences of Harry Bolton. It is he who accompanies Redburn in his return trip from Liverpool and serves as a mirror in which he can see a reflection of his earlier naïve self. Although dead at time of writing, Harry returns to take his place in the narrator's account of his first voyage:

But Harry! you live over again, as I recall your image before me. I see you, plain and palpable as in life; and can make your existence obvious to others. Is he, then, dead, of whom this may be said?

But Harry! you are mixed with a thousand strange forms, the centaurs of fancy; half real and human, half wild and grotesque. Divine imaginings, like gods, come down to the groves of our Thessalies, and there, in the embrace of wild, dryad reminiscences, beget the beings that astonish the world.

But Harry! though your image now roams in my Thessaly groves, it is the same as of old; and among the droves of mixed beings and centaurs, you show like a zebra, banding with elks. (L, 243–44)

Harry exists as the "White Doe of Truth" in a fictional forest inhabited by the strange offspring of memory and imagination, for it is his artistic resurrection which allows both the narrator and reader a momentary glimpse of the truth at the heart of the young Redburn's experience. By leaving Harry to shift for himself in the unfamiliar world of New York, Redburn discards his one remaining guide book. Like everyone else in the "wolfish world," he denies his brother, and the book which he writes is a confession of this fact. It is an answer to the unanswered question which ends it: "Harry Bolton was not your brother?" Now fully exposed to the "calamitous sea," Redburn still seeks a way to face the truth of his experiences and to avoid becoming another Jackson. This he manages through his fictive account of his first voyage.

iv

White Jacket, Melville's last experiment with first-person narration before *Moby-Dick*, is the most deceptive of the early novels. As with *Redburn*, its intense inner activity belies its placid surface. At the center of the book is an important tension between what Northrop Frye would call its "hypothetical and assertive elements."[10] Its apparently descriptive and assertive functions initially identify it as propagandistic fiction.

---

[10] *Anatomy of Criticism* (New York, 1966), p. 74.

The concern with representing conditions on a man-of-war and the hope that the representation will result in positive political action suggest that the direction of the book's meaning is outward rather than inward. *White Jacket*, like many other socially oriented quest or journey novels, seems to stress the importance and educational value of experience. The narrator's desire to see "wrong things righted, and equal justice administered to all" (LXXII, 289) apparently justifies both his journey and his book. By acquainting one with evil, experience makes change both desirable and possible.

As with Melville's other fiction, however, *White Jacket*'s landscape is a subjective one. Its ironic mode implies that what it *says* is quite different from what it *means*. As a literary structure, it is grounded in the narrator's use of the ship-world microcosm, a technique which calls the validity of its assertive claims into question. By insisting that the "Neversink" is a "city afloat" (XVIII, 82) and that he portrays *"the world in a man-of-war"* (XXXIX, 158), the narrator is able to evaluate his earlier experience by placing it within a larger structure, but, at the same time, he implies that it cannot be changed. If life on a man-of-war is indeed microcosmic, then talk of reform and change is filled with self-deception:

> As a man-of-war that sails through the sea, so this earth that sails through the air. We mortals are all on board a fast-sailing, never-sinking, world-frigate, of which God was the shipwright; and she is but one craft in a Milky-Way fleet, of which God is the Lord High Admiral. The port we sail from is forever astern. And though far out of sight of land, for ages and ages we continue to sail with sealed orders, and our last destination remains a secret to ourselves and our officers. . . . ("The End," 374–75)

As Lawrence Thompson has suggested, White Jacket is here describing his voyage allegorically as the Christian journey homeward toward God.[11] However, the end of the voyage

[11] *Melville's Quarrel with God* (Princeton, N.J., 1952), p. 94.

does not lead to a new life in a new world but strengthens

one's ties to the old one. Although at the time of writing the narrator is no longer on board the "Neversink," he still rides the other *"never-sinking,* world-frigate" (italics mine). As he relates his past experience, he also describes his present condition: "This man-of-war life has not left me unhardened. I cannot stop to weep over Shenly [a former shipmate who had died] now; that would be false to the life I depict; wearing no mourning weeds, I resume the task of portraying our man-of-war world" (LXXXIII, 325). White Jacket's inability to weep is due as much to the conditions of the world he now inhabits as it is to a commitment to realism in fiction. Like the painter of the head of Medusa, he is sickened "at what I myself have portrayed" because it is so "true to life" (XCI, 363). Nevertheless, he insists that his idealistic motives justify the creation of his artistic monster:

I let nothing slip [about the man-of-war world], however small; and feel myself actuated by the same motive which has prompted many worthy old chroniclers, to set down the merest trifles concerning things that are destined to pass away entirely from the earth, and which, if not preserved in the nick of time, must infallibly perish from the memories of man. Who knows that this humble narrative may not hereafter prove the history of an obsolete barbarism? Who knows that, when men-of-war shall be no more, *White Jacket* may not be quoted to show to the people in the Millennium what a man-of-war was? (LXVIII, 270)

Pretending to forget the implications of the "Neversinks' " name, the narrator ironically anticipates the end of the Christian journey homeward. This irony is strengthened as he considers in greater detail the "trifles" of the never-sinking ship and world. Faced with the incongruity of a captain of a gun who is also a "sincere, humble, believer," he wonders how "those hands of his begrimed with powder, could . . . break that *other* and most peaceful and penitent bread of the Supper" (LXXVI, 307–8). After concluding that "those maxims which, in the hope of bringing about a millennium, we busily teach to the heathen, we Christians ourselves disregard" (308), he points to a discrepancy between the real and ideal which makes a millennium impossible: "In view of the whole present social framework of our world, so ill-adapted to the practical adoption of the meekness of Christianity, there seems almost some ground for the thought, that although our blessed Saviour was full of the wisdom of heaven, yet His gospel seems lacking in the practical wisdom of earth" (308).

White Jacket, like Plotinus Plinlimmon, implies that the conflict between earthly and heavenly wisdom creates a condition where "a virtuous expediency . . . seems the highest desirable or attainable earthly excellence for the mass of men" (*P*, XIV, 252). This realization, like the microcosmic structure, serves to undercut the impassioned calls for social reform found at other places in the novel.

A case in point is the narrator's argument against flogging, which is made from the "lofty mast-head of an eternal principle" (*WJ*, XXXVI, 147). Flogging should be abolished, he argues, "no matter if we have to dismantle our fleets, and our unprotected commerce should fall a prey to the spoiler" (XXV, 146). As subsequent discussion will make clear, in the context of *White Jacket* any argument made from "the mast-head of an eternal principle" is suspect and dangerous. But the irony implicit in the discussion of flogging is due largely to internal contradictions. America, the narrator insists, as the nation of the future, is the "Israel of our time" (XXXVI, 151). With a new political creed of freedom and equality, it is destined to lead the world. However, its practical naval code conflicts with its idealistic political theory. To abolish flogging at the risk of the destruction of the naval and commercial fleets is to destroy the nation's ability to be a leader on the practical level. Strict adherence to a forward-looking political ideal could lead to national self-destruction.

It matters little that White Jacket goes on to show that flogging is ineffectual within the limits of the man-of-war world, since to abolish it for this reason is to remove the symptom, not to cure the disease. To note that men may be governed by the "mere memory of the lash" is but to emphasize the enormous gap between the ideal and the actual. Practical arguments for the abolition of flogging serve only to identify the weakness in the argument from "eternal principle."

The narrator's argument, then, constantly doubles back on itself and ends by ironically destroying the validity of both the social and religious quests. He first pretends to write a book for the people in the Millennium and then proves that the Millennium can never exist. Correspondingly, his pleas for social reform in a man-of-war ship serve only to point to the impossibility of that reform by revealing the existence of a man-of-war world in a man-of-war universe. Since God is the "Lord High Admiral," it is clearly useless for Congress to pass laws designed to change the nature of the man-of-war.

More important than simply following the tricky twists and turns of the narrator's argument is the more difficult task of discovering the motives which underlie this peculiar narrative strategy. As with Melville's earlier first-person narrators, White Jacket's perception at the time of writing has its beginnings in an earlier experience. Like *Typee, Mardi,* and *Redburn, White Jacket* dramatizes the education of the artist, and to understand the scope and implications of the mature vision one must understand its origins.

Because the novel is structured around the creation and destruction of the jacket, the most important difference between the time-of-action and the time-of-writing voices would seem to lie in the fact that the narrator no longer possesses the garment. Nevertheless, its influence lives on, for it furnishes both name and being to the narrator. At some indeterminate time after the end of the voyage and the destruction of the jacket, the narrator still calls himself "White Jacket." For this reason, to understand the narrator is to read the meaning of the jacket.

Critics have found the symbols of *White Jacket*, especially that of the jacket itself, nebulous and inconclusive. The obvious and important questions, why a jacket? and why white? seem unanswered in the book. The novel, however, was published less than one year before *Moby-Dick*, during which time Melville's artistic consciousness must have been developing rapidly, for all the major symbols of *White Jacket*— the maintop, the jacket, the color white— reappear in the later novel, among a host of others, clearly defined and precisely rendered. By using the chapters "The Mast-Head" and "The Whiteness of the Whale" as glosses, it is possible to read the meaning of White Jacket's man-of-war world.

Like the young White Jacket, a proud member of the maintop crew, the young Ishmael also prefers the higher regions of a ship. One important disadvantage of this predilection, however, is, as Ishmael recalls, that the higher regions of the ship are "so sadly destitute of anything approaching to a cosy inhabitiveness, or adapted to breed a comfortable localness of feeling" (*M-D*, XXXV, 153). One apparent solution to this inconvenience is to don a jacket:

To be sure, in cold weather you may carry your house aloft with you, in the shape of a watch-coat; but properly speaking the thickest watch-coat is no more of a house than the unclad body; for as the soul is glued inside of its fleshly tabernacle, and cannot freely move about in it, nor even move out of it, without running great risk of perishing (like an ignorant pilgrim crossing the snowy Alps in winter); so a watch-coat is not so much of a house as it is a mere envelope, or additional skin encasing you. You cannot put a shelf or chest of drawers in your body, and no more can you make a convenient closet of your watch-coat. (*M-D*, XXXV, 153–54)

Like the body, which is a necessary but restricting envelope for the soul, the watch coat at once both protects and confines. To wear the jacket in the masthead is to limit one's freedom of movement, but to go aloft without it is to be exposed to the "inclement weather of the frozen seas" (*M-D*, XXXV, 154). In a man-of-war world loss of freedom is a condition of survival.

The young White Jacket, however, lacks the benefits of Ishmael's wisdom. He designs his jacket with the expectation that it will both keep him warm and increase his freedom of movement:

Now, in sketching the preliminary plan, and laying out the foundation of that memorable white jacket of mine, I had had an earnest eye to all these inconveniences [the lack of privacy and the necessity of keeping all possessions in either one's bag or hammock], and resolved to avoid them. I proposed, that not only should my jacket keep me warm, but that it should also be so constructed as to contain a shirt or two, a pair of trowsers, and divers knick-knacks. . . . With this object, I had accordingly provided it with a great variety of pockets, pantries, clothes-presses, and cupboards.
. . . There were, also, several unseen recesses behind the arras; insomuch, that my jacket, like an old castle, was full of winding stairs, and mysterious closets, crypts, and cabinets. . . . (IX, 47).

The jacket, then, in addition to providing warmth, is intended to furnish its wearer with a way of circumventing the "inconveniences" of the man-of-war world. In attempting to make a convenient house of his jacket, White Jacket seeks a comfortable isolation from the world around him: "Yes: I fairly hugged myself, and revelled in my jacket" (48). But just as the soul cannot move freely within its prison of flesh, neither can the body find comfort and ease while encased by the ponderous jacket. Nature first destroys the young man's self-satisfaction as a rainstorm soaks both himself and the contents of his many pockets. Forced by the storm to spread his possessions on the deck to dry, he exposes the jacket's function to the crew, and, from that point on, he is plagued by pick-pockets.

This initial failure of the jacket is complicated by several more disturbing developments. Because the other sailors in his mess feel that he wears the garment to give himself airs, or perhaps to conceal "pilferings of tidbits," it alienates him from his shipmates. Distinguished by his jacket from the "mob of incognitoes," he is not only an object of suspicion for his peers but an easily identifiable body for officers who want "a man for any particular duty" (XXIX, 124). Hence, the white jacket, which was originally designed as a protection from the inconveniences of the man-of-war world, becomes, ironically enough, the very means of exposing the young man to the troublesome demands of that world.

More serious than any of the inconveniences the jacket causes, however, is the positive threat which it poses to the life of its wearer. Once while meditating in the top he is mistaken for a ghost by the crew, who try to dislodge him by bringing down the rigging; again, near the end of the book, he is shaken from the top of the ship as a result of the jacket's blowing over his head, and he is nearly drowned when its voluminous folds are soaked in the sea.

As the narrator is careful to make clear, the color of the jacket is responsible for most of the trouble which it causes. From the first sentence of the book ("It was not a *very* white jacket, but white enough, in all conscience, as the sequel will show") its whiteness is emphasized. The implications of this emphasis become clear in the narrator's reaction to his first narrow escape from death: " 'Jacket,' cried I, 'You must change your complexion! you must hie to the dyer's and be dyed, that I may live. I have but one poor life, White Jacket, and that life I cannot spare. I cannot consent to die for *you*, but be dyed you must for me. You can dye many times without injury; but I cannot die without irreparable loss, and running the eternal risk' " (XIX, 85). As White Jacket learns, in a man-of-war world paint is a life-preserving commodity. His jacket, which "shines of a night, like a bit of the Milky Way" (85), "shadows forth the heartless voids and immensities of the universe, and thus stabs us from behind with the thought of annihilation" (*M-D*, XLII, 193). Indeed, the color white points to the metaphysical center of the man-of-war world, for, as Ishmael reminds us, "whiteness is not so much a color as the visible absence of color, and at the same time the concrete of all colors" (*M-D*, LXII, 193). The protective colors of the "oft-painted planks" (*WJ*, "The End," 376) of the "Neversink" and the painted jackets and trousers of the sailors are, like those of Ishmael's nature, "but subtle deceits, not actually inherent in substances, but only laid on from without" which could "cover nothing but the charnel-house within" (*M-D*, LXII, 193). Since "but one dab of paint" is able to make "a man of a ghost, and a mackingtosh of a herring-net" (*WJ*, XIX, 86), only an endless supply of this miraculous substance will ensure that the "vast mass of our fabric, with all its storerooms of secrets" (*WJ*, "The End," 376), will forever remain safely hidden beneath gleaming surfaces. The whiteness of the jacket, like that of the great whale, is a reminder of the "palsied universe" (*M-D*, LXII, 194) which lies hidden just beneath the surfaces of all human fabrications, threatening with madness and death those who confront it directly. In a man-of-war world one must either be "dyed" or "die."

While his "jacket of reality" makes the young hero the center of attention and the object of suspicion in a world committed to counterfeiting, it is an aspect of his own blindness which makes it a positive threat to his life. Because of his fondness for the maintop he is constantly endangered by the cumbersome garment. He is determined, however, to remain aloft, for the men of the maintop fancy themselves the social and intellectual superiors of the other sailors. Since they are "high lifted above the petty tumults, carping cares, and paltrinesses of the decks below" (*WJ*, XII, 57), they do not consider themselves a part of the man-of-war world. Freed by their high perch from the dense, evil atmosphere of the deck, they are able to develop a metaphysics which seems to solve the problem of evil:

Besides, though we all abhorred the monster of Sin itself, yet, from our social superiority, highly rarefied education in our lofty top, and large and liberal sweep of the aggregate to things, we were in a good degree free from those useless, personal prejudices, and galling hatreds against conspicuous *sinners*—not *Sin*—which so widely prevail among men of warped understandings, and unchristian and uncharitable hearts. . . . We perceived how that evil was but good disguised, . . . how that in other planets, perhaps, what we deem wrong may there be deemed right; even as some substances, without undergoing any mutations in themselves, utterly change their colour, according to the light thrown upon them. (XLIV, 182–83)

As with the chaplain, who "had drunk at the mystic fountain of Plato" and whose "head had been turned by the Germans," the men of the maintop, although concerned with the "psychological phenomena of the soul, and the ontological necessity of . . . saving it at all hazards" (XXXVIII, 154), are able to ignore the drunkenness, fighting, flogging, and oppression of the main deck. White Jacket, however, wears a garment which reveals the true nature of the "great principle of light" (*M-D*, XLII, 193). But he ignores the truth of his colorless coat, remains faithful to the maintop vision, and almost falls to his death: "Eight bells had struck, and my watchmates had hied to their hammocks . . . and the *top* below me was full of strangers, and still almost one hundred feet above even *them* I lay entranced; now dozing, now dreaming; now thinking of things past, and anon of the life to come" (*WJ*, XIX, 84).

Like Ishmael at that "thought engendering altitude," he is "lulled into . . . an opium-like listlessness of vacant, unconscious reverie" (*M-D*, XXXV, 156). Past and present seem to blend together, as the man-of-war world disappears along with the departed watchmates. But suddenly "like lightning, the yard dropped under me, and instinctively I clung with both hands to the 'tie,' then I came to myself with a rush, and felt something like a choking hand at my throat" (*WJ*, XIX, 84). As with Ishmael's "sunken-eyed young Platonist" (*M-D*, XXXV, 156), the mystical White Jacket's "identity comes back in horror" (157) when the crew, mistaking him for a ghost, tries to shake him from the top.

The white jacket, designed as a protection from the man-of-war world but lacking the necessary coat of paint, serves as a mirror of reality for that world. Seeing in the jacket a true reflection of the carefully concealed truth of their world, the sailors are naturally frightened by the ghostly apparition. And White Jacket, carrying a symbol of truth around with him but living according to the rules of an inner, illusory world, is almost destroyed. As his adventures aloft imply, the idealistic world of the maintop is as fictitious and more dangerous than the painted world of the deck. Although both the colorful philosophy of the top and the painted objects of the deck hide the same colorless center, the latter mode of counterfeiting seems by far the more reliable one.

White Jacket, although dissatisfied with his troublesome garment, is unable to discard it. He cannot get paint to change its color, nor can he face the weather of the Cape without a coat. It is finally destroyed, however, in an act of self-preservation. Blowing up over his head while he is at work in the maintop, it causes him to pitch from the top into the sea. After surviving the fall, he is, for the second time, almost destroyed by his garment. As he tries to swim toward the ship, it pulls him under, and he frees himself only by cutting away the jacket ("as if I were ripping open myself" [*WJ*, XCII, 371]), which finally sinks to the bottom of the sea.

What then of the narrator, who has escaped the jacket but still bears its name? He certainly knows that one cannot survive in a man-of-war world without being covered with its counterfeiting paint. His unusual jacket has demonstrated this. Nevertheless, as chronicler of this world, his primary concern is with the explorations of the darkness of those secret rooms concealed beneath the colorful decks. His dilemma is clear. Those who "refuse to wear colored and coloring glasses upon their eyes" will gaze themselves "blind at the monumental white shroud that wraps all the prospect" (*M-D*, XLII, 194). The head of Medusa cannot be described if it cannot be faced.

White Jacket, however, finds a solution to his problem.

Since in fiction truths may be uttered that it would be all but madness for a man to speak in his own proper character, he resorts to a self-conscious counterfeiting or fictionalizing. In pretending to call for social reform while actually insisting that the nature of reality makes reform impossible, he is hiding his vision of whiteness under the colors of an apparently propagandistic fiction. By self-consciously translating a social and religious fiction into a literary one, he reveals its illusory nature and at the same time avoids the dangers implicit in that revelation.

It is this method of procedure which underlies the metaphoric association of the narrator's man-of-war book with the man-of-war ship and world: "Quoin, the quarter-gunner, was the representative of a class on board the *Neversink* altogether too remarkable to be left astern, without further notice, in the rapid wake of these chapters" (*WJ*, XII, 54). The implications of this apparently commonplace metaphor are broadened and deepened when the narrator insists near the end of the book that "outwardly regarded, our craft is a lie; for all that is outwardly seen of it is the clean-swept deck, and oft-painted planks comprised above the water-line; whereas, the vast mass of our fabric, with all its storerooms of secrets, forever slides along far under the surface" ("The End," 375–76). Although the narrator here is defining the relationship between the man-of-war ship and world, the pun on the word "craft" is a sign that the description fits his verbal ship as well,[12] and the word "fabric" recalls the function of the symbolic jacket. Although he is forced to destroy his "jacket of reality" in order to save himself, the narrator is able to retain and reveal the truth implicit in its white "fabric" by keeping it well below the water line of his fictional ship.

It is no wonder, then, that the narrator finds something in the devious Bland to admire, or that the reader can recognize in Bland's behavior elements of the narrator's literary method:

[12] Thompson also finds this pun important (*ibid.*, p. 94).

but who can forever resist the very Devil himself, when he comes in the guise of a gentleman, free, fine, and frank? Though Goethe's pious Margaret hates the Devil in his horns and harpooneer's tail, yet she smiles and nods to the engaging fiend in the persuasive, winning, oily, wholly harmless Mephistopheles. But, however it was, I, for one, regarded this master-at-arms with mixed feelings of detestation, pity, admiration, and something opposed to enmity. I could not but abominate him when I thought of his conduct; but I pitied the continual gnawing which, under all his deftly donned disguises, I saw lying at the bottom of his soul. I admired his heroism in sustaining himself so well under such reverses. (XLIV, 185)

Bland is an early prefiguration of the more complex and slippery cosmopolitan, and White Jacket himself is an important ancestor of the tricky creator of that "original genius." The methods of *White Jacket* are to lead, finally, to those of *The Confidence-Man*.

III

ISHMAEL AS TELLER: SELF-CONSCIOUS FORM IN *MOBY-DICK*

Queequeg was a native of Kokovoko, an island far away to the West and South. It is not down in any map; true places never are.

Moby-Dick

W ITH ITS PORTRAIT of the artist as counterfeiter, *White Jacket* apparently represents the logical conclusion of Melville's experiments with self-conscious form in the early novels, but the mode is neither fully justified nor completely mastered until *Moby-Dick*. Unlike its predecessors, *Moby-Dick* is almost completely self-contained and self-referring. Although anchored by the weight of its how-to-do-it material, it is always moving away from the objective or factual world and persistently calling attention to itself as fiction.

Ishmael's narrative strategy, as he understands, is grounded in a supreme fiction. He tells the story of his life in the form of interesting adventures, although he is aware that experience is composed of gratuitous events and disconnected sensations without significance or direction. This disturbing truth, which makes an orderly life impossible, usually remains hidden behind the many forms which man imposes on his world, since he convinces himself that they are inherent in the nature of experience itself. However, because the form of *Moby-Dick* is a self-consciously created one, the novel serves to undermine the traditional barriers which man has constructed between himself and his world. Ishmael's creative gestures are a reminder to man that whatever seems stable in experience has been put there by himself. The hierarchical social structure aboard a well-ordered ship, the constructs of science and pseudo-science, pagan and Christian religious systems, even the concepts of space and time—all of the forms which man uses to assure himself that everything which happens follows certain laws—are revealed, in *Moby-Dick*, as "passing fables."

In his short introduction to the whaling extracts which preface the novel Ishmael destroys the reassuring but naïve assumption that the world can be explained and controlled by the collection of its facts and description of its objects. No matter how "authentic" the facts compiled by the "mere painstaking burrower and grubworm of a poor devil of a Sub-Sub" may seem, they cannot be taken for "gospel cetology" (xxxix). As Ishmael will later demonstrate in detail, natural objects are a kind of hieroglyphic writing. Although apparently clear and self-explanatory, they really produce confusion rather than clarity. Their meaning is not to be found in the surfaces which they present to man, but seems to lie enigmatically behind them. You will not solve my mystery by staring at me, they seem to say; to read me you must possess something quite different from a knowledge of my surface.

For Ishmael, knowledge does not result from bringing man face to face with a collection of pure facts. It involves, paradoxically, a turning away from the factual world, a retreat into an imaginary reality where the only visible objects are literary ones, products of the imaginative realm they inhabit. As the Sub-Sub's "commentator," Ishmael seeks a more successful road to truth than those "long Vaticans and street stalls of the earth" through which the Sub-Sub has wandered "picking up whatever random allusions to whales he could anyways find in any book whatsoever, sacred or profane" (xxxix). Truth-telling books, for Ishmael, are not those which are guides to the actual world or are collections of facts about it. The Sub-Sub is mistaken in believing this. Rather, as verbal constructs, meaningful books are products of a mind which has turned away from the chaos and confusion of the world toward a contemplation of its own activity.

Surrounding and structuring Ishmael's encyclopedic treatment of whaling is the metaphor of the whale as book, a device which always serves to remind the reader that he is encountering an imaginative reality which is the invention of an isolated consciousness. Correspondingly, the experiences of Ahab, the young Ishmael, and the rest of the "Pequod"'s crew are not presented as a series of past events but, as the dramatic chapters complete with stage directions and soliloquies suggest, as part of a tragic drama composed by the mature narrator. This great play, moreover, is an obvious spatialization of a series of disconnected sensations and events. Contained within the creative consciousness of Ishmael are several versions of his past self which form an account of a self continuously developing through time. Like the image Narcissus saw in the fountain, Ishmael's inner exploration is the "key to it all." But because he seeks the "ungraspable phantom of life" (I, 3) in the mirror of art rather than in nature, choosing the role of teller rather than actor, he avoids the fatal plunge of Narcissus.

i. Ishmael as Teller

Most of the first chapter of *Moby-Dick* is, significantly, in the present tense. In the first sentence of the novel the reader is introduced to the voice of the storyteller: "Call me Ishmael. Some years ago—never mind how long precisely—having little or no money in my purse, and nothing particular to interest me on shore, I thought I would sail about a little and see the watery part of the world" (1). As Paul Brodtkorb, Jr., has noted,[1] it is significant that the narrator does not say that his name *is* Ishmael. The reader is invited to share an experience with someone who apparently, for reasons of his own, has chosen to conceal his identity behind an unlikely Biblical pseudonym. The narrator's motives do not remain wholly mysterious, however, if they are seen in the context of Melville's theory of fiction as expressed in his Hawthorne essay. For Melville the name "Ishmael" has important literary as well as Biblical associations. Its use by Cooper, Byron, Carlyle, and other nineteenth-century writers gives it overtones which make it especially useful to a man who believes that the "names of all fine authors are fictitious ones." By taking another name the author hopes to escape the tie which binds him to the "world of lies." In assuming a new name, especially one as heavily allusive as Ishmael, he leaves behind his "own proper character" along with the discarded patryonym and takes on a whole new set of possibilities—in effect, occupies a new world. Since this world, like the name which invokes it, is

---

[1] *Ishmael's White World* (New Haven, Conn., 1965), p. 123. Brodtkorb's analysis centers, as mine does, on Ishmael's function as storyteller.

an obviously literary one, the reader, from the beginning, sees the narrator within a clearly defined context.

Nevertheless, the affable invitation to the reader in the book's first sentence, with the desire for intimacy which it implies, suggests that Ishmael has been wrongly named. The "splintered heart and maddened hand" (X, 50) of the outcast Ishmael are in evidence neither in the first sentence nor anywhere else in the first chapter. Although the chapter title, "Loomings," suggests that it will deal with serious or even tragic matters, such is not the case. The narrator possesses an ironic, almost comic, vision which seems to deny the authenticity of Ishmael-ism:

> What of it, if some old hunks of a sea-captain orders me to get a broom and sweep down the decks? What does that indignity amount to, weighed, I mean, in the scales of the New Testament? Do you think the archangel Gabriel thinks anything the less of me, because I promptly and respectfully obey that old hunks in that particular instance? Who aint a slave? Tell me that. Well, then, however the old sea-captains may order me about—however they may thump and punch me about, I have the satisfaction of knowing that it is all right; that everybody else is one way or other served in much the same way—either in a physical or metaphysical point of view, that is; and so the universal thump is passed round, and all hands should rub each other's shoulder-blades, and be content. (I, 4)

In this passage the narrator emphasizes an aspect of the human condition which binds men together. As is not the case with his Biblical namesake and the related figures of Cain, Job, and Jonah, Ishmael sees his alienation as one small manifestation of the "universal thump" rather than as a fate uniquely his own. Although he is "quick to perceive a horror," he, unlike Ahab, is capable of being social with it, "since it is but well to be on friendly terms with all the inmates of the place one lodges in" (6). Inhabiting a world which, like the "sharkish sea" (XXXVIII, 167), has unknown terrors "treacherously hidden beneath the loveliest tints of azure" (LVIII, 274), a world where all men are cannibals, Ishmael exalts the pleasures of food, drink, and good companionship and jokingly maintains that "I myself am a savage; owning no allegiance but to the King of the Cannibals; and ready at any moment to rebel against him" (LVII, 270). No Byronic hero, he is an outcast in name only.

The verbal identity assumed by the narrator of *Moby-Dick*, then, seems a paradoxical one. He deliberately chooses a name with a rich Biblical and literary tradition and then goes on to deny the identity attributed to him by the name. For Ishmael identity is not imposed on man from the outside by a name or by anything else. Like the other fictitious forms with which man surrounds himself, a name appears at first glance to possess the dignity of an essence. Because it seems to await man in experience, to have been there before he knew it, he sometimes mistakenly assumes that his destiny and reality are defined by it.[2] Ishmael's name, however, is a self-assumed one, a mask which at the most serves to define a role he had once chosen to play. Since he is at the time of writing a teller rather than an actor, his name is no more than a verbal convention: it designates a self which no longer exists. At the time of writing the narrator is *called* Ishmael precisely because he no longer plays the role identified by the name. No longer actor but teller, he names himself in order to reveal that all names are pseudonyms.

By *calling* himself Ishmael, the narrator establishes his identity as a purely verbal one, and then goes on to explore the implications of his act by defining his past in obviously literary terms.

Though I cannot tell why it was exactly that those stage managers, the Fates, put me down for this shabby part of a whaling voy-

[2] I am indebted here to Jean Starobinski's discussion of pseudonymity in "Truth in Masquerade," in *Stendhal: A Collection of Critical Essays,* ed. Victor Brombert (Englewood Cliffs, N.J., 1962), pp. 115–17; translated by B. A. B. Archer from *L'Oeil vivant* (Paris, 1961).

age, when others were set down for magnificent parts in high trag-
edies, and short and easy parts in genteel comedies, and jolly parts
in farces—though I cannot tell why this was exactly; yet, now that I
recall all the circumstances, I think I can see a little into the springs
and motives which being cunningly presented to me under various
disguises, induced me to set about performing the part I did, besides
cajoling me into the delusion that it was a choice resulting from
my own unbiased freewill and discriminating judgment. (I, 5–6)

Ishmael's dramatic metaphor is suggestive because it defines
the origins, quality, and dimensions of the "Pequod"'s world.
The conventions of Shakespearean drama, which are used
throughout the novel, invoke a world where a necessity external to man ("those stage managers, the Fates") provides his
actions with direction and meaning. The tragic world which
Ahab and the young Ishmael inhabit is stable and immutable.
Here careful exploration leads to the revelation of the "springs
and motives" which lie behind human action and the operation
of nature. As actors in a traditional and ritualistic drama they
necessarily follow a set of conventional patterns of behavior.
The many allusions to the incidents and heroes of Biblical
and secular tragedy supply the pattern for the story's plot,
while the use of devices from the epic and drama provide the
elements of its form.

But it is important to note that this traditional world is a
literary one, the product of Ishmael, who, like Shakespeare,
is an actor turned dramatist. The sense of permanence and
stability is illusory because it is the product of a set of fictitious
(because wholly intellectual) bonds which the dramatist uses
to tie together a series of diverse happenings. As the soliloquies,
stage directions, and other devices from Elizabethan drama
suggest, the Fates themselves are but one of a series of dramatic
conventions from which Ishmael constructs his theatrical
world. Time and again, he exercises both "free will" and
"discriminating judgment."

If, then, to meanest mariners, and renegades and castaways, I
shall hereafter ascribe high qualities, though dark; weave round

them tragic graces; if even the most mournful, perchance the most abased, among them all, shall at times lift himself to the exalted mounts; if I shall touch that workman's arm with some ethereal light; if I shall spread a rainbow over his disastrous set of sun; then against all mortal critics bear me out in it, thou just Spirit of Equality, which hast spread one royal mantle of humanity over all my kind! Bear me out in it, thou great democratic God! who didst not refuse to the swart convict, Bunyan, the pale, poetic pearl; Thou who didst clothe with doubly hammered leaves of finest gold, the stumped and paupered arm of old Cervantes. . . . (XXVI, 114)

Placing his discussion within the context of the traditional epic invocation of the muse of inspiration, Ishmael here insists that each sailor who "comes in person on this stage" (CVII, 462) is the product of his art. The words "ascribe," "weave," "touch," and "spread" denote the creative gestures of the poet-dramatist. The metaphors of light and color, however, suggest that, for Ishmael, the invocation is a useful but empty convention. Reversing the Miltonic method, he calls the name but not the meaning.[3] He, not God, is the source of divine "ethereal light" and the creator of the rainbow. For him there is no theater standing behind and supporting his fictional stage but merely a white emptiness. The democratic God to whom he calls is "a circle, whose center . . . is every where, but his circumference . . . is noe where," or in other words a naught or a *no thing*.[4] Like the "Pequod" 's "omnitooled" carpenter who is His portrait, Ishmael's God is a "stript abstract; an unfractioned integral" (464). For this reason his call for inspiration is an ironic shout into emptiness and his art, necessarily, a creation *ex nihilo*.

Even Ahab, the character described by one critic as the

---

[3] In Book 7 of *Paradise Lost*, Milton invokes Urania, the traditional muse of inspiration, but identifies himself as a Christian poet by writing, "the meaning, not the name, I call" (line 5).

[4] As Mansfield and Vincent point out (*M-D*, 665), Melville could have found this traditional metaphor, which seems to collaborate his view of God as a positive absence, in the copy of Sir Thomas Browne's *Pseudodoxia Epidemica* which he borrowed from E. A. Duyckinck.

book's "Alpha and Omega,"[5] owes his existence to the creative voice of Ishmael. In the chapter "The Specksynder," while discussing the nature and extent of the captain's control of the "Pequod"'s crew, Ishmael, fittingly, associates him with the traditional tragic hero:

> For be a man's intellectual superiority what it will, it can never assume the practical, available supremacy over other men, without the aid of some sort of external arts and entrenchments, always, in themselves, more or less paltry and base. This it is, that for ever keeps God's true princes of the Empire from the world's hustings; and leaves the highest honors that this air can give, to those men who become famous more through their infinite inferiority to the choice hidden handful of the Divine Inert, than through their un-doubted superiority over the dead level of the mass. . . . Nor, will the tragic dramatist who would depict mortal indomitableness in its fullest sweep and direct swing, ever forget a hint, incidentally so important in his art, as the one now alluded to. (XXXIII, 144–45)

The realization that the superior man must at times mask himself with the "forms and usages" (144) of the world he despises is of central importance to an understanding of Ahab. In the chapter "The Quarter-Deck"—which begins with stage directions ("Enter Ahab: Then, all")—Ishmael, in his role of tragic dramatist, describes Ahab's use of "external arts and entrenchments" to gain control of the crew. By means of the power of his hypnotizing oratory and the appeals of a gold doubloon and large measures of grog, Ahab is able to command both souls and bodies of the crew, thereby associating himself with the traditional tragic hero.

The world of the "Pequod," structured as it is by Ishmael's self-conscious use of a number of traditional literary conventions, is obviously a fictional one. The characters who walk the decks of the stage-like ship are best described by words which the narrator applies specifically to Starbuck, "whose life for the most part was a telling pantomime of action, and not a tame chapter of sounds" (XXVI, 112). Their world, in

[5] C. N. Stavrou, "Ahab and Dick Again," *TSLL*, 3 (1961–62): 316

other words, is a literary one, and they can be understood only when seen in this context.

Ishmael's artistic task is not completed with the creation of plot, character, and dialogue. Although he uses elements from the drama, he is a novelist and is responsible, too, for the construction of the "one grand stage" where the characters play their "various parts" (CVII, 463). As any reader of *Moby-Dick* is well aware, this "stage" is not limited to the deck of the "Pequod," but in its "comprehensiveness of sweep" includes the "whole universe, not excluding its suburbs" (CIV, 452). At the center of this grand theater is the huge body of the great sperm whale. Having been "before all time" and destined to "exist after all humane ages are over," the "ante-mosaic" whale (454), "in his own osseous post-diluvian reality" (455), is, for Ishmael, that mysterious "it," the "dead, blind wall" of materiality (LXXVI, 335). This silent, heavy, ageless, mysterious mass is the ultimate fact, which man must learn to read and control if he is to survive in the alien world in which he finds himself. For this reason Ishmael regards whaling as both a philosophical and a commercial enterprise. The thinker and the consumer, the philosopher and the technologist, have similar goals. The philosopher is a whaleman because he builds systems with the intention of capturing and assimilating the mysterious other in the net of consciousness. Correspondingly, the commercial whaleman journeys to every corner of the earth seeking to destroy the other and transform it into a product made in man's own image and destined to serve him. It is the whale ship, Ishmael notes, which has been "the pioneer in ferreting out the remotest and least known parts of the earth" (XXIV, 108) and which has provided France, Britain, and America with a large part of their national incomes.

Ishmael, however, views the intellectual, political, and economic history of man as a series of imaginative constructs, each one designed as an attempt to decipher the "hieroglyphical whale." Indeed, the "high and mighty business of whaling" may be regarded "as that Egyptian mother, who bore offspring themselves pregnant from her womb" (107). Since Melville regarded Egypt as the birthplace of the gods, as well as the cradle of civilization, Ishmael's reference to Nut, mother of Isis, Osiris, and Typhon, is especially suggestive.[6] Born in the home of all mythology, the Osiris myth is the first of a number of fictions which attempt to explain the nature of the material world and man's relationship to it. Not surprisingly, Ishmael finds that the whale plays a central role not only in the seminal Egyptian myth but in the later and derivative Hebrew, Hindu, and Christian ones as well.

As he pushes his "researches up to the very spring-head" of whaling, he finds large numbers of "demi-gods and heroes, prophets of all sorts" (LXXXII, 359), all of whom are related in ways which suggest a common origin. After identifying Perseus, son of Jupiter, as the first whaleman, Ishmael goes on to associate the account of the rescue of Andromeda with the stories of Jonah, St. George and the dragon, and Hercules and the whale. This account of the "Honor and Glory of Whaling" fittingly ends with his naming as "whaleman" "the dread Vishnoo, one of the three persons in the godhead of the Hindoos" (362). From whaling, that old Egyptian mother, came the first gods pregnant with other versions of themselves.

It is important, then, that Ishmael announces with considerable gusto, "I am transported with the reflection that I myself belong, though but subordinately, to so emblazoned a fraternity" (359–60). His membership is, of course, a double one. As a "whaleman" he satisfies the primary initiation requirement, but since "the whaleman is wrapped by influences all tending to make his fancy pregnant with many a mighty birth" (LXI, 177), he is, in addition, a "whale author," another child of the old Egyptian mother born pregnant from the womb:

[6] See H. Bruce Franklin's discussion of the function of the Osiris-Typhon myth in *Moby-Dick* in *The Wake of the Gods*, pp. 53–98.

And, as for me, if, by any possibility, there be any as yet undiscovered prime thing in me; if I shall ever deserve any real repute in that small but high hushed world which I might not be unreasonably ambitious of; if hereafter I shall do anything that, upon the whole, a man might rather have done than to have left undone; if, at my death, my executors, or more properly my creditors, find any precious MSS. in my desk, then here I prospectively ascribe all the honor and the glory to whaling. . . . (XXIV, 110)

That the product of Ishmael's whaling experience is a literary one validates his claim of kinship with the "dread Vishnoo." The Hindu god of creation dives to the bottom of the sea in quest of the sacred Vedas, "whose perusal would seem to have been indispensable to Vishnoo before beginning the creation, and which therefore must have contained something in the shape of practical hints to young architects" (LXXXII, 362); and Ishmael, proclaiming himself "the architect, not the builder," swims "through libraries" in the search of an "easy outline" (XXXII, 131) which will enable him to begin his "classification of the constituents of a chaos" (129). The emphasis on books is significant. In both cases the creative act begins not with the material to be shaped but with an exploration of previous verbal plans for creation. Man's creative powers depend on the scope of his reading, and his reading, in turn, is limited to the things he has made. This circular epistemology denies man any "real knowledge" of the whale (129), since it implies that he can never impose his own order on the material world.

Ishmael's creative act, like those which precede it, is purely verbal. He attempts to write the heretofore "unwritten life" of the whale. He knows, however, that this is "a ponderous task; no ordinary letter-sorter in the Post-office is equal to it. To grope down into the bottom of the sea after them; to have one's hands among the unspeakable foundations, ribs, and very pelvis of the world; this is a fearful thing" (131). He recognizes, in other words, the limits of his architectural aspirations. Although he may "stagger . . . under the weightiest words of the dictionary" (CIV, 452), he is merely a "letter-sorter." The foundations of his construct are verbal fictions, since the material ones are unspeakable because unknowable.

So it is that his great "cetological system" not only remains unfinished but refers to nothing outside of itself. The design produced is identical with the method which creates it. By naming the main divisions of his cetological construct "Folio," "Octavo," and "Duodecimo" and calling the smaller units "Chapters," he turns whales into books. Attempting to write the "life" of the whale, he tells instead the life of a book: "And if you descend into the bowels of the various leviathans, why there you will not find distinctions a fiftieth part as available to the systematizer as those external ones already enumerated. What then remains? nothing but to take hold of the whales bodily, in their entire liberal *volume*, and boldly sort them that way. And this is the *Bibliographical* system here adopted" (XXXII, 136; italics mine). As this passage suggests, Ishmael finds it impossible to escape from his library because he tries to organize the whaling world by the same method which he (presumably) has used to order his bookish one. His attempt to "comprehend them all, both small and large" (133) is in fact a literary tour de force. He includes among his list of aliases for the sperm whale "Macrocephalus of the Long Words" (133), glosses over the mystery of the use of the Narwhale's horn with the remark that "it would certainly be very convenient to him for a folder in reading pamphlets" (139), and then goes on to amuse himself with the thoughts of other kinds of horns: "An Irish author avers that the Earl of Leicester, on bended knees, did likewise present to her highness another horn, pertaining to a land beast of the unicorn nature" (139). The phallic jokes, which are found throughout the "whaling materials," are a part of Ishmael's Rabelaisian pose, a literary convention especially popular in mid-nineteenth-century America; and, like the other conventions employed in *Moby-Dick*, it serves to emphasize the self-reflexive quality of the book's world. The jokes force the reader to turn away from the factual starting point (in the above example, the horn of the Narwhale) and to consider instead internal verbal relationships which are "full of Leviathanism, but signifying nothing" (142).

Even at moments of highest inspiration, when he is apparently overwhelmed with the wonders of the whaling world, Ishmael's primary concern is with the act of writing. "Give me a condor's quill! Give me Vesuvius' crater for an inkstand!" he cries, as he tries to "rise and swell" with his subject (CIV, 452). This artistic narcissism is nowhere more obvious than in his detailed descriptions of the sperm whale. As he examines the whale piece by piece—moving gradually from the outside to the inside—his discoveries force him to assume a more and more obviously fictional mode until, finally, he appears as the author of "fish stories."

His investigations, however, from the beginning, are literary rather than scientific, as he demonstrates in his discussion of the "thin, isinglass substance" which covers the body of the whale:

from the unmarred dead body of the whale, you may scrape off with your hand an infinitely thin, transparent substance, somewhat resembling the thinnest shreds of isinglass, only it is almost as flexible and soft as satin; that is, previous to being dried, when it not only contracts and thickens, but becomes rather hard and brittle. I have several such dried bits, which I use for marks in my whalebooks. It is transparent, as I said before; and being laid upon the printed page, I have sometimes pleased myself with fancying it exerted a magnifying influence. At any rate, it is pleasant to read about whales through their own spectacles, as you may say. But what I am driving at here is this. That same infinitely thin, isinglass substance, which, I admit, invests the entire body of the whale, is not so much to be regarded as the skin of the creature, as the skin of the skin, so to speak; for it were simply ridiculous to say, that the proper skin of the tremendous whale is thinner and more tender than the skin of a new-born child. But no more of this. (LXVIII, 304)

Faced with the mystery and wonder of a small piece of that which is not man, Ishmael retreats to the security of his library. Because books are at once material objects and products of consciousness, they provide a security not available in the "whaling world." To write or to read a whaling book is to imply that the whale itself has been assimilated by consciousness and thereby rendered harmless. Surrounded by objects which are extensions of the self and used as an aid for the self's contemplation of its own objects, the small piece of material seems to have lost both its mystery and its uniqueness.

The intellectual hunger which compels Ishmael to try to absorb the whale into his consciousness parallels the physical one which causes Stubb to "feed upon the creature that feeds his lamp, and . . . eat him by his own light" (LXV, 297). Man carves his roast beef with a bonehandled knife and picks his teeth with the feather of the goose he has just devoured for the same reason that Ishmael "reads about whales through their own spectacles." He is motivated by the primitive, cannibalistic belief that whatever he consumes he can control.

"Who is not a cannibal?" (299), asks Ishmael as he contemplates Stubb's meal, thereby implying that he is fully aware of the implications of his own acts. He knows that his whaling books give him neither understanding nor control of the great monster. Although he is able to regard the whale as a vast book, since its skin is "all over obliquely crossed and re-crossed with numberless straight marks in thick array" which are "hieroglyphical," he is unable to read its meaning. Like "those mysterious cyphers on the walls of the pyramids" or "the famous hieroglyphic palisades on the banks of the Upper Mississippi" (LXVIII, 305), the markings on the whale's skin are undecipherable. While phonetic writing suggests that man, in some way, has absorbed and transformed the thing he names, hieroglyphic writing seems merely an attempt at representation and hence is as mysterious as the thing it describes. Like Queequeg, the whale is a "riddle to unfold; a wondrous work in one volume" which is destined to remain "unsolved to the last" (CX, 477).

That technology and science, like the phonetic alphabet, are useless to man when he faces the mystery of the great whale is demonstrated by Ishmael when he turns from a discussion of its skin to a consideration of its head. Assuming the roles of physiognomist and phrenologist, he attempts to read the meaning of the "Battering-Ram." As with the markings on the skin, however, the cranial and facial characteristics of the whale prove undecipherable. All sciences and pseudo-sciences are pure fictions:

> Champollion deciphered the wrinkled granite hieroglyphics. But there is no Champollion to decipher the Egypt of every man's and every being's face. Physiognomy, like every other human science, is but a passing fable. If then, Sir William Jones, who read in thirty languages, could not read the simplest peasant's face in its profounder and more subtle meanings, how may unlettered Ishmael hope to read the awful Chaldee of the Sperm Whale's brow? (LXXIX, 345)

Science, like religion, is a fictive creation of man, born of his attempts to penetrate beneath the surfaces of an enigmatic world— symbolized here by Egypt, birthplace of the gods and of hieroglyphic writing as well. Like a hieroglyph, the whale's "broad firmament of a forehead" is "pleated with riddles," and like the "deified . . . crocodile of the Nile," its "pyramidical silence" indicates that it is tongueless (345). At first glance it seems a reflection of man's consciousness: like a book it presents him with a surface which asks to be read. But this clarity of surface confuses rather than clarifies, "for you see no one point precisely; not one distinct feature is revealed; no nose, eyes, ears, or mouth; no face; he has none, proper" (345). Ishmael's view of the whale as a hieroglyph, then, is a profound comment on both the operation of consciousness and the nature of the material world. It points to man's attempt to make everything an object of consciousness, and, at the same time, suggests that he must necessarily fail because material objects are "dead, blind wall[s]" of silence (LXXVI, 335). They resist the transforming powers of the phonetic alphabet and may be represented only by enigmatic figures.

Although he associates himself with the scientific seekers of truth, Ishmael differs from them in at least one important way. He knows that his system is the result of his turning away from the world rather than of a comprehensive classification of its facts. "Dissect him how I may, then, . . . I know him not, and never will" he writes (376), when confronted by the faceless, tongueless enigma which is the largest, most dangerous thing alive and yet at the same time is a "no thing." "But I cannot completely make out his back parts; and hint what he will about his face, I say again he has no face" (377). Moreover, the deeper he probes into the body of the whale, "using my boat-hatchet and jack-knife, and breaking the seal and reading all the contents" (CII, 445), the more he comes to associate it with absence and silence. Hence he turns away from the enigmatic material world and immerses himself in his own verbal one:

That for six thousand years—and no one knows how many millions of ages before—the great whales should have been spouting all over the sea, and sprinkling and mistifying the gardens of the deep, as with so many sprinkling or mistifying pots; and that for some centuries back, thousands of hunters should have been close by the fountain of the whale, watching those sprinklings and spoutings—that all this should be, and yet, that down to this blessed minute (fifteen and a quarter minutes past one o'clock P.M. of this sixteenth day of December, A.D. 1851), it should still remain a problem, whether these spoutings are, after all, really water, or nothing but vapor—this is surely a noteworthy thing. (LXXXV, 367)

The most striking aspect of this passage is the unusual reference to the exact time of writing, a technique which serves to overshadow the practical problem of determining the nature of the composition of the whale's spoutings with the more immediate concern of literary composition. This is, however, as it should be because the "answer" to the age-old mystery is discovered and justified through literary activity. Since "among whalemen, the spout is deemed poisonous" and is said to be blinding "if the jet is fairly spouted into your eyes," Ishmael recognizes that the "wisest thing the investigator can do . . . is to let this deadly spout alone" (371). For this reason he turns away from the dangerous and mysterious object to a fictional hypothesis about it:

My hypothesis is this: that the spout is nothing but mist. . . . He [the whale] is both ponderous and profound. And I am convinced that from the heads of all ponderous profound beings . . . there always goes up a certain semi-visible steam, while in the act of thinking deep thoughts. While composing a little treatise on Eternity, I had the curiosity to place a mirror before me; and ere long saw reflected there, a curious involved worming and undulation in the atmosphere over my head. The invariable moisture of my hair, while plunged in deep thought, after six cups of hot tea in my thin shingled attic, of an August noon; this seems an additional argument for the above supposition.

And how nobly it raises our conceit of the mighty, misty monster, to behold him solemnly sailing through a calm tropical sea; his vast, mild head overhung by a canopy of vapor. . . . (371–72)

Ishmael has turned from the blinding mists of the sperm whale to the comforting vapors of the mind, from the material object to a literary conceit. Within this purely fanciful realm the mystery may be solved poetically, for here whales are mirror images of man—not merely objects of consciousness, but conscious beings themselves, who present no dangers to the eyes of the man who would read them.

In an even more whimsical mood, Ishmael justifies his knowledge of the skeletal dimensions of the whale by referring to uniquely preserved statistics which he obtained from personal observation of a skeleton on Tranque, one of the Arsacides:

The skeleton dimensions I shall now proceed to set down are copied verbatim from my right arm, where I had them tattooed; as in my wild wanderings at that period, there was no other secure way of preserving such valuable statistics. But as I was crowded for space, and wished the other parts of my body to remain a blank page for a poem I was then composing . . . I did not trouble myself with the odd inches; nor, indeed, should inches at all enter into a congenial admeasurement of the whale. (CII, 448–49)

Here at last Ishmael takes his literary account of the whale to the extreme of a "fish story," as he turns himself into a "wondrous book in one volume." As always, however, his method is a Joycean "joco-serious" one. His identity, like his world, is a purely verbal one; he exists only as the teller of a story —a story which has as its aim the portrayal of the world as it exists beneath man's fictive creations. But how is this to be done when, apparently, what remains after man's veil of forms is lifted is indescribable facelessness and silence? The answer lies in Ishmael's treatment of the great white whale. Unlike whales in general, Moby-Dick has a physical characteristic which may be used as a starting point for the imaginative investigator. Moby-Dick is white.

Whiteness is, first of all, a paradoxical sensible experience. Although nominally a color, it is perceived as "the visible absence of color" (XLII, 193), in the same way that perfect silence is sometimes experienced as the audible absence of sound. In the presence of pure whiteness man does not experience colorlessness abstractly or imaginatively as that which would remain if all colors suddenly disappeared. A confrontation with whiteness is a positive and direct encounter with blankness.

Unlike Conrad's darkness, which it resembles in part, Melville's whiteness initially is experienced as a quality belonging to an object. But, as Ishmael's discussion of this "expressive hue of the shroud" suggests (189), the white object is immediately swallowed up by its color. Whiteness does not serve, as other colors do, to emphasize the thing-ness of objects by calling attention to their forms and textures. Because it is a "visible absence of color," it tends to rob things of their individuality by absorbing their forms into its colorlessness. The white objects in Ishmael's encyclopedic list have their individual forms swallowed up by the color which they all share. It is no accident that the great whale himself is lost in Ishmael's "white-lead chapter about whiteness" (192). Although the first and largest, he is but one of a number of terrifying white objects.

The white object differs from all others in that its meaning does not seem to lie within or behind it. It does not present man with a clearly defined profile which invites him to probe beneath its surface but "by its indefiniteness . . . shadows forth the heartless voids and immensities of the universe" (193). It is a "dumb blankness, full of meaning" precisely because it does not appear to man as an enigmatic hieroglyph. Unlike the gold doubloon and all other colored objects, the white object neither requires nor invites interpretation but, through its "visible absence," seems to threaten the now useless interpreter with destruction. It "stabs" him "from behind with the thought of annihilation" (193).

Whiteness, then, is the "intensifying agent in things the most appalling to mankind" (193) because it is a positive threat to consciousness. Confronted with whiteness, the mind is deprived of its objects and becomes, necessarily, "a blankness in itself" (XLIV, 200). Whiteness is especially terrifying, Ishmael notes, "when exhibited under any form at all approaching to muteness or universality" (XLII, 191). Passivity, rest, and silence are all linked to whiteness, and all are potential threats to the verbal wanderer Ishmael or, for that matter, to every man.

But white objects are more than appalling empty spots in a colored world. They are also an indication, which is even more frightening, that color itself is an illusion:

And when we consider that other theory of the natural philosophers, that all other earthly hues—every stately or lovely emblazoning—the sweet tinges of sunset skies and woods; yea, and the gilded velvets of butterflies, and the butterfly cheeks of young girls; all these are but subtile deceits, not actually inherent in substances, but only laid on from without; so that all deified Nature absolutely paints like the harlot, whose allurements cover nothing but the charnel-house within; and when we proceed further, and consider that the mystical cosmetic which produces every one of her hues, the great principle of light, for ever remains white or colorless in itself, and if operating without medium upon matter, would touch all objects, even tulips and roses, with its own blank tinge—pondering all this, the palsied universe lies before us a leper; and like wilful travellers in Lapland, who refuse to wear colored and coloring glasses upon their eyes, so the wretched infidel gazes himself blind at the monumental white shroud that wraps all the prospect around him. (193–94)

The traditional view of color as the imperfection of white radiance is given here a uniquely Melvilleian twist. The colors of nature (the Many) usually associated with the imperfection and mortality characteristic of earthly existence would seem the logical symbol for the "charnel-house" of this world.[7] For Ishmael, however, disease and death are associated with white light (the One), while color—traditionally understood as the imperfect individualization of the One—is seen as the mask with which white light hides its destructive nature. Colored objects, then, like the attractive but diseased harlot, both allure and destroy. They invite familiarity and plead to be understood, but they threaten with syphilitic blindness and death the man who attempts to know them intimately. To the "wilful travellers" who attempt to read the mysteries with which the world presents them, all objects are in essence white.

Having destroyed his quadrant, which "was furnished with colored glasses" (CXVIII, 493), Ahab, facing the spouting whale for the last time, cries: "I grow blind; hands! stretch out before me that I may yet grope my way" (CXXXV, 563). As Ishmael makes clear in his description of his captain's

[7] For example, see Earl R. Wasserman's discussion of Shelley's use of light and color in *Adonais* in *The Subtler Language* (Baltimore, 1959), pp. 336–42.

frenzied attempts to escape his "vivid dreams of the night" (XLIV, 199), his blindness, like that of the travelers in Lapland, is the result of his "sheer inveteracy of will":

For, at such times, crazy Ahab, the scheming, unappeasedly steadfast hunter of the white whale; this Ahab that had gone to his hammock, was not the agent that so caused him to burst from it in horror again. The latter was the eternal, living principle or soul in him; and in sleep, being for the time dissociated from the characterizing mind, which at other times employed it for its outer vehicle or agent, it spontaneously sought escape from the scorching contiguity of the frantic thing, of which, for the time, it was no longer an integral. But as the mind does not exist unless leagued with the soul, therefore it must have been that, in Ahab's case, yielding up all his thoughts and fancies to his one supreme purpose; that purpose, by its own sheer inveteracy of will, forced itself against gods and devils into a kind of self-assumed, independent being of its own. Nay, could grimly live and burn, while the common vitality to which it was conjoined, fled horror-stricken from the unbidden and unfathered birth. Therefore, the tormented spirit that glared out of bodily eyes, when what seemed Ahab rushed from his room, was for the time but a vacated thing, a formless somnambulistic being, a ray of living light, to be sure, but without an object to color, and therefore a blankness in itself. (199–200)

This difficult and widely discussed passage is of crucial importance in understanding Ahab's relationship to Ishmael's white whale. The captain's determination to "chase and point lance at such an apparition" (XLI, 178) has totally disrupted the ordinary activities of his consciousness. "Thoughts and fancies"—products of the "characterizing mind" which usually furnishes objects for the soul (a "ray of living light") to color—are willfully replaced by a material object which is a "mystic sign" of the "heartless voids and immensities of the universe." When the mind is forced to surrender its creative powers, the soul is deprived of the fictional objects which protect it from its own blankness. Hence, while the will sleeps, both soul and mind ("the common vitality") flee in horror from the material thing which Ahab has made the object of consciousness.

Whereas Ishmael retreats from the white world to a private one composed of his own "thoughts and fancies," Ahab tries to make that white world his own. He acts out the role of the tragic hero, who, finding himself in a world where he does not belong, tries to reach and change its hidden essence. Moby-Dick is an appropriate object for his hate since it is the one thing in his experience which does not mirror "back his own mysterious self" (XCIX, 428) but threatens him with dismemberment and death. While Ishmael's vision begins with the whale and expands, Ahab's vision gradually becomes more concentrated until he can see only Moby-Dick. By piling "upon the whale's white hump the sum of all the general rage and hate felt by his whole race from Adam down," he has taken that "intangible malignity . . . to whose dominion even the modern Christians ascribe one-half of the worlds," and has reduced it to a still large but now "practically assailable" cancer-like center (XLI, 181). Moby-Dick, therefore, becomes for Ahab the "unreasoning" wall of materiality (XXXVI, 161), the "inscrutable thing" (162) which he must master and destroy. But, as Ishmael knows, Moby-Dick is but one white object in a white universe; and the color white is evidence enough for the imaginative man that material objects can never be "visible image[s] of that deep, blue, bottomless soul" (XXXV, 157) because they are "visible absence[s]" which must be carefully avoided. As the "Samuel Enderby"'s Captain Boomer wisely observes, "Moby Dick doesn't bite so much as he swallows" (C, 438).

ii. Ishmael as Actor

What then of the young Ishmael? Even the man without Ahab's will to power, his determination to know and control material objects, is not safe. Pip, who "loved life, and all life's peaceable securities" (XCIII, 410), is by chance momentarily abandoned in the middle of a "heartless immensity" (412) and has the conscious self destroyed. From the time of his rescue until his death he refers to himself in the third person, as he seeks to find "a little negro lad, five feet high, hang-dog look, and cowardly" (CXXIX, 526). That the young Ishmael's situation is similar to Pip's is suggested by the narrator's reference to the "like abandonment [which] befell myself" (XCIII, 413). Like Pip, who "saw God's foot upon the treadle of the loom, and spoke it; and therefore his shipmates called him mad" (413), the abandoned Ishmael is also concerned with the speaking of truth. As the epigraph to the Epilogue emphasizes, he escapes "alone to tell" ("Epilogue," 567).

There is, however, a significant and obvious difference between Pip's selfless (and hence insane) speaking and the self-conscious telling of Ishmael. As Ishmael repeatedly reminds us, to gaze into the mysterious sea or into the enigmatic surfaces of objects is to be drawn by the "ungraspable phantom of life" toward the empty white voids of the universe. To survive one must turn away from the real world toward the "thoughts and fancies" of an imaginative one. At first glance, however, this strategy seems doomed to failure. Ishmael's tendency to retreat from the realm of objects to a verbal realm of his own creation would seem to imprison him in a world as solipsistic as Ahab's. Nevertheless, as the experiences of the young Ishmael aboard the "Pequod" demonstrate, the narrator's language and the truth which lurks behind it put him in touch with other men. His self-conscious lies, like the one told by Marlow at the end of "Heart of Darkness," although leaving a "taint of death, a flavor of mortality,"[8] keep the heavens from falling and provide the first link in the chain of conversation which binds men together.

As many of *Moby-Dick*'s critics have noted, the experiences of the young Ishmael which are described in the chapters "A Squeeze of the Hand" and "The Try-Works" point to his rejection of Ahab's intellectual quest and his acceptance of the "wife, the heart, the bed, the table, the saddle, the fire-side, the country" (XCIV, 415). This shifting of one's "conceit

[8] *Youth and Two Other Stories* (New York, 1915), p. 93.

of attainable felicity" (415), however, is not so easy as it first appears, as the other appearances of the young Ishmael suggest. His discovery of the destiny which he shares in common with other men is one result of his movement from actor to teller. Only when he comes to regard his life as a story he is telling does he discover and communicate with other men. In this sense, language is the very basis of his existence.

It is significant that when the young Ishmael is for the first time distinguished from the crew which had taken the "oaths of violence and revenge" (XLI, 175), he, with the aid of Queequeg, is self-consciously weaving a sword-mat:

I say so strange a dreaminess did there then reign all over the ship and all over the sea . . . that it seemed as if this were the Loom of Time, and I myself were a shuttle mechanically weaving and weaving away at the Fates. There lay the fixed threads of the warp subject to but one single, ever returning, unchanging vibration, and that vibration merely enough to admit of the crosswise interblending of other threads with its own. This warp seemed necessity; and here, thought I, with my own hand I ply my own shuttle and weave my own destiny into these unalterable threads. Meantime, Queequeg's impulsive, indifferent sword, sometimes hitting the woof slantingly, or crookedly, or strongly, or weakly, as the case might be; and by this difference in the concluding blow producing a corresponding contrast in the final aspect of the completed fabric; this savage's sword, thought I, which thus finally shapes and fashions both warp and woof; this easy, indifferent sword must be chance—aye, chance, free will, and necessity—no wise incompatible —all interweavingly working together. (XLVII, 212–13)

Here Ishmael first considers the possibility of creating the pattern of his own life rather than giving himself up to the workings of the universal loom. With the "ball of free will" in his hands, he refuses to allow the Fates to knit him into the design of their fabric. Instead he weaves "away at the Fates," thereby achieving "the last featuring blow at events" (213). This initial experience, however, is only momentary, for he drops the ball of free will and is caught up again in the flow of experience as soon as the first whale is sighted.

So in the chapter "The Monkey-rope" the reader finds the young Ishmael in actuality involved in the workings of the universal loom. Here he watches Queequeg, who, surrounded by the dangers of the "whaling world," "only prayed to his Yojo, and gave up his life into the hands of his gods" (LXXII, 320). And Ishmael, bound by the monkey-rope to both Queequeg and his threatening world, seems in a "sad pickle and peril" (320). The monkey-rope and the even more dangerous whale line are indications of the "silent, subtle, ever-present perils of life" (LX, 281). "All men live enveloped in whale-lines. All are born with halters round their necks" (281). These two lines, along with all the other ropes and threads in *Moby-Dick*, form the "mingled, mingling threads of life" (CXIV, 486) from which the destinies of the characters are woven; they, like Queequeg, place themselves in the hands of the weaving Fates. For this reason Fedallah's assurance to Ahab that "hemp only can kill thee" (CXVII, 492) is not so much a prophecy as it is a statement of the necessary result of man's involvement in the world.

It is just this involvement which Ishmael hopes to avoid by weaving his own destiny. He retains the loom metaphor to describe his creative gestures ("weave round them tragic graces") and invokes it, appropriately, in the title of the novel's first chapter, "Loomings." The necessity of creating one's own loom is dramatized both by the fate of Pip, "who saw God's foot upon the treadle of the loom," and by Ishmael's encounter with the universal loom as he examines the whale's skeleton in the Arsacides:[9]

[9] See Daniel Hoffman, *Form and Fable in American Fiction* (New York, 1965), pp. 272–78, for a differing interpretation of the weaving metaphor.

the trees stood high and haughty, feeling their living sap; the in-
dustrious earth beneath was as a weaver's loom, with a gorgeous car-
pet on it, whereof the ground-vine tendrils formed the warp and
woof, and the living flowers the figures. . . . Through the lacings
of the leaves, the great sun seemed a flying shuttle weaving the
unwearied verdure. . . . The weaver-god, he weaves; and by that
weaving is he deafened, that he hears no mortal voice; and by that
humming, we, too, who look on the loom are deafened; and only
when we escape it shall we hear the thousand voices that speak
through it. For even so it is in all material factories. The spoken
words that are inaudible among the flying spindles; these same
words are plainly heard without the walls, bursting from the
opened casements. . . .

Now, amid the green, life-restless loom of that Arsacidean wood,
the great, white, worshipped skeleton lay lounging—a gigantic idler!
Yet, as the ever-woven verdant warp and woof intermixed and
hummed around him, the mighty idler seemed the cunning weaver;
himself all woven over with vines . . . but himself a skeleton.
(CII, 446–47)

Here, as in the chapter "The Whiteness of the Whale,"
Ishmael points to the dangers inherent in an exploration of
the natural world. To question the weaver-god is to expose
oneself to the threat of deafness, for just as the colors of
nature are illusory cosmetics which hide a blinding blankness,
so too its sounds are a disguise for an awful deafening silence.
Both the movement of the loom and the colors of its product
belie the nature of the "mighty idler" who is "himself a
skeleton." Only by escaping from the loom of nature is man
able safely to recognize the truth inherent in its "flying spindles." This Ishmael manages by weaving a world of words
which allows him to approach the sounds and sights of the
world indirectly. Recognizing that "material factories" are
no places for men, he builds a house of fiction and through its
magic casements hears the "sane madness of vital truth."

Since Ishmael's vision is the product of "many prolonged,
repeated experiences" (XCIV, 415), it develops gradually. As
a young man, who momentarily dropped the "ball of free
will" and resigned his life "into the hands of him who steered

the boat" (XLIX, 226), he reacts to the shock of his "first lowering" by weaving an account of his death rather than of his life. At this point, regarding the "whole voyage of the Pequod, and the great White Whale its object" with a "free and easy sort of genial, desperado philosophy" (226), he makes his will and prepares to take a "cool, collected dive at death and destruction" (227).

It may seem strange that of all men sailors should be tinkering at their last wills and testaments, but there are no people in the world more fond of that diversion. This was the fourth time in my nautical life that I had done the same thing. After the ceremony was concluded upon the present occasion, I felt all the easier; a stone was rolled away from my heart. Besides, all the days I should now live would be as good as the days that Lazarus lived after his resurrection; a supplementary clean gain of so many months or weeks as the case might be. I survived myself; my death and burial were locked up in my chest. I looked round me tranquilly and contentedly, like a quiet ghost with a clean conscience sitting inside the bars of a snug family vault. (227)

By anticipating his own death and imprisoning that event in words, Ishmael has apparently turned the threatening future into a harmless phantom and has successfully removed himself from the dangerous reality of the present. Fictive suicide, however, is only a temporary answer. The fictive "will" is finally destined to become the real one. It, like the resurrection of Lazarus, only postpones the inevitable. Several chapters later, in "The Try-Works," young Ishmael is suddenly overwhelmed by "a stark, bewildered feeling, as of death" (XCVI, 421), as his "snug family vault" is filled with the stink of materiality, an odor "such as may lurk in the vicinity of funereal pyres" (420).

As with his initial use of the loom metaphor, however, Ishmael's early and partial resurrection is a step in the right direction. He will resurrect himself again, this time by providing himself with a fictive life rather than a death. The figure who survives "to tell" at the end of the novel is not the ghost of an old self but a new one who will inhabit a world of words rather than objects Because he is a *teller*, he lives not in experience but in an illusory realm where sharks wear "padlocks on their mouths" and sea hawks sail with "sheathed beaks" ("Epilogue," 567).

The portrait of the artist as a young man which is partially painted in the narrator's descriptions of young Ishmael is completed by Ishmael's account of himself as he was after the voyage but before the period of creative authorship. This transitional Ishmael appears in the chapter "The Town-Ho's Story," as a result of the narrator's unusual way of describing the circumstances surrounding the meeting of the "Pequod" and the "Town-Ho." The chapter's subtitle, "(As told at the Golden Inn)," distinguishes its narrative mode from that of the rest of the novel and indicates that the account presented is but one of several versions of the same story. Originally told in confidence to Tashtego by three sailors from the "Town-Ho," it is revealed to the crew of the "Pequod" when the harpooner talks in his sleep. It is subsequently narrated by Ishmael at the Golden Inn, and this version is repeated by him at the time of writing: "For my humor's sake, I shall preserve the style in which I once narrated it at Lima, to a lounging circle of my Spanish friends, one saint's eve, smoking upon the thick-gilt tiled piazza of the Golden Inn. Of those fine cavaliers, the young Dons, Pedro and Sebastian, were on the closer terms with me; and hence the interluding questions they occasionally put, and which are duly answered at the time" (LIV, 241). Clearly, this is another example of Ishmael's use of self-conscious form. The emphasis which he places on his own method of narration as well as his description of other versions of the same events calls attention to the story as story. Moreover, as a story within a story, it is but part of a longer and more complex fiction. In answer to a question by Don Sebastian concerning the identity and history of Moby-Dick, Ishmael replies, "A very white, and famous, and most deadly immortal monster, Don;—but that would be too long a story" (257). The story exists in the interior of the novel, and the meaning of the shorter fiction depends on a set of literary correspondences between it and the longer one. In other words, its form becomes its content, since the way it is told is its meaning.

The young Ishmael escapes "alone to tell," and, as "The Town-Ho's Story" demonstrates, he fulfills his destined role, although he does not remain alone. Surrounded by friends, he drinks, smokes, and talks—denying the implications of his name and hence creating a new self as well as a new story. As he organizes his fiction by "interweaving in its proper place this darker thread [the secret part of the tale] with the story as publicly narrated on the ship" (241), he both recalls his weaving experience aboard the "Pequod" and anticipates his novelistic use of the loom metaphor.

Anticipating the novel, too, is the fact that the story is woven against a white background. Told in Lima, the city which "has taken the white veil" and is characterized by the "whiteness of her woe" (XLII, 191), it is an early example of Ishmael's remarkable ability to avoid the dangers of the whiteness which surrounds him. When he refers to the "Venetianly corrupt" life of the area of the Great Lakes (LIV, 248), one of his auditors comments on the delicacy of his metaphor: " 'A moment! Pardon!' cried another of the company. 'In the name of all us Limeese, I but desire to express to you, sir sailor, that we have by no means overlooked your delicacy in not substituting present Lima for distant Venice in your corrupt comparison. Oh! do not bow and look surprised; you know the proverb all along this coast—'Corrupt as Lima' " (249).

It is important that Ishmael acknowledges neither this comment nor the later observation of Don Pedro ("No need to travel! The world's one Lima" [250]) but in each case returns immediately to his story. The motives which cause him to avoid such an obvious metaphor, however, are probably different from those which precipitate the "strange delicacy" shown by the crew of the "Pequod" when they keep the

"Town-Ho" 's secret "among themselves so that it never tran-
spired abaft the Pequod's main-mast" (241). In "The Town-
Ho's Story," Moby-Dick seems "to step in to take out of his
[Steelkilt's] hands into its [Heaven's] own the damning thing
he would have done" (257), and his act thus belies Ahab's
interpretation of him as either the agent or principle of injustice, thereby introducing ambiguities which the "Pequod" 's
captain would have been incapable of tolerating.

Ishmael's self-preserving delicacy deprives no one of the
knowledge of his story, although it does influence his choice
of metaphors. Protected for the moment from the white
world which surrounds him, by the atmosphere of the Golden
Inn, he is careful to approach the truth of his situation indirectly by choosing "distant Venice" for his "corrupt comparison." Indeed, he shows a remarkable ability to ignore
sinister Lima altogether. He safely preaches heresy in a mili-
tantly Catholic city and blasphemously fulfills the empty
boast made by every barroom storyteller, when, in the company of a priest, he places his hand on the Holy Book and
swears to the truth of his narrative. Although he is telling a
"wicked story," he seems "spotless as a lamb" (L, 142).

"The Town-Ho's Story," then, is a rehearsal of the later and
longer book. By reproducing the story "as told at the Golden
Inn," Ishmael once again calls attention to his fiction as fiction
—this time directing the reader's attention to the osmotic relationship between two aesthetic bodies. Here, as in the novel
as a whole, he affirms the central thesis of "Hawthorne and
His Mosses": "the names of all fine authors are fictitious
ones."

Ishmael's achievement in *Moby-Dick* is the result of a vic-
tory of art over life. Finding the natural world a place which
at first enchants, then confuses and terrifies, and recognizing
that human constructs fail to explain or control it, he removes
himself from both nature and society by retreating to a fanciful world of his own creation. Here his self-conscious ges-

tures distinguish his creative venture from the unconscious acts of god-making and society-making which characterize the "world of lies." His relationship to other people is that of a storyteller to his audience, in touch with them through his words but removed from their meaningless masquerade. From this position he is able to face and describe safely the truth which the world's empty forms conceal.

IV

THE FAILURE OF THE AUTHOR-HERO: NARRATIVE FORM IN *PIERRE* AND *ISRAEL POTTER*

I shudder at idea of the ancient Egyptians. It was in these pyramids that was conceived the idea of Jehovah. . . . Moses learned in all the lore of the Egyptians. The idea of Jehovah born here.

.   .   .   .   .

Man seems to have had as little to do with it as Nature. It was that supernatural creature, the priest. . . . And one seems to see that as out of the crude forms of the natural earth they could evoke by art the transcendent mass & symetry & . . . . . of the pyramid so out of the rude elements of the insignificant thoughts that are in all men, they could rear the transcendent conception of a God.

JUS, pp. 58, 64

Craftsmen, in dateless quarries dim,
Stones formless into form did trim,
Usurped on Nature's self with Art,
And bade this dumb I AM to start
    Imposing him.

"The Great Pyramid"

A FTER THE COMPLETION of *Moby-Dick* Melville immediately began to work on *Pierre*, the book which announced a new and important stage in his career as a writer. Here for the first time he steps outside the form of the first-person narrative. The familiar Melvilleian author-hero is conspicuously absent in *Pierre*. In his place is a nameless, intrusive author who at first seems in no way connected with the events of the story he tells. Accompanying this innovation in point of view is the use of a new subject and locale. With its country-city setting and its concern with the issues of love and money —problems which result from man's involvement in society— *Pierre* is in the tradition of the domestic novel, a popular form with Melville's contemporaries but one which up to this point in his career he had carefully avoided.

Present within this alien form, however, is a familiar Melvilleian theme. Although young Pierre is concerned with the several important social issues which are raised by his discovery that he has an illegitimate sister, his problems are complicated by the fact that he is a writer. As a practitioner of the "great Art of Telling the Truth," he faces the troublesome task of defining the writer's relationship to the pseudo-reality which is society and to the conventions and formulas which structure it. This is, of course, the problem which Ishmael's method allows him to avoid altogether. Because he is unwilling to be an actor in the world's play, Ishmael retreats from both nature and society by becoming a teller of stories. For him it is necessary that the writer remove himself from the prison of "hereditary forms and world-usages" (*P*, V, 104), which cut him off from the truth of the universe.

Pierre, however, is not the narrator of his own story. He is too tightly entangled in the world's net of circumstances to make the leap from actor to teller. His is the story of the necessary failure of the author-hero. As Melville himself had done, Pierre attempts to write a book by using his own experience "to fill out the mood of his apparent author-hero" (XXII, 356) but is able to produce only a pile of unrelated scraps.

But while the customary movement of the hero to author is missing in *Pierre*, other familiar elements of self-conscious form remain. Here, as in *Moby-Dick*, the action of the plot is subservient to the activities of a self-reflexive narrator at the time of writing. His methodological metaphors form a special area around the events of the story where the writer sits brooding over the problems of his craft and linking the meaning of his story to the methods which produce it.

Like Ishmael's figurative loom, the narrator's metaphors define the writer's relationship to both the fictional and the material world. In *Pierre* the mountain replaces the whale as the central image of materiality, and rocks and stones rather than lines and ropes define the threatening environment in which man is imprisoned. The novel is dedicated to "the majestic mountain, Greylock," the "sovereign lord and king" of the "amphitheatre over which his central majesty presides," and important roles are given to Mount Sinai, meeting place of God and Moses; the "divine mount," the site of Christ's famous sermon; and Bunyan's Delectable Mountains, from which the Celestial City may be seen. Like the whale in *Moby-Dick*, the mountain in *Pierre* is the mute, material other which man attempts to control and transform in his effort to humanize the world. As H. Bruce Franklin and others have noticed, in *Pierre* man builds with rocks and stones.[1] Human institutions as well as buildings are described in stony terms. Christ's church is built on imperishable rock, and "an immense mass of state-masonry is brought to bear as a buttress" (I, 10) in the upholding of man's less enduring political institutions.

The narrator, however, is haunted by the "foreboding and prophetic lesson taught, not less by Palmyra's quarries, than by Palmyra's ruins. . . . The proud stone that should have stood among the clouds, Time left abased beneath the soil" (I, 7). Man's "brick and mortar" cities (XVI, 271), as well as his stony values and institutions, are subject to decay and de-

---

[1] See for example Stern, *The Fine Hammered Steel of Herman Melville*, pp. 150–205; Saburo Yamaya, "The Stone Image of Melville's 'Pierre,'" *Selection*, 34 (1957):31–58; and Franklin, *The Wake of the Gods*, pp. 99–125.

struction not only because they are artificial products but because the material from which they are made is itself insubstantial and illusory. As the narrator discovers when he probes beneath the world's surfaces, the social fiction is a result of the ontological one:

But, as far as any geologist has yet gone down into the world, it is found to consist of nothing but surface stratified on surface. To its axis, the world being nothing but superinduced superficies. By vast pains we mine into the pyramid; by horrible gropings we come to the central room; with joy we espy the sarcophagus; but we lift the lid—and no body is there!—appallingly vacant as vast is the soul of a man! (XXI, 335)

The violent and apparently illogical conflation of the two mining metaphors points directly to the central problem of *Pierre*. The crucial idea here is not merely that the pyramids of the soul and the mountains of the world conceal a similar emptiness, but that the constructs of the soul are built with materials taken from the "superinduced superficies" of the world. Pyramids are man-made mountains, empty forms built on the crust of a hollow but multi-layered ball. Within these artificial structures is conceived the "idea of Jehovah" as well as all those institutions and values which compose civilization. But the problem is not simply that God and culture are human fictions. This is the truth which Ishmael accepts and uses as a basis for his art. The really frightening discovery is the realization that apparently subjective illusions have their origins in a material fiction. The pyramids own their existence as much to the mountains which provide their substance and shape as they do to the mind which apparently conceived them. It is this truth implicit in the narrator's strange metaphor which suggests a logical but radical solution to his hero's central problem—the reconciling of "this world with his own soul" (244).

Sooner or later in this life, the earnest, or enthusiastic youth comes to know, and more or less appreciate this startling solecism:

—That while, as the grand condition of acceptance to God, Christianity calls upon all men to renounce this world; yet by all odds the most Mammonish parts of this world—Europe and America—are owned by none but professed Christian nations, who glory in the owning, and seem to have some reason therefor. (XIV, 243)

To the young enthusiast whose soul is filled with the "stream of tenderness" which flows from Christ's "divine mount," the human world seems "saturated and soaking with lies" (243). Man's "brick and mortar" cities are "depraved and accursed" places (244), filled with "sneaking burglars, wantons, and debauchees; often in actual pandering league with the most abhorrent sinks" (XVI, 272). This is the city of Mammon rather than that of God, a place where the "infinitely sweet and soothing" words of Christ (XIV, 243) are useless. Only "fine coats and full pockets can whip such mangy hounds into decency" (XVI, 273). Faced with this knowledge, "two armies" come to the shock within him, and "unless he can find the talismanic secret, to reconcile this world with his own soul, then there is no peace for him" (XIV, 244).

As the narrator's mixed metaphor implies, however, this conflict is more apparent than real. The objects of the soul and the things of Mammon have a common source. Both the rough, cold pavingstones of the city streets and the soothing words of Christ have their origins in the mountains. The Delectable Mountain is also the Mount of the Titans. Behind its purple promise and Christian name are found the barren rocks which are used in the construction of the "Titanic" tower in which Pierre lives, as well as in the other buildings which surround it. But to know this is but to see through the "first superficiality of the world," not to discover the "unlayered substance" (XXI, 335). The final truth is not just that the words of Christ and the things of Mammon have a common source but that both words and things are equally fictitious. Both soul and world consist of "surface stratified on surface," and the "unlayered substance" in each case is emptiness—infinite, uncreated nothingness.

This knowledge, however, is available only to the man who, like the narrator, mines deep beneath the rocky surfaces of both soul and world: "Deep, deep, and still deep and deeper must we go, if we would find out the heart of a man" (340). His penetrating of surfaces gives him access to a truth which is denied to his mountain-climbing hero, who hopes through Isabel to be "lifted to exalted mounts" and who tries "to climb Parnassus with a pile of folios on his back" (334). The empti-ness which he discovers at the center of man and the world suggests an image of divinity which is the reverse of the transcendent deity who traditionally speaks to man on moun-tain tops:

Yea, in silence the child Christ was born into the world. Silence is the general consecration of the universe. Silence is the invisible laying on of the Divine Pontiff's hands upon the world. Silence is at once the most harmless and the most awful thing in all nature. It speaks of the Reserved Forces of Fate. Silence is the only Voice of our God. . . . Like the air, Silence permeates all things, and pro-duces its magical power, as well during that peculiar mood which prevails at a solitary traveler's first setting forth on a journey, as at the unimaginable time when before the world was, Silence brooded on the face of the waters. (XIV, 239)

The world is not the product of Logos or of divine speech but rather of a brooding Silence. Like the painting of the Stran-ger's Head by the "unknown hand," it seems to have had nei-ther creator nor original. It is an "enigma, a mystery, an imaginative delirium" (XXVI, 416), an absurd fiction which has emerged in some inexplicable way from the empty air. For man, the "solitary traveler" who journeys through this nightmare world, the realization that "it is all a dream" (XIX, 322) offers no sense of relief, for it in no way frees him from the "superinduced superficies." He finds himself "placed at cross-purposes, in a world of snakes and lightnings, in a world of horrible and inscrutable inhumanities" (VI, 144). Like the "shivering pasture elms" which grow near the Ulver farm-house, he is "standing in a world inhospitable, yet rooted by inscrutable sense of duty to [his] place" (128). He is bound by that "all-controlling and all-permeating wonderfulness, which, when imperfectly and isolatedly recognized by the generality, is so significantly denominated The Finger of God[.] But it is not merely the Finger, it is the whole outspread Hand of God; for doth not Scripture intimate, that He holdeth all of us in the hollow of His Hand?—a Hollow, truly!" (VII, 163–64).

The reference to the finger of God is especially important in a book which associates divine speech with mountain tops. God "gave unto Moses, when he had made an end of communing with him upon mount Sinai, two tables of testimony, tables of stone, written with the finger of God" (Exodus 31: 18). The laws written on those tables of stone are to form the basis of society: they regulate not only man's relationship to God but to other men as well. Their authenticity, however, is questionable, for the narrator reinterprets the Biblical symbol of God's presence and action in the same way as he does the Genesis account of The Creation. Just as he reveals God's creative voice to be a silence, so he turns His substantial finger into a hollow void. The attributes of infinite space have become the attributes of God.

The tables of stone, like the world itself, are counterfeit because they are the supposed product of a silent emptiness which is incapable of speaking or writing. Nevertheless, they not only endure but are embellished with the passing of time. Christ, the establisher of the new law and new covenant, also invokes the finger of God, maintaining that it furnishes him with the power to give speech to the dumb (Luke 11:14–20). Both Moses and Christ, then, insist that they are able to get a voice out of silence, and therefore they are like "certain philosophers" who pretend to have found the "Talismanic Secret" which will reconcile man with the world:

Now without doubt this Talismanic Secret has never yet been found; and in the nature of human things it seems as though it never can be. Certain philosophers have time and again pretended to have found it; but if they do not in the end discover their own delusion, other people soon discover it for themselves, and so those philosophers and their vain philosophy are let glide away into practical oblivion. Plato, and Spinoza, and Goethe, and many more belong to this guild of self-imposters, with a preposterous rabble of Muggletonian Scots and Yankees, whose vile brogue still the more bestreaks the stripedness of their Greek or German Neoplatonical originals. That profound Silence, that only Voice of our God . . . from that divine thing without a name, those impostor philosophers pretend somehow to have got an answer; which is as absurd, as though they should say they had got water out of stone; for how can a man get a Voice out of Silence? (XIV, 244)

The allusion to Moses' ability to obtain water from stone (Numbers 20:10–13) further identifies him with this "guild of self-impostors" and makes the narrator's position clear.[2] In *Pierre*, as in *Mardi*, "truth is voiceless," and any act of speaking or writing is therefore a lie. Because there is a "universal lurking insincerity" in even the "greatest and purest written thoughts" (XXV, 399), the truest man is the silent one and the truest book the unwritten one. It is the "Wonderful Mutes"—not Moses or Christ—who inhabit the "vast halls of Silent Truth," where the "Poetic Magi discuss, in glorious

[2] Melville may have in mind here that famous but mysterious atheistic book *De tribus impostoribus*, which was supposed to have been a polemic against the three major religions of Europe. Attributed to Frederick II by Pope Gregory IX at the beginning of the thirteenth century, the book was said to have described the way in which the world was deceived by three tricksters, Mohammed, Moses, and Christ. Robert Burton writes in *The Anatomy of Melancholy* that "Frederick the emperor, as Matthew Paris records, *licet non sit recitabile* [though it is not fit to be repeated] (I use his own words) is reported to have said, *Trēs praestigiatores, Moses, Christus, et Mahomet, uti mundo dominarentur, totum populum sibi contemporaneum seduxisse* [three swindlers, Moses, Christ, and Mahomet, seduced all their contemporaries, in order that they might rule over the world]" (see the three-volume Everyman's Library edition of the *Anatomy*, used here throughout [New York, 1964], 3:389). Melville acquired his copy of Burton in 1848 (Sealts, *Melville's Reading* entry 102, p. 45). For an account of the history of *De tribus impostoribus*, see Don Cameron Allen, *Doubt's Boundless Sea* (Baltimore, 1964), pp. 224–43.

gibberish, the Alpha and Omega of the Universe" (XVII, 287).

But what then of *Pierre*'s verbose, self-conscious narrator and his "book of sacred truth" (V, 127)? His metaphysics appear to preclude the possibility of a viable aesthetics. Nevertheless, the mining metaphor which he uses to describe his narrative method seems at first to distinguish him from the impostor philosophers who are associated with mountain climbing and tower building, and this distinction is maintained when he extends the figure to describe the education and development of the young writer:

But while Nature thus very early and very abundantly feeds us, she is very late in tutoring us as to the proper methodization of our diet. Or,—to change the metaphor,—there are immense quarries of fine marble; but how to get it out; how to chisel it; how to construct any temple? Youth must wholly quit, then, the quarry, for a while; and not only go forth, and get tools to use in the quarry, but must go and thoroughly study architecture. Now the quarry-discoverer is long before the stone-cutter; and the stone-cutter is long before the architect; and the architect is long before the temple; for the temple is the crown of the world. (XVIII, 302)

Writing is seen as both an external and internal mining, a digging down toward the "axis of reality." But if the writer's method distinguishes him from the impostor philosophers, his product binds him to them. He too builds marble temples from the stones of his experience. For this reason, the wise writer constructs his temples only to destroy them. Just as "in digging for precious metals in the mines, much earthy rubbish has first to be troublesomely handled and thrown out; so, in digging in one's soul for the fine gold of genius, much dullness and common-place is first brought to light." Because he has no built-in "receptacle" for this rubbish, the writer, like the man who lives in a house without a cellar, must deposit it "in the street before his own door, for the public functionaries to take care of" (303). "No common-place is ever effectually got rid of, except by essentially emptying one's self of it into a book; for once trapped in a book, then the book can be put into the fire, and all will be well. . . . Nor will any thoroughly sincere man, who is an author, ever be rash in precisely defining the period, when he has completely ridded himself of his rubbish, and come to the latent gold in his mine" (303).

Only if the writer creates in order to destroy does he practice the "great Art of Telling the Truth." Constructed from stony materials, his book, if allowed to exist, would take its place among the other structures in the "world of lies." Although "positively distasteful" to its author, it might become the "foolish glory of the world" (303) and thereby entangle him all the more in the net he seeks to escape. Fire, however, "like ultimate Truth itself, of which it is the eloquent symbol, consumes all, and only consumes" (XV, 258). Hence it is in the destruction rather than in the creation of a book that the writer comes closest to truth.

Ishmael, conceiving of experience as a chaos of dangerous lines and ropes inexplicably woven together by the operation of the universal loom, snatches up his ball of free will, turns his back on the loom, and weaves a world of his own. For the narrator of *Pierre* this solution is fugitive and unstable. As his mining and architectural metaphors suggest, the writer cannot escape experience. He is a miner rather than a weaver because he knows that the "infinite entanglements of all social things . . . forbids that one thread should fly the general fabric, on some new line of duty, without tearing itself and tearing others" (XII, 225).

The world of *Pierre* makes any distinction between actor and teller impossible. Because the writer is trapped within an artificial world based on money, his book is "born of unwillingness and the bill of the baker" (XVIII, 303): "Let not the short-sighted world for a moment imagine, that any vanity lurks in such minds [those driven by the hard constraints of some social necessity]; only hired to appear on the stage, not voluntarily claiming the public attention; their utmost life-redness and glow is but rouge, washed off in private with bitterest tears; their laugh only rings because it is hollow; and the answering laugh is no laughter to them" (304). Money, however, is neither the first nor the strongest link in the chain which binds the writer to the world's stage and forces him to paint his face and participate in the empty masquerade. He is also bound by his materials themselves: "For though the naked soul of man doth assuredly contain one latent element of intellectual productiveness; yet never was there a child born solely from one parent; the visible world of experience being that procreative thing which impregnates the muses; self-reciprocally efficient hermaphrodites being but a fable" (304-5). No author, then, is original in the sense that he is capable of creation *ex nihilo*. "Had Milton's been the lot of Caspar Hauser, Milton would have been vacant as he" (304).

The "visible world of experience"—the earth's rocky crust and the products invented and accumulated by man—make it impossible for any true man ever to "pretend that his slightest thought or act solely originates in his own defined identity" (X, 207). When examined closely, the drama of the mind is found to be a reproduction of the realm where truth is concealed first by materiality itself and further obscured by a crust of social formulas and conventions. What the writer thinks—indeed, what he is—is determined by the forms and usages which surround him, not the least of which is language itself.

For the narrator of *Pierre* words are shadows of substance which do not help to free man from his enslavement to the world but instead bind him more tightly to its artificiality. "For as the breath in all our lungs is hereditary, and my present breath at this moment, is further descended than the body of the present High Priest of the Jews, so far as he can assuredly trace it; so mere names, which are also but air, do likewise revel in this endless descendedness" (I, 8-9). Names, as a matter of fact, turn out to be more artificial than the institutions or objects to which they obstensibly refer.

"When the substance is gone, men cling to the shadow" (XIX, 314), writes the narrator as he contemplates the Church of the Apostles, an institution whose history illustrates the "endless descendedness" of names and their relationship to artificial institutions:

Places once set apart to lofty purposes, still retain the name of that loftiness, even when converted to the meanest uses. It would seem, as if forced by imperative Fate to renounce the reality of the romantic and lofty, the people of the present would fain make a compromise by retaining some purely imaginative remainder. The curious effect of this tendency is oftenest evinced in those venerable countries of the old transatlantic world; where still over the Thames one bridge yet retains the monastic title of Blackfriars; though not a single Black Friar, but many a pickpocket, has stood on that bank since a good ways beyond the days of Queen Bess. . . . (314)

Associated through its name with Christ and the Apostles, through its heavy stone walls with Peter in particular, and through its heaven-aspiring tower with the otherworldliness of the Sermon on the Mount, the Church of the Apostles was originally built as a symbol of man's ability to communicate directly with God. But while it enjoys its "days of sanctification and grace," it gradually gives way to the worldly forces of Mammon and is "divided into stores; cut into offices" (312). So successful is this conversion that the churchyard is "invaded for a supplemental edifice," a worldly tower made from the same materials and almost as tall as the original one. But in spite of the change in function the name of the building remains the same. Moreover, the name is "transferred" by society to the lawyers who initially occupy the offices as well as to the "adventurers and artists, and indigent philosophers" who replace them. "So it came to pass, that in the general fashion of the day, he who had chambers in the old church was familiarly styled an *Apostle*" (315).

As a result of this "waggishness in the public," the church, which was named for a set of impostors whose delusions are revealed through its change in function, creates in its turn another such group. Referred to by others as "Apostles," the inhabitants of the building are "attracted toward each other by a title common to all," and they proceed to form a society vaguely connected with the advance of "some unknown great political and religious Millennium" (315). In pretending to have gotten a voice from silence, Christ created a pseudo-reality which then perpetuates and embellishes itself, forming, as the years pass, a web of "myriad alliances and criss-crossings" which makes any distinction between "empty nominalness" and "vital realness" (XII, 225) impossible.

The writer, then, is necessarily compressed and oppressed by the world's usages, and his books are the products of his experiences:

And in the inferior instances of an immediate literary success, in very young writers, it will be almost invariably observable, that for that instant success they were chiefly indebted to some rich and peculiar experience in life, embodied in a book, which because, for that cause, containing original matter, the author himself, forsooth, is to be considered original; in this way, many very original books, being the product of very unoriginal minds. (XVIII, 304)

Henry Murray has suggested that Melville may have written these words with his experiences with *Typee* and *Omoo* in mind.[3] If in fact this is the case (and other autobiographical elements in the novel tend to support Murray's assertion), the personal reference is functional rather than digressive. It is important to recall that *Pierre* is Melville's first departure from the first-person narrative, a mode which emphasizes the movement from the living of an experience to the inventing of it. With the exception of *Mardi*, the novels from *Typee* through *Moby-Dick* demonstrate that to turn personal experience into a story is to assert man's ability to stand outside the stream of time, to escape the "eternal tides of time and fate" (VII, 166). Melville's fictional first-person narrators indicate both the pos-

[3] Explanatory Notes, *P*, 482.

sibility and the necessity of separating his books from their "ostensible author," and the author-hero method itself reaffirms this goal by dramatizing the narrator's escape from his experience. It is precisely these assumptions which are denied by *Pierre*'s narrative form as well as by the career of its hero.

Pierre is at once a satiric appraisal of Melville's own career as a writer, of the American literary scene in general, and, finally, of the nature of fiction. The Pittsfield setting, the thinly veiled familial and personal details, and the ironic dedication all serve to connect the novel with the name on its title page. And the inability of the *writer* to free himself from the *man* and the "world of lies" he inhabits is reflected in *Pierre*'s subject and style. While the narrator parodies the style and content of "countless tribes of common novels" in his account of Pierre's career (166), his novel reflects his inability to escape his literary milieu. The country-city contrast, the incest theme, the light and dark girls, the use of the letter as a dramatic plot device, and the employment of such standard romantic symbols as the guitar and portrait tie *Pierre* to the domestic sentimental novel which it mocks. This is not accidental. The form and style of the book are not the result of Melville's sudden loss of his novelistic powers or of his too close identification with the vision of his hero; they represent a self-conscious re-evaluation of the relationship between art and life. As the concluding paragraph of the narrator's discussion of fiction and life makes clear, he is well aware of his own limitations:

> There is infinite nonsense in the world on all of these matters; hence blame me not if I contribute my mite. It is impossible to talk or to write without apparently throwing oneself helplessly open; the Invulnerable Knight wears his visor down. Still, it is pleasant to chat; for it passes the time ere we go to our beds; and speech is further incited, when like strolling improvisatores of Italy, we are paid for our breath. And we are only too thankful when the gapes of the audience dismiss us with the few ducats we earn. (XVIII, 305)

129

Like Plotinus Plinlimmon, the narrator knows that in the world any act of speaking or writing makes one an unwilling participant in society's masquerade. Plinlimmon's self-interested passivity, or what the narrator calls his "non-Benevolence" (XXI, 341), is essentially a refusal to respond to anything, since "to respond is a suspension of all isolation" (345). His face is a "face of repose,—repose neither divine nor human, nor any thing made up of either or both—but a repose separate and apart—a repose of a face by itself" (343). He maintains this "apartness" by refusing to become involved with the world in any way. He will not work with his hands, will not write, and has never been known to open a book. Although he lives among other men, he refuses to become involved with them.

The narrator, however, lacking the Apostle's frightening if logical "non-Benovolence," is drawn toward other men by inclination and profit. Nevertheless, it is quite clear that fiction can no longer be defined as the "great Art of Telling the Truth." At the best, it is a not unprofitable role for a man who for one reason or another finds himself unable to remain silent.

Consequently, *Pierre* is a sneering condemnation of a counterfeit world and a horrifying assertion of the writer's necessary tie to it. The narrator is agonizingly aware that he is as much an impostor as Plato, Moses, and Christ. When, in his Dedication, he "devoutly kneel[s], and render[s] up [his] gratitude" for the "bounteous and unstinted fertilizations" that he has received from "his central majesty," he implies that he too has been inspired by a divine mountain, that his voice flows from silent rock. Also linking him to the impostors he hates is his talent for obtaining water from stone, an achievement he explicitly labels as "absurd." He berates his hero for failing "to wrest some final comfort" from his dream of Enceladus by flogging "this stubborn rock as Moses his, and [forcing] even aridity itself to quench his painful thirst," and then proceeds to "smite" the rock himself, forcing it to seem to yield a "stream" (XXV, 408). Indeed, imagery of water is found throughout this arid, rocky book. The characters' minds, souls, and lives flow like "currents," "streams," and "rivers." They are "whelmed" by "billows" (V, 122), "plunged" into "wide sea[s] of trouble" (103), "shipwrecked and cast on the beach" (III, 75). These individual rivers and streams are collectively embodied in the narrator's description of his procedural method ("But I shall follow the endless, winding way, —the flowing river in the cave of man; careless whither I be led, reckless where I land" [V, 126]), as well as in his reference to his book as a "deep-heady Hudson" (XVIII, 304).

The unresolved tension which exists between the metaphors and images of water and voyaging on the one hand and those of rocks and mining on the other is one literary manifestation of the writer's inability to escape the "world of lies." More obvious and yet more complicated, however, is the effect of his imprisonment on the web of events which constitute the novel's plot. It is to this inner drama that one must look if one is fully to discover the artistic repercussions of the writer's inability to forget the world which lies beyond the walls of his fiction.

That the world of Saddle Meadows to which the reader is introduced at the beginning of *Pierre* is a realm ruled by appearances is made clear by Pierre's naïve idealism, his mother's commitment to empty social forms, and the Reverend Falsgrave's pragmatic Christianity. The Glendinning family is dedicated to the preservation and celebration of a feudalistic heritage and is committed to the questionable ethics of Grandfather Glendinning, an owner of slaves but a "sweethearted charitable Christian" whose deeds include the annihilation of "two Indian savages by making reciprocal bludgeons of their heads" (II, 33). As suggested by the narrator's constant use of the word "seems" to describe it, this is a world of surfaces.

The young Pierre, however, in his animal-like innocence, accepts the world as it appears to him: he is proud of the heroic deeds of his ancestors, regards his dead father as a god, and assumes that the face which his mother presents to others is a true mirror of her soul. Both the hypocrisy of the Saddle Meadows world and the nature of Pierre's youthful idealism, however, have been adequately discussed by others and need not be treated in detail here.[4] What is important for the purpose of the present study is the role which books play in the shaping of both Pierre's naïve and his enlightened visions, for like his creator he is incapable of separating the realms of art and life. His growth begins with destruction of one book and the discovery of another; his progress is charted through his development of a more sensitive eye for significant literary detail; and his maturity is defined by his decision to abandon one form of literary activity in favor of a more profound one.

It is appropriate that in Pierre's almost perfect prelapsarian world the realms of art and life, like those of the ideal and actual, the subjective and the objective, should be as one:

So perfect to Pierre had long seemed the illuminated scroll of his life thus far, that only one hiatus was discoverable by him in that sweetly-writ manuscript. A sister had been omitted from the text. He mourned that so delicious a feeling as fraternal love had been denied him. Nor could the fictitious title, which he so often lavished upon his mother, at all supply the absent reality. This emotion was most natural; and the full cause and reason of it even Pierre did not at that time entirely appreciate. For surely a gentle sister is the second best gift to a man; and it is first in point of occurrence; for the wife comes after. He who is sisterless, is as a bachelor before his time. For much that goes to make up the deliciousness of a wife, already lies in the sister. (I, 6)

Like a stone dropped in water, this passage creates a series of concentric circles which gradually move through the events at the interior of the novel and extend, finally, into the special area inhabited by the self-conscious narrator. For young Pierre life imitates art. Like love, it is "a volume bound in rose-leaves, clasped with violets, and by the beaks of humming-

---

[4] See especially Stern's essay, cited above.

birds printed with peach-juice on the leaves of lilies" (II, 38). At this point in his career grief is "still a ghost-story" (47), and human relationships are unambiguous. "Read me through and through," says Lucy to her lover, "I am entirely thine" (45).

This lucid transparency, however, is partially obscured in the case of Pierre's relationship to his mother, since he provides her with a "fictitious title" in an attempt to bridge the one small gap which exists between his experience and his desire. In this instance the realms of art and life are discontinuous, for the "absent reality" remains intrusive. What is even worse, not only does his fictionalizing fail to capture the missing ideal, but it also calls into question parts of his experience which had previously seemed perfect. The ambiguity present in the narrator's comments on the relationship of sister and wife is deepened by Pierre's unusual view of his mother, obscuring his almost perfect life with veiled suggestions of incest.

These ambiguous complications continue to develop as the book metaphor enlarges its sphere of influence. With the arrival of Isabel's letter, "the fit scroll of a torn, as well as bleeding heart" (III, 75), the fictive sister becomes an actual one, the ghost story grief, a poignant reality, and the "illuminated scroll of his life," a fraudulent, empty fiction. Overcome suddenly by truth's "black billow" (75), Pierre now sees that "all the objects which [previously] surrounded him were concealingly deceptive" (V, 104). Now he believes he sees only truth: "From all idols, I tear all veils; henceforth I will see the hidden things" (III, 76). To have escaped one fiction, however, is not necessarily to have come to the "unlayered substance." Although he has cast aside one false manuscript, he still sees his life in bookish terms: "I remember now those first wise words, wherewith our Saviour Christ first spoke in his first speech to men:—'Blessed are the poor in spirit, and blessed they that mourn.' Oh, hitherto I have but piled up words; bought books, and bought some small experiences, and builded me in libraries; now I sit down and read" (V, 106–7). Pierre turns from the fictions of Mammon to the apparently profound truths of the "Creator's and Saviour's gospel to mankind" (II, 38). As yet unaware that Christ is an impostor who pretends to get a voice from silence, he uses the Christian message as a basis for his response to the "one poor book of Isabel" (VIII, 183). His sister, however, presents a special set of problems. Unlike Lucy, she is opaque and difficult to read:

In her life there was an unraveled plot; and he felt that unraveled it would eternally remain to him. No slightest hope or dream had he, that what was dark and mournful in her would ever be cleared up into some coming atmosphere of light and mirth. Like all youths, Pierre had conned his novel-lessons; had read more novels than most persons of his years; but their false, inverted attempts at systematizing eternally unsystemizable elements; their audacious, intermeddling impotency, in trying to unravel, and spread out, and classify, the more thin than gossamer threads which make up the complex web of life; these things over Pierre had no power now. . . . By infallible presentiment he saw, that not always doth life's beginning gloom conclude in gladness; that wedding-bells peal not ever in the last scene of life's fifth act; that while the countless tribes of common novels laboriously spin veils of mystery, only to complacently clear them up at last; and while the countless tribe of common dramas do but repeat the same; yet the profounder emanations of the human mind, intended to illustrate all that can be humanly known of human life; these never unravel their own intricacies, and have no proper endings; but in imperfect, unanticipated, and disappointing sequels (as mutilated stumps), hurry to abrupt intermergings with the eternal tides of time and fate. (VII, 165–66)

Once again it is important to recognize that Pierre's mode of perception has remained essentially the same. Although he no longer sees human life as a "sweetly writ" and uncomplicated manuscript, he still views it novelistically, replacing the vision of the sentimental novel with that of one of the "profounder emanations of the human mind." In short, he still is unable to look at the "object itself," but instead views its "reflection" in the "mirror" of a book (XXI, 334). For this reason, the book metaphor expands its area of influence to include Pierre's own "desperate career," which also ends in an unanticipated "sequel" (XXV, 396). The "armless trunk" of rock on the Mount of the Titans, which in Pierre's dream wears "his own duplicate face and features" (407), is the "mutilated stump" which symbolically brings to a close the fifth act of the play which is his life. Here too there are no wedding bells, but rather incest, murder, and suicide, for "the curtain inevitably falls upon a corpse" (XII, 232).

The truth, however, transcends the boundaries of Pierre's defective vision, as the ever-expanding metaphor of the book suggests. Not even the narrator can offer an escape from the web of fictions which surround his hero, for he, too, is an actor in a similar drama. In his analysis of Pierre's response to Isabel's letter his creator writes:

Pierre! thou art foolish; rebuild—no, not that, for thy shrine still stands; it stands, Pierre, firmly stands; smellest thou not its yet undeparted, embowering bloom? Such a note as thine can be easily enough written, Pierre; impostors are not unknown in this curious world; or the brisk novelist, Pierre, will write thee fifty such notes, and so steal gushing tears from his reader's eyes; even as *thy* note so strangely made thine own manly eyes so arid; so glazed, and so arid, Pierre—foolish Pierre! (IV, 81)

The suggestion that Isabel may be an impostor is enough to call into question Pierre's belief that he now sees only truth. But the reminder that the note is the product of a novelist is even more destructive, for it reduces the reality of Pierre's adventures to the vapors of the narrator's mind. His story, like Hamlet's, "though a thing of life, was, after all, but a thing of breath, evoked by the wanton magic of a creative hand" (IX, 199). The world occupied by the narrator and the reader, however, is no more real than the novelistic one, for it too is filled with impostors and fictions of all kinds. As the narrator's use of a technique associated with the sentimental novel suggests, he is entangled in an artificial web as imprisoning as the one which surrounds his hero. Although his book is written against the products of the "brisk novelist," it carries them within it and is unable to escape their poisonous influence.

Pierre's tendency to see the world through the mirror of a book is only one aspect of his difficult entanglement. He further complicates his situation by looking to literature for a solution to his problems. Indeed, he even allows his reading to influence his response to Isabel's plea for recognition. With the loss of his youthful blindness comes an ability to recognize the "superficial and purely incidental lessons" of *Hamlet*, although he remains incapable of understanding "the hopeless gloom of its interior meaning." Because the play teaches him that "all meditation is worthless, unless it prompt to action; . . . that in the earliest instant of conviction, the roused man must strike" (199), he acts without considering the consequences. In his determination to avoid Hamlet's indecisiveness, he allows his enthusiasm to distort his vision and mistakenly believes that by pretending marriage to Isabel, he can live a "planned and perfect Future" (X, 202).

Hamlet, however, is a fiction, "a thing of breath, evoked by the wanton magic of a creative hand, and as wantonly dismissed at last into the endless halls of hell and night" (IX, 199). It is no wonder, then, that Pierre's decision leads him into the manufactured intricacies of "Cretan labyrinths" (X, 206) rather than into a realm of unadorned truth. Because he is driven to action by a superficial understanding of a fiction, he rushes into a "fictitious alliance" which, "though in reality but a web of air, yet in effect would prove a wall of iron; for the same powerful motive which induced the thought of forming such an alliance, would always thereafter forbid the tacit exposure of its fictitiousness" (205).

Pierre's reading of *Hamlet*, however, is responsible only for his destructive eagerness and intensity. The decision itself has its origins in another more superficial fiction.

For surely no mere mortal who has at all gone down into himself will ever pretend that his slightest thought or act solely originates in his own defined indentity. The preamble seems not entirely unnecessary as usher of the strange conceit, that possibly the latent germ of Pierre's proposed extraordinary mode of executing his proposed extraordinary resolve—namely, the nominal conversion of a sister into a wife—might have been found in the previous conversational conversion of a mother into a sister; for hereby he had habituated his voice and manner to a certain fictitiousness in one of the closest domestic relations of life; and since man's moral texture is very porous, and things assumed upon the surface, at last strike in—hence, this outward habituation to the above-named fictitiousness had insensibly disposed his mind to it as it were. . . . (207–8)

Like Taji, Pierre is tied to his past and doomed to repeat it. The very method he hopes to use to escape the artificial world of Saddle Meadows binds him more tightly to it. His solution to his problem does not originate within himself but is invented by someone else and comes to him from the outside. The narrator's description of the Glendinning heritage and its relationship to the obviously artificial peerage system of the old world implies that domestic relations, like religious and political systems, are artificial forms and usages which have been constructed by man. And Pierre's "nominal" and "conversational" conversions of these apparently essential forms explicitly reveal "the mere imaginariness of the so supposed solidest principle of human association" (VII, 167). By innocently departing from the "arbitrary lines of conduct" established by the "common world" (X, 207), he breaks through man's surface of forms and finds himself in an absurd realm where mothers and sisters, sisters and wives, and lovers and cousins are interchangeable, and the atmosphere is polluted by the crimes of adultery, incest, matricide, and parricide. His self-conscious role playing, in short, exposes him to the truth that all life is a masquerade and the world a house of fictions, a labyrinthine enclosure with mirrors instead of windows.

It is this "miserably neglected Truth" which Pierre hopes to reveal to the world by writing a novel. His goal, however, is a hopeless one, for he is bound to the "profound events which had lately befallen him, and the unprecedented situation in which he now found himself" (XXI, 333). As a result, he is unable to move from actor to teller or to maintain the necessary distance between himself and his fictional surrogate. As the narrator notes when he peeps over the young author's shoulder—once again placing himself within the interior of his book and creating a Chinese box of fictions—he "seems to have directly plagiarized from his own experiences, to fill out the mood of his apparent author-hero, Vivia" (XXII, 356). The word "plagiarized," of course, is especially appropriate in this context because Pierre's experience is composed of a series of literary fictions. Bound as it is to its author's personal situation, his book does not reveal the "sane madness of vital truth" but instead adds another strand to the web of fictions which enclose him. As he comes to realize, its "leaves," like "knavish cards," are "covertly packed" (XXV, 399), and its author, an "unwilling states-prisoner of letters" (400), is a "coiner" and a "swindler" (XXVI, 421).

Overwhelmed at last by this knowledge, Pierre abandons his book, although he retains his literary vision to the very end: "Here, then, is the untimely, timely end;—Life's last chapter well stitched into the middle! Nor book, nor author of the book, hath any sequel, though each hath its last lettering" (424). Nevertheless, his story forms the center of a completed book, and his "untimely end" provides its "disappointing sequel." His final position is not that of his creator.

The best measure of the distance which exists between the narrator and his hero is provided by Isabel, the character responsible for the destruction of Pierre's naïve world and the object of his newly developed goals and desires. Surrounded by darkness and mystery, she seems as ambiguous as the universe itself. An important clue to the function of that "poor book," however, is found in the fact that in several places she is associated with the narrator and his literary methods. Her ghost-like face, which is "vaguely historic and prophetic;

backward, hinting of some irrevocable sin; forward, pointing
to some inevitable ill" (III, 49), seems an analogue to the movement of the novel itself, which "goes forward and goes backward, as occasion calls" (62). Like one of those "profounder
emanations of the human mind," which end in "unanticipated
and disappointing sequels," her autobiographical story ends in
an "abrupt and enigmatical obscurity" (VII, 160). And, like
the narrator, who follows "the endless, winding way,—the flowing river in the cave of man; careless whither I be led, reckless where I land" (V, 126), Isabel "speak[s] straight on, in all
my thoughts, heedless whither they may flow, or what things
they may float to me" (VIII, 182).

Because Isabel has grown up outside of human institutions,
without knowledge of her family and free from contact with
the doctrines of impostor philosophers or priests, she is capable of detaching herself from her own thoughts:

> I have had no training of any sort. All my thoughts well up in me;
> I know not whether they pertain to the old bewilderings or not;
> but as they are, they are, and I can not alter them, for I had noth-
> ing to do with putting them in my mind, and I never affect any
> thoughts; . . . but when I speak, think forth from the tongue,
> speech being sometimes before the thought; so, often, my own
> tongue teaches me new things. (VI, 144)

Isabel understands that thoughts and language do not originate
in the individual but come to him from the outside. Her consciousness stands removed from both her thoughts and her
words and is affected by neither the one nor the other. For this
reason not even her "inmost and truest thoughts" have any
"operative effect" on her. She stands outside their artificiality,
and senses that silence and "motionlessness" (140) are truer
than either thought, speech, or action. For this reason she accepts the essential mysteriousness of things and refuses to
assert anything definite concerning the nature of reality. To
her "mysteries" are "far sweeter" than "surmises," for "though

the mystery be unfathomable, it is still the unfathomableness of fullness; but the surmise, that is but shallow and unmeaning emptiness" (VIII, 180).

Only one thought violates the mystery of her consciousness, and it is born out of her first association with other human beings. When at the age of ten she experiences family life for the first time, she discovers that "all good, harmless men and women were human things, placed at cross-purposes, in a world of snakes and lightnings, in a world of horrible and inscrutable inhumanities" (VI, 144). It is this feeling of "my humanness among the inhumanities" (145) which causes Isabel to involve herself in man's "hereditary forms and world usages." Drawn to the mysterious gentleman who calls himself her father, she resolves to learn to read in order that she may decipher the "talismanic word" (VIII, 172) written in the middle of his book-like handkerchief. It is, of course, the knowledge that this word provides which leads Isabel to make the one surmise of her life—that Pierre is her brother—and thereby to involve herself in the world's net of circumstances: "Thy hand is the caster's ladle, Pierre, which holds me entirely fluid. Into thy forms and slightest moods of thought, thou pourest me; and I there solidify to that form, and take it on, and thenceforth wear it, till once more thou moldest me anew. If what thou tellest me be thy thought, then how can I help its being mine, my Pierre?" (XXIV, 381).

Drawn by love to other human beings, Isabel absorbs the destructive knowledge of the alphabet in an attempt to establish lines of communication with her own kind. Once she communicates with her brother, however, her saving "apartness" is ended forever. An unbreakable "monkey-rope" ties her to him and to the artificial forms which are his cultural inheritance. For this reason, his failure is also hers, and she is led by his mistaken vision to incest and suicide.

Just as Isabel's vision is analogous to the narrator's, so the story of her relationship with her brother is a dramatic re-enactment of the aesthetic conflict which takes place within the narrator's mind. Like Isabel he recognizes the authenticity and attractiveness of silence and motionlessness. But he is drawn to the world, as she is to her brother, finding a life of Plinlimmon "repose" unattractive and cruel. Like Isabel, he speaks and writes although he knows that silence is more profound and true, and like Isabel's note and story, his product brings degradation, heartache, and tears. But whereas Isabel is destroyed by her involvement with the world, the narrator continues to live in a state of unrelieved despair.

Pierre is a book with a bad conscience but not an apocalyptic or suicidal one, as exemplified in, for example, *The Confidence-Man*. It is this condition which is responsible for its stylistic inconsistencies and which produces the peculiarly horrifying effect experienced by so many of its readers. *Pierre* presents us with the grotesque and frightening image of a writer who understands that he must become the "canting showman" (XXV, 396) he despises but who is unwilling either to accept the role or to relapse into silence. Because society is composed of other men, he speaks to make contact with it; because that act necessarily involves him in its artificiality, he speaks with violence, hoping to break through the fictive layers which surround him. But social forms are invincible, and he is led to a confession of failure but not to total surrender. Hence his expression is at once futile and unremitting, and his form is that of an unresolved crisis.

ii

Bridging the gap between the unresolved despair of *Pierre* and the apocalyptic laughter of *The Confidence-Man* is *Israel Potter*, a book which does much to explain and define the relationship between the two works which bracket it. More than a whimsical account of American history, it, like Melville's other novels, is acutely self-reflexive. Like *Pierre*, it dramatizes the failure of the author-hero, but in this case a solution is found to the artistic crisis which the failure precipitates. Because the narrator is an editor rather than an original creator, he is able to avoid the web of fictions which surrounds his hero and to remain ironically detached from its confusing intricacies.

Crucial to an understanding of the book's narrative mode is its ironic dedication, which, like that of *Pierre*, is addressed to a mass of solid rock. The narrator of *Pierre*, by means of his genuflection to that presiding "central majesty," "The Most Excellent Purple Majesty of Greylock," suggests his own relationship to that creative "Hollow Hand" which the writer of fiction must emulate and describe. Similarly, the narrator of *Israel Potter*, with his celebration of the "Great Biographer," "his Highness the Bunker Hill Monument," establishes an example for himself to follow. As the dedication suggests, he regards himself as a biographer of a very special type. Unwilling to commit himself to creative or fictional biography, he merely edits the autobiographical story of another.

> I am the more encouraged to lay this performance at the feet of your Highness, because, with a change in the *grammatical person*, it preserves, almost as in a *reprint*, Israel Potter's autobiographical story. Shortly after his return in infirm old age to his native land, a little narrative of his adventures, forlornly published on sleazy gray paper, appeared among the peddlers, written, probably, not by himself, but taken down from his lips by another. But like the crutch-marks of the cripple by the Beautiful Gate, this blurred record is now out of print. From a tattered copy, rescued by the merest chance from the rag-pickers, the present account has been drawn, which, with the exception of some expansions, and additions of historic and personal details, and one or two shiftings of scene, may, perhaps, be not unfitly regarded some thing in the light of a dilapidated old tombstone retouched. (v-vi, italics mine)

Because the narrator knows that the writer's imagination is necessarily tied to his own experiences, he seeks a literary form which will require little or no contribution from that faculty. Because the story he tells is not his own imaginative product but is taken from the "blurred record" of another's experience, he hopes to be able to penetrate the surfaces of that experience and, at the same time, retain his ironic detachment. By limiting his creative activities to the addition and expansion of details and the shifting of narrative point of view, he seeks to attain the indifference of the Bunker Hill Monument and to reveal the meaning of that "Great Biographer" 's silence.

This is made possible not only by his lack of imaginative commitment but by the nature of biography itself: "Biography, in its purer form, confined to the ended lives of the true and brave, may be held the fairest meed of human virtue—one given and received in entire disinterestedness—since neither can the biographer hope for acknowledgment from the subject, nor the subject at all avail himself of the biographical distinction conferred" (v). Here, of course, is a method of writing which is far removed from the autobiographical mode of Melville's earlier novels. Even more forcibly than Pierre's abortive attempts at authorship, Israel Potter's autobiography illustrates the failure of the author-hero. Forced to dictate his story to another and incapable of understanding its implications, Israel tells it in order to dramatize his need for a pension. But it fades "out of print" as Israel fades "out of being" (XXVII, 241), and it is left to the ironic voice of the editor to rescue it from the rag-pickers.

With some "additions" and "expansions" the editor is able to reveal the total meaninglessness of Israel's wandering life and thereby point to the truth which lies behind the "sleazy gray paper" of his story and the gray face of the "Great Biographer." Finding ironic significance in Israel's name and in the fact that he wandered for "more than forty years . . . in the wild wilderness of the world's extremest hardships and ills" (I, 6), he structures his account of his hero's wanderings around a set of Biblical analogues. Israel is the "prodigal son" (II, 11), "Jonah in the belly of the whale" (III, 18), Daniel in the lion's den (V, 38), a Christ-like "bescarred bearer of a cross" (XXVII, 239). He is associated with the Israelites as he labors in the "English Egypt" (XXIV, 224), wanders in the "London deserts," with the London fog "before him the ever-present cloud by day, but no pillar of fire by the night, except the cold column of the monument, . . . on whose top . . . the shiverer . . . often laid down" (XXVI, 229), and returns, finally, "with the shared Benjamin of his old age" to the illusory "Canaan beyond the sea" (236).

But the Biblical metaphors are ironic. Unlike his scriptural counterparts Israel is to die as he has lived, with "his scars . . . his only medals" (XXVII, 241). Taking his initial clue from his hero's name, the narrator, through an extended use of Biblical allusion, makes it quite clear that for Israel the finger of God is truly the hollow of His hand. One of God's chosen people, he lives and dies an exile. His failure, however, in no way involves the well-being of the disinterested narrator, who has invented neither Israel nor the events of his life. He stands removed from the fiction which is his hero's name and comically calls attention to its meaninglessness by revealing the emptiness which lies behind it. For example, his additive and expansive hand turns Israel's brief and straightforward account of his association with Squire Woodcock into an ironic religious experience. "Buried alive" in a "tomb" with a "cavernous gate," he is told by the good squire, "your resurrection will soon be at hand" (XII, 94). But the god-like Squire dies suddenly in the meantime, and as no one else knows of Israel's presence, he remains entombed for more than three days. Eventually driven to an attempt to force his way out, he discovers accidentally that "the jamb was ajar" (101), and, dressing in the dead Squire's clothing so that he "would well pass for Squire Woodcock's genuine phantom" (XIII, 105), he makes his ghostly escape.

But as Israel's subsequent actions suggest, his burial and resurrection have been symbolically meaningless. After leaving the Squire's house he exchanges clothes with a scarecrow and is immediately mistaken for a scarecrow himself: "Waiting until the man momentarily disappeared in a little hollow, Israel ran briskly to the identical spot where the scarecrow had stood, where, standing stiffly erect, pulling the hat well over his face, and thrusting out his arm, pointed steadfastly towards the Squire's abode, he awaited the event" (110). Israel manages to make his escape and his wandering continues; his life is to no degree affected by his Christ-like experience, nor by any of his adventures which seem to be symbolically meaningful. Unlike the Biblical figures with whom he is so often associated, his physical pain and suffering is no preparation for spiritual cleansing and rebirth. Providence in the world of *Israel Potter* is imaged by the gray, disinterested face of the "Great Biographer."

Thus it is that the editor, following the creative example of the "Great Biographer" and anticipating the demands of twentieth-century critics, consciously avoids artistic intercession in Israel's life:

Well aware that in your Highness' eyes the merit of the story must be in its general fidelity to the main drift of the original narrative, I forbore anywhere to mitigate the hard fortunes of my hero; and particularly towards the end, though sorely tempted, durst not substitute for the allotment of Providence any artistic recompense of poetical justice; so that no one can complain of the gloom of my closing chapters more profoundly than myself. (vi)

The narrator's editorial changes, then, are in no way intended to reshape the events of Israel's life in order to suggest meaning where none existed. In fact, as his additions of the Biblical analogues suggest, his intention is to reveal the absence of meaning in Israel's life of wandering. Indeed, it is his devotion to truth which has governed his choice of subject:

But these experiences [in London], both from their intensity and his solitude, were necessarily squalid. Best not enlarge upon them. For just as extreme suffering, without hope, is intolerable to the victim, so, to others, is its depiction without some corresponding delusive mitigation. The gloomiest and truthfulest dramatist seldom chooses for his theme the calamities, however extraordinary, of inferior and private persons; least of all, the pauper's; admonished by the fact, that to the craped palace of the king lying in state, thousands of starers shall throng; but few feel enticed to the shanty, where, like a pealed knuckle-bone, grins the unupholstered corpse of the beggar. (XXVI, 229–30)

Although he approaches the truth behind Israel's life with care, the narrator refuses to participate in the act of "delusive mitigation." Because the objects and titles which surround the life of a socially prominent person give that life an illusory sense of seriousness and meaning in the same way that an artificially preserved corpse gives an appearance of life to death, he chooses a beggar for his hero. As a result of his low social status, Israel retains none of the trappings of the socially superior and public person and therefore is not surrounded by any of the fictitious seriousness which is derived from empty social forms. For this reason, his life furnishes a perfect example of the comically pathetic life of Everyman and permits the narrator to avoid the fictions which surround the death of a king and to bring the reader closer to the truth-containing shanty of the beggar.

In order to avoid grotesque over-emphasis, however, he does not describe in detail the "starveling's wrangling with rats for prizes in the sewers; or his crawling into an abandoned door-less house in St. Giles', where his hosts were three dead men, one pendant" (230). Avoiding the madness implicit in direct description of Israel's "unupholstered" life, the narrator, as his use of Biblical analogues demonstrates, finds other, more indirect, ways of approaching the truth. Enabled by his detachment to penetrate the fictions with which man surrounds himself, he exposes with amused disinterestedness not only the void which exists behind Israel's seemingly meaningful name, but the emptiness behind everything else as well. Behind the sage-like, practical mask of the aged diplomat, Benjamin Franklin, is revealed the smiling face of a confidence man who, "having carefully weighed the world, . . . could act any part in it" (VIII, 66); and John Paul Jones, the famous naval hero, is shown to be a man "civilized in externals but a savage at heart" (XIX, 170).

Like *Pierre, Israel Potter* reduces all of man's activities to the level of role playing, but in the later novel the narrator is never drawn into the masquerade. As his account of the battle between the "Bon Homme Richard" and the "Serapis" demonstrates, he remains offstage and reveals the central truths of man, his world, and his God. In his description he emphasizes the artificial aspects of the conflict, even going so far as to suggest that the dramatic unities of time and place are carefully followed: "Several circumstances of the place and time served to invest the fight with a certain scenic atmosphere casting a light almost poetic over the wild gloom of its tragic results. The battle was fought between the hours of seven and ten at night; the height of it was under a full harvest moon, in view of thousands of distant spectators crowding the high cliffs of Yorkshire" (171). The setting is important because it has poetic application to the battle itself. The English coast "wears a savage, melancholy . . . aspect" as a result of the attacks of the "wasteful desert of the sea" on the land, which "succumbs to the Attila assaults of the deep." Because of this eternal war, the coast seems in a state of "incessant decay," and "nowhere is this desolation more marked than for those fifty miles of coast between Flamborough Head and the Spurm" (171), the site of the battle between the "Richard" and the "Serapis." Hence the "crowds of the islanders" (176) who witness the engagement see a mirror image of the conflict which is being waged by the sea on the land just below them.

As suggestive as the location of the battle is the time of its occurrence. Although begun in darkness, "when objects [are] perceived with difficulty" (173), the battle is soon bathed in the "half demoniac glare" of a newly risen moon, and the "objects before perceived with difficulty, now glimmered ambiguously." The moon, which is placed on the horizon by an "invisible hand" (175) and which serves as a "great foot light" (174), adds to the cosmic significance of the battle which is raging on the water:

Through this sardonical mist, the face of the Man-in-the-Moon—looking right towards the combatants, as if he were standing in a trap-door of the sea, leaning forward leisurely with his arms complacently folded over upon the edge of the horizon—this queer face wore a serious, apishly self-satisfied leer, as if the Man-in-the-Moon had somehow secretly put up the ships to their contest, and in the depths of his malignant old soul was not unpleased to see how well his charms worked. There stood the grinning Man-in-the-Moon, his head just dodging into view over the rim of the sea:—Mephistopheles prompter of the stage. (175)

The "invisible hand"—no doubt related to the "Hollow Hand" of *Pierre*—seems a suitable image for divinity in a world where the warring elements both echo and inspire the efforts of man, and the divine gift of footlight and prompter to aid in the enactment of the earthly drama suggests that both man and nature are following a cosmic script. Living in a stage-like world absurdly created by an invisible and hollow hand, man plays his meaningless and barbaric role and in so doing loses his humanity. The fleet of English ships flutter like "chickens . . . under the wing of the shore" (170); the "Serapis" circles the "Richard," "hate causing her to act not unlike a wheeling cock about a hen, when stirred by a contrary passion"; the two ships are like a "hawk and crow . . . clawing and beaking" (174); the sailors resemble "swallows about barn-eaves" (180), "fauns and satyrs," and are "thinned out . . . like spring radishes" (185).

But if the narrator's revealing metaphors imply that he stands outside this world of meaningless gestures, they also point to the severe artistic limitations which this stance entails. His "expansions and additions" do not violate his anonymity by involving him in Israel's pathetic life, but they do define his role as a custodial one. *Israel Potter* is, in fact, a "dilapidated old tombstone retouched." The narrator is capable of revealing truth, but, as he knows, his vehicle precludes the possibility of "great Art."

V

THE NOVELIST AS IMPOSTOR:
SUBVERSIVE FORM IN
THE CONFIDENCE-MAN

To see a man turn himself into all shapes like a chameleon, or a Proteus, omnia transformans sese in miracula rerum [*who transformed himself into every possible shape*], *to act twenty parts and persons at once for his advantage, to temporize and vary like Mercury the planet, good with good, bad with bad; having a several face, garb, and character for every one he meets; of all religions, humours, inclinations; to fawn like a spaniel,* mentitis et mimicis obsequiis [*with feigned and hypocritical observance*], *rage like a lion, bark like a cur, fight like a dragon, sting like a serpent, as meek as a lamb, and yet again grin like a tiger, weep like a crocodile, insult over some, and yet others domineer over him, here command, there crouch, tyrannize in one place, be baffled in another, a wise man at home, a fool abroad to make others merry.*

To see so much difference betwixt words and deeds, so many parasangs betwixt tongue and heart, men like stage-players act variety of parts, give good precepts to others, [to] soar aloft, whilst they themselves grovel on the ground.

$$. \qquad . \qquad . \qquad . \qquad .$$

We have women politicians, children metaphysicians; every silly fellow can square a circle, make perpetual motions, . . . interpret Apocalypsis, *make new theorics, a new system of the world, new logic, new philosophy, etc.* Nostra utique regio, *saith Petronius, "our country is so full of deified spirits, divine souls, that you may sooner find a god than a man amongst us," we think so well of ourselves. . . .*

ROBERT BURTON, *The Anatomy of Melancholy*
The literary career seems to me unreal, both in its essence and in the rewards which one seeks from it, and therefore fatally marred by a secret absurdity.

MAURICE DE GUERIN,
quoted by MATTHEW ARNOLD in *Essays in Criticism*
Melville marks and comments: "This is the first verbal statement of a truth which everyone who thinks in these days must have felt."

MERTON M. SEALTS, *Melville's Reading*

MELVILLE FINALLY, with *The Confidence-Man*, abandons his search for the form which will provide the truth-seeking novelist with a means of escape from the ontological and social lies. Instead, he accepts and affirms the necessity which makes the teller an actor by using it as his central formal principle. *The Confidence-Man*, which is apparently designed to conceal rather than to reveal, presents a world where the real and fictitious are indistinguishable and interchangeable. Structured around the metaphor of the world as stage, the book is filled with references to costumes, transformations, disguises, dramatic performances, and characters from various plays. Here is a realm of appearances ruled over by a multi-formed impostor who asks to be judged by the clothes he wears, the objects he carries, and the words he speaks; a realm where one is "at a loss to determine where exactly the fictitious character had been dropped, and the real one, if any, resumed" (XLI, 253). Reality here may be viewed as at best the mere recurrence of certain appearances, and the presence of inconsistent characters capable of playing many roles at times seems to preclude even this limited definition.

Here, then, is a fiction which is ostensibly inaccessible to the careful eye of the ideal reader described in "Hawthorne and His Mosses," for the world of this book is that of "the tricky stage." Its reader finds himself in a position remarkably similar to that of the confidence man's numerous victims. Like the cynic with the wooden leg he may suspect every character —victim as well as victimizer—of acting in bad faith, but his "discerning eye" is as unsuccessful at penetrating the painted surfaces as is the one-legged man's "gimlet one" (VI, 35). Plagued by suspicions but led on by such conventional literary clues as puns, complex patterns of imagery, and suggestive allusions to important people, events, and products of human history, the reader is tempted time and again to try to bring to the surface the meaning and order which seem to lie concealed behind the actions and words of the novel's characters. But the "sacred white doe" remains hidden in the "woodlands," for each newly discovered clue, each new operative pattern or allusion, leads not beneath the verbal surface but across it to another mystery or, more often, to an example which subverts the implications of the original pattern. For example, the reader is confronted near the beginning of the novel with what H. Bruce Franklin calls a "patterned conflict" between the advocates of trust and distrust and the wild and domestic animals which are associated with each. Juxtaposed to Black Guinea, who is described as a "black sheep" (II, 10), is the cynical one-legged man who wants to leave "the streaks of these fingers on his [the Negro's] paint, as the lion leaves the streaks of his nails on a Caffre" (VI, 35–36).[1] The reader, in other words, is asked to associate sheep with confidence and lions with distrust and to read the book, which is filled with animals, with this apparently meaningful distinction in mind. As he nears its end, however, his literary confidence is severely shaken when he hears the knowledgeable barber maintain that "truth sometimes is sheepish. Lies, lies, sir, brave lies are the lions" (XLIII, 263).

The Confidence-Man takes advantage of a set of assumptions which readers of fiction make concerning the novelistic world and its relationship to the actual one in the same way that its hero plays upon his victim's commitment to accepted social forms and conventions. The book's carefully woven surface pattern testifies to the presence of an omniscient manipulator who possesses the secret to its complex design. Indeed, he sometimes appears in his own person as if to assure the reader that the secret of his "tangled web" (XIV, 78) will at last be revealed. Only the most confident lover of fiction, however, can read far in the novel without beginning to "suspect" (VI, 33) that "even were truth on his tongue, his way of speaking it would make truth almost offensive as falsehood" (34). Just as the cosmopolitan doesn't "exactly see how Shakespeare meant the words he put in Polonius' mouth" (XXX, 194), so even the "nicest critics" are unable to be sure of the true "sentiments" (XXVIII, 179) of either the narrator or his characters. Even when the motive of a character seems clear, as

[1] *The Wake of the Gods,* pp. 180–81.

in the case of the crippled cynic, equivocations are always introduced. The reader, for example, is not allowed to hear the cynic's illustrative story of distrust told in his "porcupine way, and with sarcastic details," but must be content with the narrator's "good-natured version" (VI, 33).

This kind of suspicious authorial manipulation, which is characteristic of *The Confidence-Man*, raises a number of aesthetic problems. What is the nature and purpose of fiction? Does it entertain or teach? Is the novel a mimetic or an autonomous form? What kind of reality does it have? These questions are not ignored, for the narrator of *The Confidence-Man*, like those of Melville's other novels, is deeply interested in such important theoretical matters. He too draws attention to his fiction as fiction by obtruding technical matters upon the reader. This is accomplished chiefly in two ways: direct commentary by an intruding narrator, and the use of the technique of the fiction within a fiction. In three important chapters (XIV, XXXIII, and XLIV) the narrator breaks into the action of the novel to defend his artistry against imagined attacks by critics. In addition to these intrusions there are at least ten other digressions in the form of stories of varying lengths told either by the characters or by the narrator himself.

These two kinds of digressions, the intruding narrator and the story within a story, while similar in the sense that both demand a readjustment to the reader's relationship to the novel, apparently have quite different effects. The narrator's discussion of technical matters would seem to remind the reader of the story's fictitious nature, of its unreality, and to imply a solider reality occupied by both narrator and reader. In *The Confidence-Man*, however, the solidity of this realm is immediately undercut by the narrator's insistence that it too is a stage filled with characters playing roles similar to those enacted within the novel itself. But this does not, as one might suppose, serve to remove reality one step further and to imply the existence of a more real realm behind the stage of nature. Just the reverse is true. *The Confidence-Man* radically conflates the supernatural, natural, and artistic realms, placing them all on one plane. Among other things, the book is a demonstration that man's vision of a supernatural realm is as much a fiction as the world in which he lives and the books which he writes.

The three digressions by the narrator, then, which seem attempts on his part to break out of his fictional maze and appear to stand as a reality against which the rest of the novel can be measured, are themselves an intimate part of the novel's complexity. Because the narrator's theories and language are incorporated in twisted and distorted forms into the texture of the fictive narrative itself, there is created a realm where fiction and real life are indistinguishable.

The device of the story within a story seems at first to counteract the effects of the narrator's discussion of technique. Because it diverts the reader's attention to another fictive level, it should make the larger story of which it is a part seem more real. The confidence man listening to and telling stories should appear less of a fictional character himself. Indeed, the reader approaches the smaller story with the expectation that its relationship to the larger one will help him to define the relation of the larger one to the real world. As is the case with most other traditional critical assumptions, this confidence is betrayed by the novel. The stories which are told and interpreted in *The Confidence-Man* are twisted to fit the roles which the characters are at that time playing. A story which is at one point considered real may at another be described as fictitious, because the confidence man himself makes no distinction between the two realms.

i. Fiction as an Imitation of Nature: Chapter XIV

In the first of the three digressive chapters the narrator directly confronts the complex problem of the relationship between fiction and reality. Anxious to retain the critic's admiration and confidence, he stops the action of the novel in order to defend his representation of Henry Roberts, the gullible merchant, who, having been duped by the confidence man three times in succession, finally displays his lack of confidence just before disappearing from the book. An author, the narrator argues, should not be blamed for the creation of inconsistent characters. The critic's demand for consistent ones seems to him to conflict with another equally important aesthetic dictum—"fiction based on fact should never be contradictory to it." And as "in real life, a consistent character is a *rara avis*," the "distaste of readers to the contrary sort in books, can hardly arise from any sense of their untrueness. It may rather be from perplexity as to understanding them" (XIV, 76).

That fiction, where every character can, by reason of its consistency, be comprehended at a glance, either exhibits but sections of character, making them appear for wholes, or else is very untrue to reality; while, on the other hand, that author who draws a character, even though to common view incongruous in its parts, as the flying-squirrel, and, at different periods, as much at variance with itself as the butterfly is with the caterpillar into which it changes, may yet, in so doing, be not false but faithful to facts.
If reason be judge, no writer has produced such inconsistent characters as nature herself has. . . . When the duck-billed beaver of Australia was first brought stuffed to England, the naturalists, appealing to their classifications, maintained that there was, in reality, no such creature; the bill in the specimen must needs be, in some way, artificially stuck on. (76–77)

The controlling assumption in this passage, as in the entire chapter, is that the novel is a mimetic form which is to be judged by something external to itself. Its truth must be discussed not in terms of its internal consistency but rather by reference to nature, the realm which it seeks to imitate. This credo, however, raises several important problems. To begin with, it seems to deny the possibility of significant form. Writers who "represent human nature not in obscurity, but transparency" (77) and thereby achieve harmony of form

155

and character are guilty of counterfeiting. Especially suspect of misrepresenting nature are those "psychological novelists" who "challenge astonishment at the tangled web of some character, and then raise admiration still greater at their satisfactory unraveling of it." Their "ingenuity," which has as its end the "revelation of human nature on fixed principles," leads to a complex design but not to a truthful rendering. The "studious youth," after careful study of the "best novels professing to portray human nature, . . . will still run risk of being too often at fault upon actually entering the world" because his guides distort human nature by oversimplifying it. These books are defective mirrors. Had the youth "been furnished with a true delineation, it ought to fare with him something as with a stranger entering, map in hand, Boston town; the streets may be very crooked, he may often pause; but, thanks to his true map, he does not hopelessly lose his way" (78).

The problem here is more complex than it first appears. Initially, the narrator seems simply to be saying that the aesthetic elements of the novel are necessarily limited by its human content, by the demand that it imitate a realm of inconsistent flux. But contained within his figures of speech is the hint that the natural realm itself is a fiction. The examples of the flying-squirrel, the caterpillar-butterfly, and the duck-billed beaver identify a masquerade in nature comparable to that which occurs aboard the "Fidèle." Moreover, the problem is complicated further by the narrator's denial of a knowable, essential, or ideal order behind nature's unreal and inconsistent flux. "Divine nature," like human nature, "is past finding out" (77). This view of nature, of course, makes any imitative literary activity morally and intellectually fraudulent, as it involves the pretense that the world man inhabits is the real one.

The circularity of the chapter's title, "Worth the Consideration of Those to Whom It May Prove Worth Considering," is reflected in its argument, which begins with the suggestion that we judge fiction in terms of what it is not—that is, reality —and ends by suggesting that the apparently real world is itself a fiction. And the reader's bewilderment increases when he returns to the story and discovers that the narrator's theoretical digression is a part of the narrative complexity which it seeks to clarify. The caterpillar's metamorphosis into a butterfly becomes the basis for one of the confidence man's tricky analogies. While engaged in an attempt to dupe the cynical Coonskins, the P.I.O. man offers an illustration of man's constant progress toward the good and the beautiful: "Madam, or sir, would you visit upon the butterfly the sins of the caterpillar? In the natural advance of all creatures, do they not bury themselves over and over again in the endless resurrection of better and better? Madam, or sir, take back this adult; he may have been a caterpillar, but is now a butterfly" (XXII, 141). But Coonskins, convinced that the P.I.O. man "pun[s] with ideas as another man [the narrator?] may with words" (141), is not convinced by such an analogy: "Pun away; but even accepting your analogical pun, what does it amount to? Was the caterpillar one creature, and is the butterfly another? The butterfly is the caterpillar in a gaudy cloak; stripped of which, there lies the impostor's long spindle of a body, pretty much worm-shaped as before" (141).

Present in this argument are two contradictory explanations for the inconsistency which the narrator finds in nature. People and insects change, the P.I.O. man suggests, because they are constantly evolving toward a higher form. Inconsistency is the sign of moral and intellectual development. Coonskins, on the other hand, implies that nature's inconsistency is an indication of its deceitfulness. The butterfly represents no development but is merely the caterpillar in a bright coat. Both of these theories seem relevant to the confidence man, the novel's most inconsistent character. Coonskin's description of the butterfly as a worm-like impostor in a gaudy cloak suggests the serpent-like confidence man in his role as cosmopolitan, hiding his satanic motives beneath his multicolored coat and seeming as attractive as the butterfly. Nonetheless, the more optimistic theory of the P.I.O. man also seems to describe the novel's polymorphic hero. Because the book is divided into two equal parts, with one half devoted to the first seven avatars of the confidence man and the second dominated by his final and most perfect incarnation, the cosmopolitan invites comparison with his less entertaining predecessors. His relationship to the off-white, black, gray, and snuff-colored avatars, all of whom are conservatively dressed and most of whom are slightly shabby, seems to parallel the butterfly's relation to his prosaic original.

The cosmopolitan himself suggests the nature of his connection to the earlier avatars when he comments on the P.I.O. man's dress: "a rather sensible fellow, by the way; much of my style of thinking; would, for his own sake, he were of my style of dress. Grief to good minds, to see a man of superior sense forced to hide his light under the bushel of an inferior coat" (XXIV, 152). According to the cosmopolitan a "vesture barred with various hues" (149) best expresses the true light of a man of "superior sense." For this reason he views the drab costume of the P.I.O. man as an unfortunate disguise and regards his own colorful garments as a true expression of his proper identity. This philosophy of clothes, however, is at best equivocal. To expose its ambiguities one has only to recall Ishmael's analysis of that "great principle of light," which produces all "earthly hues," including the "gilded velvets of butterflies," but "forever remains white or colorless in itself." If colors are regarded as "subtile deceits, not actually inherent in substances, but only laid on from without" (*M-D*, XLII, 193), the cosmopolitan's remarks take on an ironic doubleness, since they leave open the possibility that he may be unmasking himself.

This suspicion is strengthened when one recalls that the confidence man first appears on April Fools' Day at sunrise and is associated with Manco Capac, a child of the sun.[2] Dressed in a yellowish-white suit and wearing a white fur hat, the deaf and dumb lamb-like man is the silent, almost colorless principle from which the verbose and colorful cosmopolitan derives. Resplendent in his coat of many colors, appearing at twilight to "dispense a sort of morning through the night" (XLV, 273), he seems the child of the sun in his most highly evolved but most artificial form. Nevertheless, on the surface the two men seem to have very little in common. The "plumagy aspect" of the talkative cosmopolitan (XXIV, 149) is the antithesis of the "linty" appearance of the deaf-mute (I, 5), and the tendency of the lamb-like man neither to court nor shun regard is in obvious contrast with the behavior of the cosmopolitan, a "mature man of the world" (XXIV, 150) to whom "no man is a stranger" (151). Still, there are a number of important similarities between them. As the first avatar it is the job of the lamb-like man to prepare the way for those who will follow him. This he does by diverting the attention of the passengers from a poster which describes a mysterious impostor from the East and offers a reward for his capture, and by offering the text from which all the other avatars draw their sermons on charity. The narrator's description of him as he seems to fall asleep "in a retired spot on the forecastle" (I, 4) suggests that he has had his effect on the "Fidèle":

His aspect was at once gentle and jaded, and, from the moment of seating himself, increasing in tired abstraction and dreaminess. Gradually overtaken by slumber, his flaxen head drooped, his whole lamb-like figure relaxed, and, half reclining against the ladder's foot, lay motionless, as some sugar-snow in March, which, softly stealing down over night, with its white placidity startles the brown farmer peering out from his threshold at daybreak. (5)

[2] Elizabeth Foster points out that Manco Capac was a Peruvian god, a child of the sun (*C-M*, 289–90).

Although the lamb-like man disappears, the narrator's later description of the "Fidèle" as a "whitewashed fort" (II, 7) and "snowy boat" (XX, 114) as well as the success of the later avatars, is evidence that his sugar-snow message is effective. The extent of his success may be measured by comparing him to the less ambitious person in "quaker dress" (X, 57) who "snowed the odes" (58) of charity about the cabin and to the less subtle crippled soldier of fortune who maintains that "woes, when told to strangers for money, are best sugared" (XIX, 110).

Like much of the narrator's figurative language, however, the sugar-snow simile points in two directions. As the words "white placidity" suggest, snow is more than an apt figure for the confidence man's mode of operation. At the same time that it artificially sweetens and falsifies human life, it reveals the blank emptiness which lies behind all the forms of that life. The real crime of the confidence man is not that he takes money from his victims but that he robs them of their belief in the authenticity of their own roles as well as of the illusion that divine acts and appearances can only be sustained by divinity. The "advent" of the lamb-like man (I, 1) equivocates the authenticity of Christ's; and the serpentine avatars which follow him yoke together the two archetypal disguises, the serpent and the incarnation, the one no less deceptive than the other.

Deaf and dumb and associated with that "colorless all color," white, the lamb-like man combines most of Melville's favorite images for divinity. However, his heavenly humility and his yellowish-white suit, an earthly version of the color of the "very veil of the Christian's Deity" (M-D, XLII, 193), make him an object of suspicion on the worldly "Fidèle." The other passengers sense that he is "trying to enlist interest" and feel that they must "beware of him" (II, 6). But when he disguises his silent whiteness with the colors, voice, and gestures of the world, they are ready to believe in his Protean easychair and to have their names recorded in his transfer book.

For this reason the lamb-like man courts "oblivion" (7) by going to sleep under a "cross-wise balcony" like an "enchanted man in his grave" (6) and waits until the "last transient memory" of him is gone (7) before he begins a series of resurrections. Having had his message of charity rejected by mankind, he undergoes a painless crucifixion and is reborn at least seven times to test the extent of man's Christian charity.

In *The Confidence-Man*, then, the order of the two archetypal disguises is reversed in a significant way. The lamb-like man arrives not to mitigate the satanic effects of the serpent but to prepare the way for his many wiles. The appearance of the cosmopolitan, a man who has "confidence in the latent benignity of that beautiful creature, the rattle-snake" (XXXVI, 213), is necessitated by the failure of his prosaic original. While the lamb-like man was unable to cope with the barber's sign of "No Trust," which he encountered at sunrise, the cosmopolitan succeeds, near the end of the day, in getting the sign temporarily removed and gets a free shave for his efforts. Armed with the "double shields" of his genial hands (XXIV, 155), he proves a worthier foe for man's distrust than did the deaf-mute, who was protected only by his "shield-like" slate (I, 3). It is little wonder that the passengers who regard the confidence man in his original form as something of a "simpleton" (4) label him in his most highly evolved one, "QUITE AN ORIGINAL" (XLIII, 269).

The confidence man certainly seems to participate in the "natural advance of all creatures"; the butterfly-like figure of the worldly cosmopolitan appearing at twilight in its "various hues" completes the journey begun by the lamb-like man at sunrise. Dressed in his coat of many colors he is better able to conceal the nature of the "mystical cosmetic . . . the great principle of light" (*M-D*, XLII, 193) which has fathered him, for he is "sunshiny" (*C-M*, XXIV, 155) and tries to federate, "in heart as in costume, something of the various gallantries of men under various suns" (151). Arriving on the "Fidèle" in the middle of "one *cosmopolitan* and confident tide"

(II, 8; italics mine), the divine impostor finds it necessary to hide his telltale whiteness under a series of shabby coats until he finally evolves to his highest, most brightly colored form.

The novel, then, appears to suggest two contradictory ways of understanding the relationship between the first and final avatars of the confidence man. On the one hand, the cosmopolitan seems merely the lamb-like man disguised by the "subtle deceits" of his gaudy coat, while on the other, he appears to be a more highly evolved form of his ineffective original. This apparent contradiction is a central problem of the novel, and its solution reveals the metaphysical basis of Melville's comedy.

The key to the problem lies in the book's obviously Biblical structure. Because the "Fidèle" is filled with "all kinds of that multiform pilgrim species, man" (II, 8), it is clearly a spatial microcosm. But it is a temporal one as well. The events which occur on the decks of the ship in one day imply a period of time which stretches at least from the birth of Christ to the Apocalypse.[3] The cosmopolitan, in the three final chapters of the novel, achieves revenge on those who had rejected the Christ-like deaf-mute; and in the midst of echoes from Revelation he puts out the solar lamp and brings the novel to its comically apocalyptic close.

Although a fiction, *The Confidence-Man*, as its Biblical structure implies, is also gospel truth. Religion, the novel suggests, is, like the figure of the cosmopolitan, at once the greatest fiction and the highest reality. It is this truth which lies behind the relationship of the first and final avatars and which provides the rationale for the latter's philosophy of life: "Life is a pic-nic *en costume;* one must take a part, assume a character, stand ready in a sensible way to play the fool. To come in plain clothes, with a long face, as a wiseacre, only makes one a discomfort to himself, and a blot upon the scene. Like your jug of cold water among the wine-flasks, it leaves

[3] In Chapter XLIV the narrator suggests an even wider temporal frame by indirectly associating the novel's beginning with Genesis.

you unelated among the elated ones" (XXIV, 152). At once a commentary on his earlier prosaic disguises, the cynical misanthropes who remain unduped, and the method of the book itself, the cosmopolitan's words justify his creator's production of inconsistent characters. Because the world is a stage where all men play many roles, the best actors achieve the highest reality. And in a literary fiction the character which is most inconsistent and "at variance with itself" is most faithful to the facts of life. In a world where "to do, is to act" (VI, 35), where men fashion their selves and their gods out of a blank emptiness, any distinction between actuality and a fictive realm with its own internal laws of operation is spurious. In this sense the narrator's imitative theory of fiction is a matter of necessity rather than choice.

Leaving the reader with the sense that he has said more than he intended but less than he knows, the narrator concludes his apology for "whatever may have seemed amiss or obscure in the character of the merchant" and turns back to his comedy, or, rather, passes "from the comedy of thought to that of action" (XIV, 79). The extent to which both realms are comic is immediately suggested as the confidence man, who seems to have overheard the narrator's discussion, also passes from thought to action:

> The merchant having withdrawn, the other remained seated alone for a time, with the air of one who, after having conversed with some excellent man, carefully ponders what fell from him, however intellectually inferior it may be, that none of the profit may be lost; happy if from any honest word he has heard he can derive some hint, which, besides confirming him in the theory of virtue, may, likewise, serve for a finger-post to virtuous action. (XV, 80)

The immediate effect of this passage is to confuse the narrator's address to the reader with the confidence man's conversation with the merchant. The narrator, one must remember, has just finished distinguishing his Protean world from the consistent ones of the psychological novelists, which fail in the attempt to provide the "studious youth" with a "true map" to the crooked streets of reality. In the light of this failure, it is significant that the inconsistent merchant provides the thoughtful confidence man with a "fingerpost" which guides him through "a sort of corridor, narrow and dim, a by-way to . . . the emigrants' quarters" (80), in which he finds his next victim.

Although occupied by human travelers, these quarters seem more suited to birds. The bunks are arranged as "nests in the geometrical towns of the associate penguin and pelican" and are "pendulous" like "the cradle of the oriole" (80). This enormous birds' nest has a suitable inhabitant, an old miser, who has arms like "wasted penguin-flipper[s]" (81) and a "buzzard nose" (82). Obviously another of the narrator's duck-billed characters, hardly human but true to life, he is taken for "ten hoarded eagles" (84) by the most inconsistent character of all. As was the case with the butterfly-caterpillar analogy, a factual example used by the narrator in his non-fictional digression becomes a central metaphor in his fictional world. A factual duck-billed beaver becomes a fictional one, and both are equally artificial. As the miser later demonstrates when he pays the herb doctor with worthless coins, he, too, is a confidence man.

But what is the reader's relationship to this intricate web of facts and fiction? In what sense does he "profit" from the narrator's "honest words"? The answer to this question may lie in the fact that the reader of a book, like the merchant and the miser, invests both his money and his confidence in the author's integrity and knowledge. For this reason, the reader of *The Confidence-Man* can hardly be at ease when the narrator's discussion of the problems of "representing" characters is followed by a chapter entitled, "An Old Miser, upon Suitable Representation, Is Prevailed upon To Venture an Investment." Nor is his uneasiness relieved when in Chapter XVI an herb doctor appears and, like the narrator, insists that all men should have "confidence in my art" (XIX, 113) because it is "nature's own" (XVI, 91). As a matter of fact, both the herb doctor and his immediate successor, the P.I.O. man, like the narrator, "proceed by analogy from the physical to the moral" (XXII, 137). Such reasoning, although effective, is obviously equivocal. In his attack on "atheistical science," which has produced a book blasphemously titled *Nature in Disease*, the herb doctor employs a metaphor which subverts both his and the narrator's mimetic premises:

A title I cannot approve; it is suspiciously scientific. "Nature in Disease"? As if nature, divine nature, were aught but health; as if through nature disease is decreed! But did I not before hint of the tendency of science, that forbidden tree? Sir, if despondency is yours from recalling that title, dismiss it. Trust me, nature is health; for health is good, and nature cannot work ill. (XVI, 91)

The reference to the "forbidden tree" gives the reader valid cause for suspicion, reminding him that the fruit which brought sin, disease, and death into the world came from nature. And if unfallen nature was dangerous, the fallen one will be more so. Hence consumption of natural medicines and a devotion to mimetic fiction may be equally perilous. Coonskins' assertion—"Nature made me blind and would have kept me so. My oculist counterplotted her" (XXI, 123)—is hardly consoling, therefore, to the reader who has placed his confidence in the narrator's imitative theory of fiction.

ii. Fiction as a Self-Contained World: Chapter XXXIII

Like the herb doctor, the narrator seems to believe that "distrust is a stage to confidence" (XVI, 94), for at the moment when the novel's fallen world threatens to destroy the reader's confidence in its moral and artistic validity, he returns with another and different plea for confidence. As he had done in Chapter XIV, he begins his pitch by defending the behavior of an apparently "unreal" character, the harlequin-like cos-

165

mopolitan. This time, however, his apology is based on an autonomous rather than an imitative theory of fiction. He finds it "strange" that a "severe fidelity to real life should be exacted by any one, who, by taking up such a work, sufficiently shows that he is not unwilling to drop real life, and turn, for a time, to something different" (XXXIII, 206):

> There is another class, and with this class we side, who sit down to a work of amusement tolerantly as they sit at a play, and with much the same expectations and feelings. They look that fancy shall evoke scenes different from those of the same old crowd round the custom-house counter, and same old dishes on the boarding-house table, with characters unlike those of the same old acquaintances they meet in the same old way every day in the same old street. And as, in real life, the proprieties will not allow people to act out themselves with that unreserve permitted to the stage; so, in books of fiction, they look not only for more entertainment, but, at bottom, even for more reality, than real life itself can show. Thus, though they want novelty, they want nature, too; but nature unfettered, exhilarated, in effect transformed. In this way of thinking, the people in a fiction, like the people in a play, must dress as nobody exactly dresses, talk as nobody exactly talks, act as nobody exactly acts. It is with fiction as with religion: it should present another world, and yet one to which we feel the tie. (206-7)

Here then is a theory which emphasizes neither the novelist's fidelity to nature nor his role as guide or teacher but rather his duty to divert and entertain. The value of his art lies in its ability to make the reader forget the human realm, which is regarded as monolithic, monotonous, and dull, by immersing him in a vital and amusing world of make-believe. But this novelistic realm is not only more entertaining than the natural one; it is also more real. Like religion, it enables the reader to escape the shadow realm of appearances by giving him access to a higher reality.

Apparently the narrator has abandoned the Aristotelian view which he had espoused in Chapter XIV in favor of a Schopenhauerian one. Fiction, he now maintains, is more real than nature. In dealing with *The Confidence-Man*, however, such impulsive critical decisions are always dangerous. As a matter of fact, the narrator's comments do not imply the existence of a realm of ideas which is accessible to the pure mind of the artist. Just the reverse is true. For him the novelistic world is a "higher" reality precisely because it allows uninhibited role playing. The fictive harlequin performing his "capers" in his "parti-colored" coat is larger than life because he embodies and expresses more completely and successfully than is possible for an ordinary man an essential truth about life—that it is a dramatically enacted thing. In "real life," performances are limited by the "proprieties." The official values of society impose limitations on dress, talk, and manner, and man must avoid or conceal any thoughts which are inconsistent with these values. He must remain inside the boundaries of customhouse, boarding house, and street if his role is to be accepted as an authentic one. In short, all real-life performances are limited by the dictates of propriety and decorum.

In spite of the reassuring tone, the narrator's argument, like those of the confidence man, is an ontologically subversive one. Fiction and religion are linked not because they both serve as bridges between the shadows of this world of appearances and the divine reality above or behind it but because they both imply purely artificial realms. The realization that the greatest fiction is the highest reality negates the possibility of an essential identity and destroys all connection between a legitimate authorization to play a role and one's capacity for playing it. In the fictive and religious realms the actor, man, released from the restrictions of social decorum, may give himself up to his dramaturgic instincts and play both archetypal roles at once. The cosmopolitan, a satanic harlequin with a Christian message, is "charming" in one place and "serious" in another.

The narrator's autonomous theory, however, seems at first to have positive as well as negative effects. Since the fictive world is easily recognized as such and is designed to divert

167

and entertain rather than to instruct, it apparently presents no threat to the reader's well-being; in fact, it may allow him to return to real life with a more profound understanding of its structure. But, once again, as the reader moves from the narrator's theory to his practice, he becomes progressively more uneasy. While it is true that the unreal and colorful cosmopolitan is always free to "create a scene" (V, 26), the man with the weed, when he receives a monetary gift from the merchant, is prevented by the "cold garb of decorum" from "giving warmly loose to his genuine heart" (27). The implications of this contrast are disturbing. Since the "proprieties" demand that men give homogeneous performances with careful attention to fitness and decorum, real life seems to require more professional acting ability than does the stage. Here the actor must play his role "to the life" (XXXII, 205), that is, must convey the impression that his performance is reality itself and not an intentional product of his skill. The fictive harlequin, on the other hand, may perform his capers with complete freedom, since he does not have to conceal the fact that he is playing a role.

Meditation over kindness received seemed to have softened him [the man with the weed] something, too, it may be, beyond what might, perhaps, have been looked for from one whose unwonted self-respect in the hour of need, and in the act of being aided, might have appeared to some not wholly unlike pride out of place; and pride, in any place, is seldom very feeling. But the truth, perhaps, is, that those who are least touched with that vice, besides being not unsusceptible to goodness, are sometimes the ones whom a ruling sense of propriety makes appear cold, if not thankless, under a favor. For, at such a time, to be full of warm, earnest words, and heart-felt protestations, is to create a scene; and well-bred people dislike few things more than that; which would seem to look as if the world did not relish earnestness; but, not so; because the world, being earnest itself, likes an earnest scene, and an earnest man, very well, but only in their place—the stage. See what sad work they make of it, who, ignorant of this, flame out in Irish enthusiasm and with Irish sincerity, to a benefactor. . . . (V, 26)

The narrator here, as he does in Chapter XXXIII, distinguishes between two kinds of performances, one to be taken seriously, the other unseriously. It is the former, of course, which makes the greater demand on the actor, for the usages of his society do not allow him to "flame out in Irish enthusiasm" and play the earnest man to the hilt. To do this would be to reveal the dramaturgic nature of human relationships and thereby to destroy the foundation for the confidence man's game of charity, as it depends on a concept of an absolute identity which can be neither denied nor altered.

Only after his benefactor has gone does the man with the weed shed the "cold garb of decorum," and give "loose to his genuine heart," thereby transforming himself "into another being." The resulting "melancholy unreserved," which is "at variance with propriety" (27), apparently identifies one of the narrator's entertaining and diverting characters who reveals "even more reality, than real life itself can show." But the confidence man does not divert merely to entertain. His melancholy air seems designed to attract the attention of "another pensive figure," who, because he is standing nearby, cannot help overhearing the earnest words of his "murmuring neighbor" (27). The new identity is another mask and the "melancholy unreserved" another real-life role created to appeal to the pensive sophomore.

Once again the reader begins to feel uneasy as he finds himself faced with another situation which equivocates his relationship with the narrator. His invitation to "drop real life, and turn, for a time, to something different" is uncomfortably similar to the man with the weed's repeated plea to the bored student to "drop Tacitus" and "carry" instead Akenside's *Pleasures of Imagination* (29). One begins to suspect that the narrator's distinction between fiction and reality is a counterfeit one and that fiction and religion are linked because they both lure the innocent victim into an otherworldly realm which leaves him helpless to function in the real one. This suspicion certainly seems confirmed when Egbert, Mark Winsome's practical disciple, maintains that "any philosophy that, being in operation contradictory to the ways of the world, tends to produce a character at odds with it, such a philosophy must necessarily be but a cheat and a dream" (XXXVII, 223). Egbert's comment subtly links not only the figures of the otherworldly Christ and the cosmopolitan confidence man but that of the narrator as well, since it recalls his discussion of unreal characters in Chapter XXXIII.

But is it possible, one wonders, for a novelist to ruin his reader as Christ and the confidence man do their followers by leading him to either the "mad-house" or the "poor-house" (224)? Unfortunately for the reader's peace of mind, this very question is raised and answered only three chapters prior to the narrator's second plea for confidence. The discussion of the problem, which is a part of an extended conversation between two confidence men, each of whom is trying to get the other drunk on elixir of logwood masquerading as port wine, begins innocently enough. Charles Arnold Noble playfully deceives the cosmopolitan—who calls himself in this instance Frank Goodman—by deliberately confusing the wine press and the free press: " 'You deceived me,' smiled the cosmopolitan, as both now resumed their seats; 'you roguishly took advantage of my simplicity; you archly played upon my enthusiasm. But never mind; the offense, if any, was so charming, I almost wish you would offend again. As for certain poetic left-handers in your panegyric, those I cheerfully concede to the indefinite privileges of the poet' " (XXX, 189–90).

Like the narrator's defense of the cosmopolitan's unreality, Frank's justification of his friend's deception is based on its charming and diverting qualities. But what seems innocent fun here will soon assume a more sinister aspect. The harlequin-like cosmopolitan is later described as "very charming" because he has "the power of holding another creature by the button of the eye . . . despite the serious disinclination, and, indeed, earnest protest, of the victim" (XLIII, 265). And as the careful Egbert's experience reveals, a "story-teller" has this same man-charming ability; his intellect has the "power to impose itself upon another, against its best exerted will, too" (XXXIX, 233). The "more indulgent lovers of entertainment" (XXXIII, 207), then, seem to run the risk of being duped as well as diverted.

This suggestion is substantially strengthened when the conversation between Frank and Charlie turns to the question of "how Shakespeare meant the words" (XXX, 194) he puts in his characters' mouths and to the related problem of the effect of his characters on the readers of his plays. Here again the reader's attention is called to the subversive aspects of the narrator's association of fiction and religion. Shakespeare, "a kind of deity" (195), who has a "hidden sun . . . about him, at once enlightening and mystifying" (194), seems a combination of God and the "Mississippi operator" (XXXVI, 220); he "opens [people's] eyes and corrupts their morals in one operation" (XXX, 194). Moreover, the characters produced by this sinister deity are remarkably similar to those created by the narrator. On the one hand there is the "irreligious warner" (193), the "time-serving old sinner" (196), Polonius, who takes his place alongside the novel's advocates of distrust; and on the other there is the harlequin, Autolycus, the "devil's drilled recruit" as "joyous as if he wore the livery of heaven" (195), who resembles the cosmopolitan.

But how can such fictive creatures either open eyes or corrupt morals since they exist only "in the powerful imagination which invoked" them (195)? The cosmopolitan suggests a frightening answer to this question as he ponders the character of Autolycus:

It may be, that in that paper-and-ink investiture of his, Autolycus acts more effectively upon mankind than he would in a flesh-and-blood one. Can his influence be salutary? True, in Autolycus there is humor; but though, according to my principle, humor is in general to be held a saving quality, yet the case of Autolycus is an exception; because it is his humor which, so to speak, oils his mischievousness. The bravadoing mischievousness of Autolycus is slid into the world on humor, as a pirate schooner, with colors flying, is launched into the sea on greased ways. (195–96)

Autolycus' effectiveness lies precisely in the fact that he exists in a work which purports to entertain. Usually humor is a "blessed . . . thing," a "catholicon and charm," which "redeem[s] all the wicked thoughts, though plenty as the populace of Sodom" (XXIX, 184). In the hands of the man-charming writer, however, its effect is the reverse of salutary. The "Fidèle," like Autolycus, is "launched into the sea on greased ways" because the narrator diverts and charms in order to mislead and corrupt. In this sense he is the confidence man *par excellence*, for he attacks the reader's castle at its "south side, its genial one, where Suspicion, the warder, parleyed" (XXXIII, 148). As Charlie's experience with the genial cosmopolitan proves, "those trusty knights of the castle" (148) philosophy, knowledge, and experience are no match for the artful wiles of the storyteller. When Frank tells an "absurd story of . . . being in need" (XXXII, 204), Charlie, mistaking the fiction for reality, places himself in a position where his performed character cannot be sustained: "go to the devil, sir! Beggar, impostor!—never so deceived in a man in my life" (XXXI, 203). "While speaking or rather hissing these words, the boon companion underwent much such a change as one reads of in fairy-books. Out of old materials sprang a new creature. Cadmus glided into the snake" (XXXII, 204).

Having penetrated the impostor's disguise and exposed his "long spindle of a body" (XXII, 141), the cosmopolitan immediately falls into the role of necromancer, casts a "successful charm" by enclosing the boon companion with a magic circle of coins, and, in the process, replaces the "hideous apparition" with Noble's "blest shape" (XXXII, 204). Upon regaining his "lost identity" and "self-possession," Charlie attempts to save face by pretending to have been playing a role: "My dear Frank, what a funny man you are; full of fun as an egg of meat. How could you tell me that absurd story of your being in need? But I relish a good joke too well to spoil it by letting on. Of course, I humored the thing; and, on my side, put on all the cruel airs you would have me. Come, this little episode of fictitious estrangement will but enhance the delightful reality" (204–5). That one instant when the boon companion forgets to act is quickly deemed fictitious and is contrasted to "delightful reality," which is based on the careful playing of roles. As the cosmopolitan is quick to note, Charlie has played his role "to the life" (205).

As a commentary on the entire episode, the cosmopolitan decides to tell a story, and, after being briefly interrupted by the narrator's discussion of the relation between fiction and real life, he relates an episode in the life of Charlemont, the gentleman-madman. The theme of the story as well as the name of the character adds to Charlie's uneasiness because it concerns a man whose understanding of human nature causes him to exile himself rather than ask his friends for money. The cosmopolitan, however, "Strikingly Evinces the Artlessness of His Nature" (XXV, 211) by denying the truth of his story and, at the same time, prepares to make another attempt to borrow money:

"Well, what do you think of the story of Charlemont?" mildly asked he who had told it.

"A very strange one," answered the auditor, who had been such not with perfect ease, "but is it true?"

"Of course not; it is a story which I told with the purpose of every story-teller—to amuse. Hence, if it seem strange to you, that strangeness is the romance; it is what contrasts it with real life; it is the invention, in brief, the fiction as opposed to the fact. For do but ask yourself, my dear Charlie," lovingly leaning over towards him, "I rest it with your own heart now, whether such a forereaching motive as Charlemont hinted he had acted on in his change—whether such a motive, I say, were a sort of one at all justified by the nature of human society? Would you, for one, turn the cold shoulder to a friend—a convivial one, say, whose pennilessness should be suddenly revealed to you?" (211)

Obviously, the confidence man is here articulating a theory of fiction remarkably similar to the narrator's. The change which Charlemont undergoes is an ironic reversal of the boon companion's metamorphosis. Because he understands human nature, the Christ-like Charlemont resolves "to be beforehand with the world, and save it from a sin by prospectively taking the sin to [himself]" (XXXIV, 210). He turns from affability to moroseness rather than witness the same change in his friends. As it stands, then, the cosmopolitan's story is an imitation of real life, portraying through its central character the "inconsistencies" of human nature. But the subtle storyteller cleverly reverses fact and fiction. By maintaining that his story was told only to amuse, that Charlemont's motives have no basis in the real world, he tries to charm the fictitious friend into playing the role of a real one. And Charlie, unwilling to provide the properties which the role demands, once again drops his mask, blurts out a condemnation of the wine, and retires in defeat to his bed.

The cosmopolitan's mode of operation is similar to Shakespeare's, and both are related in turn to the narrator's. All three are professionals because they are capable of playing the roles of either realist or romancer. The narrator begins his justification of the cosmopolitan's unreal behavior by insisting that he is a fictitious character created solely for the purposes of amusement and therefore logically invested with a strangeness which contrasts him with real life. Near the end of his discussion, however, as he parenthetically comments on the inconsistency of the character's behavior, he refers the reader back to Chapter XIV, where inconsistency in fiction is defended on realistic premises. The reader, therefore, is faced on one side with a fallen, poisonous natural world and on the other with an equally dangerous imaginative one, each of which is controlled by a polymorphic impostor who asks for confidence in order to betray it.

iii. Fictions within a Fiction: Three Interpolated Stories

Just as *The Confidence-Man* destroys its reader's confidence in the authenticity and solidity of the world which exists outside its borders, so it carries within itself a series of smaller fictions which subvert its own validity. As the previous discussion of the story of Charlemont suggests, these interpolated fictions shatter the thin veneer of the novel's narrative surface and break the enchantment cast by the man-charming storyteller by exposing his "long spindle of a body." While there are at least ten occasions on which the action of the novel is interrupted by a short story or anecdote, the accounts of the "Unfortunate Man," "A Man of Questionable Morality," and "China Aster," spaced as they are near the beginning, middle, and end of the novel, serve nicely for purposes of illustration.

The story of the "Unfortunate Man" is complicated by the fact that it is the product of the sinister and inventive mind of the confidence man and that it exists in several versions. Although told initially by the man with the weed to the gullible merchant and confirmed and expanded by the man in gray, the reader is denied access to it until the merchant repeats it to the representative from the Black Rapids Coal Company, another avatar of the confidence man. Moreover, this already confusing situation is complicated by the narrator's decision "to tell it in other words than his [the merchant's], though not to any other effect" (XI, 64). This story, in other words, is presented specifically as a *story*, a situation which puts its authenticity into question from the beginning.

Adding to this problematical context are the ironic circumstances which result in the telling of the story. After investing some money in the Black Rapids Coal Company, the merchant, feeling that his experiences aboard the "Fidèle" have opened his eyes to reality, laments the pain and sorrow which seem to lie hidden beneath the gaiety which he sees around him. Before introducing the situation of the "Unfortunate Man," he uses two other related examples to justify his newly developed cynicism. When he refers first to the old miser who is himself a third-rate cheat and one of the confidence man's most unsympathetic victims, the reader, along with the B.R.C. man, feels that the merchant envinces a "jaundiced sentimentality" (64). The fact that Black Guinea provides his second illustration, however, points to an even more dangerous fault in the merchant's vision. As the B.R.C. man indicates in his ironic analysis of the Negro's condition, the merchant may be mistaking fiction for reality: "But his companion suggested whether the alleged hardships of that alleged unfortunate might not exist more in the pity of the observer than the experience of the observed. He knew nothing about the cripple, nor had seen him, but ventured to surmise that, could one but get at the real state of his heart, he would be found about as happy as most men, if not, in fact, full as happy as the speaker himself" (64).

Although on one level the B.R.C. man seems to be continuing his defense of a bright view of life, on another level he is implying a secret connection between himself and Black Guinea. His irony, while undetected by the merchant, furnishes another equivocal hint to the reader that there may be an undeclared connection between the various characters who move across the decks of the "Fidèle." This suspicion becomes even stronger when the merchant ventures "still a third case, that of the man with the weed" (64). The subversive aspects of the story, then, are not limited to its effect on the merchant. Upon hearing the story of this unfortunate man the reader is "betrayed into [a] surprise incompatible with [his] own good opinion of [his] previous penetration" (XIII, 70).

In his account of the wicked Goneril it is significant that the narrator employs a pottery metaphor. She has a complexion which would have been "naturally rosy, . . . but for a certain hardness and bakedness, like that of the glazed colors on stoneware" (XII, 65). In addition, she is partial to "little dried sticks of blue clay" (66) and is possessed by a "calm, clayey, cakey devil" (67). The figure is an appropriate one, for it links the unfortunate man to the story which he tells. He himself uses this same metaphor when he suggests an explanation for the merchant's extraordinary loss of memory: "You see, sir, the mind is ductile, very much so; but images, ductilely received into it, need a certain time to harden and bake in their impressions, otherwise such a casualty as I speak of will in an instant obliterate them, as though they had never been. We are but clay, sir, potter's clay, as the good book says, clay, feeble, and too-yielding clay" (IV, 21). The baked figure of Goneril, clearly the product of either the narrator's or the confidence man's potter's wheel, is deeply etched on the memory of the feeble and too yielding merchant, who allows the void of his experience to be filled by the sculptural artistry of the confidence man. The use of the baker metaphor, however, is not limited to the narrator and the man with the weed. Black Guinea, too, seems the product of the sun, a baker who "bakes . . . black bread in his oven, alongside of his nice white rolls" (III, 10), a fact which associates him not only with the man with the weed but with the cream-colored man as well, since he is also a child of the sun. And later in the novel Coonskins attempts to discourage the "baker-kneed" P.I.O. man (XXII, 129) by demanding that he not "intrude that man-child upon me too often. He who loves not bread, dotes not on dough" (139). Hence the story of the "Unfortunate Man" undermines the reader's confidence in the authenticity of the novelistic world by implying a set of secret relationships between characters whom the narrator presents as individual and unique.

Like the story of the "Unfortunate Man," the account of Colonel Moredock, the Indian-hater, is intended as a commentary on life, as it is told with the intention of illuminating the personality of the queer Coonskins. Taken at face value it seems both factual and revealing, for it seems to provide a lesson in how to defeat a confidence man. The Indian-hater stands as an example of a man who is not susceptible to his cunning wiles. "Lonely," "thoughtful," and "self-willed," the backwoodsman is a man who "less hearkens to what others may say about things, than looks for himself, to see what are things themselves" (XXVI, 163). Although naturally taciturn and cynical, he is "not without some fineness to his nature" (164). In spite of his hatred of Indians he has a "heart more generous than the average" (XXVII, 175).

This factual story of the practical man, however, is told by men with questionable motives. The reader, along with the cosmopolitan, hears it from Charles Arnold Noble, a second-rate confidence man whose vest flushes his cheek in a "fictitious way" and whose "teeth were too good to be true" (XXV, 159). He uses the story as a means of establishing a relationship which he hopes will eventually become strong enough to support the weight of an appeal for a loan. But the account of Colonel Moredock does not originate with Noble. It is his "impressible memory" which allows him to capture the "methodic" style of Judge James Hall, the original narrator, who, as he told his story, "seemed talking for the press" (161). Unfortunately, the motives of the good judge are as questionable as Noble's. Many people maintain that the press is either a "paid fool" or a "conceited drudge" which is "pledged to no cause but his in whose chance hands it may be" (XXIX, 187), and it is not unlikely that the Judge's story, like his "impressive manner," may be designed to further personal political ambitions.[4]

Moreover, as the rest of *The Confidence-Man* implies, the complex human situation does not allow such an unambiguous analysis of trust and distrust as the Judge's story presents. The reader shares the confidence man's abhorrence of such figures as the cynical cripple with the gimlet eye, Mark Winsome, and Egbert his disciple because they seem to have sacrificed their humanity to save their money. In many ways

[4] For a detailed account of Melville's attitudes toward James Hall, see Edwin Fussell, *Frontier: American Literature and the American West* (Princeton, N.J., 1965), pp. 320–26.

they seem more dangerous than their antagonists. This observation is equally true of Colonel Moredock, as he appears in Melville's version of Hall's account. Although the Judge is methodical and factual, his story reveals a fondness for metaphor, a weakness which unmasks both himself and his hero. The Indian-hater *par excellence* settles his "temporal affairs" with the "solemnity of a Spaniard turned monk" and prepares to act upon a "calm, cloistered scheme of . . . lonesome vengeance" (XXVI, 170). The "diluted" Indian-hater, on the other hand, is drawn at times by the "soft enticements of domestic life" from the "aescetic trail; a monk who apostatizes to the world at times" (170). "It is with him as with the Papist converts in Senegal; fasting and mortification prove hard to bear" (170-71). Hence he is driven by his intense solitude to "relaxing his vow" (171).

Colonel Moredock appears to have given himself to the service of God, for his "retributive spirit" speaks of the "trepidations" of the Indians "like the voice calling through the garden" (XXVII, 174). And he, like the Old Testament prophets "was not unaware that to be a consistent Indian-hater involves the renunciation of ambition, with its objects—the pomps and glories of the world; and since religion, pronouncing such things vanities, accounts it merit to renounce them, therefore, so far as this goes, Indian-hating . . . may be regarded as not wholly without the efficacy of a devout sentiment" (176).

Both the "methodic" judge and his hero are engaged in a masquerade. Not unlike the cream-colored garb of the lamb-like man, the figurative monastic robes of the Indian-hater are used to lend a devout sentiment to a sinister occupation. Colonel Moredock is a false prophet, another devil in divine clothing.

Skilled as he is in the art of masking, the cosmopolitan is quick to catch the implications of the Judge's religious metaphors. As he observes, Moredock is a pagan masquerading as a Christian. "Though, like suicide, man-hatred would seem peculiarly a Roman and a Grecian passion—that is, Pagan, yet, the annals of neither Rome nor Greece can produce the equal in man-hatred of Colonel Moredock, as the judge and you have painted him" (XXXVIII, 177–78). For this reason he rejects as inconsistent both the character and the story: "That story strikes me with even more incredulity than wonder. To me some parts don't hang together. If the man of hate, how could John Moredock be also the man of love? Either his lone campaigns are fabulous as Hercules'; or else, those being true, what was thrown in about his geniality is but garnish. In short, if ever there was such a man as Moredock, he, in my way of thinking, was either misanthrope or nothing" (177).

The cosmopolitan attacks the account of the Indian-hater in its most vulnerable spot. It is, he maintains, either pure fiction or garnished fact and hence contradictory to real life. Moredock is an amateur, the "genial misanthrope" half evolved. He is only partially capable of hiding "under an affable air" a "misanthropical heart" because he has not yet taken on "refinement and softness" (XXX, 201). Like the Bible, which it in many ways resembles, the account of Colonel Moredock is another fiction which is swallowed up and replaced by *The Confidence-Man*. Its central character is "prevailingly local, or of the age" (XLIV, 271), and he pales into nothingness when he is placed alongside the "original" cosmopolitan.

"China Aster," the final interpolated story in *The Confidence-Man*, differs in two important ways from those which precede it. It is, first of all, an undisguised fiction. As the names of its characters suggest, it is an allegorical fable. The absence of an identifiable author also distinguishes it from its counterparts. Although told by Egbert, the practical disciple of Mark Winsome, it is the product of a nameless but influential storyteller: "I will tell you about China Aster. I wish I could do so in my own words, but unhappily the original story-teller here has so tyrannized over me, that it is quite impossible for me to repeat his incidents without sliding into his style. I forewarn you of this, that you may not think me so maudlin as, in some parts, the story would seem to make its narrator" (XXXIX, 233). But no matter how greatly influenced he may be by the story's style, Egbert's "neuter" instincts make him impervious to its theme, and he distorts its meaning by maintaining that it shows "the folly, on both sides, of "a friend's helping a friend" (XLI, 250). For "China Aster" is only superficially concerned with the conflict between the celestial candlemaker, "whose trade would seem a kind of subordinate branch of that parent craft and mystery of the hosts of heaven, to be the means, effectively or otherwise, of shedding some light through the darkness of a planet benighted," and the terrestial shoemaker, "whose calling it is to defend the understandings of men from naked contact with the substance of things" (XL, 234). Orchis is an unreliable friend but hardly a man-charming confidence man, as his eventual marriage and religious conversion make clear. The deceiver in this story is the smiling angel with the bright face, the "beautiful human philanthropist" (239) who appears in China Aster's dream. It is she who is responsible for the candlemaker's fall, and, even more significant, it is she who provides the cosmopolitan with a new mode of operation. After hearing the story of "China Aster," he pronounces a "benediction" over the sleeping barber in "tones not unangelic" (XLII, 254), introduces himself as a philanthropist, charms the barber into signing an agreement of trust, and cheats him out of the price of a shave. And as the cosmopolitan replaces the angel, so an "original" storyteller replaces *the* original one by creating a cosmos which takes the place of the "benighted planet" of China Aster, extinguishing the light of its spermaceti candles and substituting a new method of illumination.

iv. The World as Fiction: Chapter XLIV

As he nears the end of his book, the narrator, apparently recognizing "how bootless it is to be in all cases vindicating one's self" (XXXIII, 207), drops his defensive pose and, in the final digressive chapter, tries to qualify what appears to be a perfect artistic solution to the central problem of the book. An important question is raised on the first page of the novel by the "Wanted" poster which describes the confidence man as "an original genius" but does not specify "wherein his originality consisted." This question is ostensibly answered when, at the end of Chapter XLIII, the barber's friends pronounce the cosmopolitan "QUITE AN ORIGINAL" on the basis of his "mancharming" abilities.

The narrator, however, with a newly developed modesty, does not wish to claim that he has created a truly original character, at least not in the sense that Hamlet, Don Quixote, and Milton's Satan are original. For this reason, he "endeavour[s] to show, if possible, the impropriety of the phrase, *Quite an Original*, as applied by the barber's friends" (XLIV, 271). But the reader of *The Confidence-Man* is well aware that to be "at variance with propriety" (V, 27) is not necessarily to be untrue, since a "ruling sense of propriety" (26) at times may mask one's real feelings. Perhaps the humility which the narrator shows in criticizing the "impropriety" of the barber's friends is the result of his assumption of the "cold garb of decorum" (27). This is a likely but disquieting possibility. For he has argued in Chapter XXXIII that fiction releases man from the demands of propriety and hence provides not only more entertainment, but "more reality, than real life itself can show" (206).

In any case, the question of the cosmopolitan's originality is placed squarely in the lap of the reader. At first glance the issue seems a relatively simple one; he appears to be just the reverse of original. As the last of a series of impostors, he can hardly be considered *primary* or *originative*. The complex series of relationships which the novel establishes between the confidence man's first and final avatars clearly shows that the cosmopolitan is derived from, if not dependent on, the ambiguous lamb-like man. As a matter of fact, the very existence of a "mysterious impostor" capable of playing any number of striking roles raises a disturbing question: which role is the authentic or original one? This genius may subvert the entire concept of originality—he may have no real or enduring self at all but may be merely a set of changing profiles.

Nevertheless, the confidence man possesses several of the important attributes of the truly original character. In addition to having "original instincts" (XLIV, 270) which "make him almost as much of a prodigy there [in the fiction], as in real history is a new law-giver, a revolutionizing philosopher, or the founder of a new religion" (271), the original character is the creative center of the fiction in which he exists:

> Furthermore, if we consider, what is popularly held to entitle characters in fiction to being deemed original, is but something personal—confined to itself. The character sheds not its characteristic on its surroundings, whereas, the original character, essentially such, is like a revolving Drummond light, raying away from itself all round it—everything is lit by it, everything starts up to it (mark how it is with Hamlet), so that, in certain minds, there follows upon the adequate conception of such a character, an effect, in its way, akin to that which in Genesis attends upon the beginning of things.
> For much the same reason that there is but one planet to one orbit, so can there be but one such original character to one work of invention. Two would conflict to chaos. (271)

The confidence man is, of course, always at the center of the novel's action, and the passengers on the "Fidèle" are drawn like insects to his artificial light of charity and confidence. Moreover, the structure of the novel suggests that the narrator himself possesses one of those minds capable of creating a fictional world around an original chracter. In Genesis, following the beginning of things,

> the earth was without form, and void; and darkness was upon the face of the deep. And the Spirit of God moved upon the face of the waters.
> And God said, Let there be light: and there was light.

And God saw the light, that it was good: and God divided the light from the darkness.

And God called the light Day, and the darkness he called Night. (1:2–5)

With the appearance of the lamb-like man at sunrise, as "suddenly as Manco Capac at the lake Titicaca" (I, 1), the narrator's fictional world begins. And, like that of Genesis, it is equally divided into day and night, darkness and light. Because of the peculiar nature of the narrator's original character, however, there also follows in his world an effect akin to that which in Revelation attends upon the end of things. As the apocalyptic overtones of the final chapter suggest, in *The Confidence-Man* the day of creation is also the day of destruction. Because the hero has no real self, the world he calls into being is an absurd one, with several planets in one orbit. Hence the novelist's quest for truth and the reader's quest for meaning are ridiculous ventures. Cosmos is chaos, the orderly and entertaining verbal realm a prosaic and smoky confusion: "In the endeavour to show, if possible, the impropriety of the phrase, *Quite an Original,* as applied by the barber's friends, we have, at unawares, been led into a dissertation bordering upon the prosy, perhaps upon the smoky. If so, the best use the smoke can be turned to, will be, by retiring under cover of it, in good trim as may be, to the story" (XLIV, 271).

The narrator, however, returns to his story only to end it, and the final chapter offers no escape from the smoky darkness. Here the cosmopolitan puts out the smoking solar lamp and leads his final victim, as the narrator has led the reader, into the resultant darkness. But while this final and most difficult chapter of the novel hardly restores the reader's confidence in his guide, it does expose most of the implications of the subversive journey, for it is here that the shocking nature of the mysterious impostor's originality is finally revealed. Centered around the cosmopolitan's extinguishing of the solar lamp, on the shade of which are the images of a horned altar and a robed man with a halo, and filled with echoes from Revelation, the chapter hints at some kind of Apocalypse. The peculiar nature of the cosmopolitan's divinity, however, seems to preclude the one described in the vision of St. John. Newly groomed from his trip to the barber's shop and dispensing a sort of "morning through the night" (XLV, 273), the worldly cosmopolitan is not likely to end his "pic-nic *en costume*" (XXIV, 152). Although he enters the cabin of the symbolic light "as any bridegroom tripping to the bridal chamber might come" (XLV, 273), one feels sure that he is not in search of the Holy City, the traditional bride of the Lamb.[5] For he arrives as an iconoclastic, pagan Apollo, a "principle of beneficent force and light," to replace the "mock" sun with the "true" one (XXIX, 188).

The solar lamp, with its images of the horned altar of Moses (Exodus 27:1–2) and the figure of Christ, is clearly an icon of the Hebraic-Christian faith, the last survival of the world's religions, as represented by those "barren planets, which had either gone out from exhaustion, or been extinguished" (XLV, 272).[6] It is significant that the images are not the sources of the lamp's light but merely filters which refract and color it as it passes through them. To change the quality and meaning of its illumination one has only to change the shade. Moreover, like the "artificial fire" of the try-works (*M-D*, XCVI, 422), the light produced by the smelly solar lamp is impure, colored, terrestial light, the light of burning matter.

Cleanly shaven and freshly scented, the cosmopolitan arrives in his "vesture barred with various hues" (XXIV, 149) with "original conceptions designed to eclipse" (XXX, 196) the stinking lamp. For his light is that of the original character, the powerful and dazzling white light produced by the incan-

---

[5] Revelation 21:1–14 describes the descent of the "Holy city, new Jerusalem . . . prepared as a bride for her husband."
[6] This interpretation was first suggested by Foster, p. lxxiv.

desence of quicklime.[7] Because incandescent light is at once more artificial and more pure than oil light, it is the proper illumination for the unreal but highly evolved cosmopolitan, as well as an apt metaphor for the novelist's world. It is, then, the pure white light of the original character which illuminates the gentlemen's cabin in the final chapter of *The Confidence-Man* and "touch[es] all objects . . . with its own blank tinge" (*M-D*, XLII, 194).

Not only does the cosmopolitan extinguish the solar lamp, he also demonstrates the absurdity of the book which is the source of the icons on its shade. Like *The Confidence-Man* itself, the Bible seems deliberately designed to confuse rather than clarify.

"Ah!" cried the old man, brightening up, "now I know. Look," turning the leaves forward and back, till all the Old Testament lay flat on one side, and all the New Testament flat on the other, while in his fingers he supported vertically the portion between, "look, sir, all this to the right is certain truth, and all this to the left is certain truth, but all I hold in my hand here is apocrypha."

"Apocrypha?"

"Yes; and there's the word in black and white," pointing to it. "And what says the word? It says as much as 'not warranted;' for what do college men say of anything of that sort? They say it is apocryphal. . . ."

"What's that about the Apocalypse?" here, a third time, came from the berth. (XLV, 275)

Not only does the Bible have the true and false "bound up together" (275), but the names for each part are similar enough to be confused. Since the salvation of one's soul is at stake, the possibility of innocently mistaking "apocrypha" ("conceal") for "Apocalypse" ("reveal") is indeed a frightening one. Even more terrifying, however, is the realization that

[7] The Drummond light, invented by Captain Thomas Drummond (1797–1840), is brilliant white light produced by the incandescence of quicklime (see *The American Cyclopaedia* [New York, 1881] 2:271–72).

the names may have been originally misapplied. Perhaps the Church Fathers made a horrible mistake when they questioned the practical wisdom of the Son of Sirach but accepted as authentic the visionary dreams of Revelation. The thesis that the Apocalypse of St. John is the product of one Corinthus, who "by means of revelations, which he pretended were written by a great apostle falsely introduces wonderful things to us, as if they were showed to him by angels," is one that Melville could have found in both Kitto's *Cyclopaedia* and Bayle's *Dictionary*.[8]

Even if John is accepted as the authentic author of Revelation, however, the enigmatic book still presents complicated interpretive problems. Kitto, in his discussion of John's view of the Second Coming, introduces a possibility which would have attracted Melville's blasphemous eye: "Far be it from us to entertain the idea that the sacred writer was a wilful deceiver. But it is not inconsistent with his apostleship to believe that both he and the rest of the early apostles supposed the time of the Lord's return to be near at hand."[9] Most commentators, however, prefer the less disturbing allegorical approach to the book, and both Bayle and Kitto mention a few of the many unsuccessful attempts which have been made to unlock and explicate its meaning.[10]

It is fitting, of course, that the final chapter of *The Confidence-Man* should focus on this possibly fraudulent and certainly obscure text, for it is behind the arguments of both the believers in confidence and the advocates of distrust. Both groups seek to protect themselves from the destruction and damnation which is to follow the Second Coming. Their

[8] John Kitto, *A Cyclopaedia of Biblical Literature*, ed. William Lindsay Alexander (Edinburgh, 1870), 3:659. Also see Pierre Bayle, *A General Dictionary*, trans. John Peter Bernard, Thomas Birch, John Lockman, et al. (London, 1734), 4:246.

[9] *Cyclopaedia*, 3:670.

[10] See *ibid.*, pp. 674–75, and Bayle, *Dictionary*, 4:47, 648.

rivalry derives from the fact that the Bible, like the account of Colonel Moredock, has "some parts" which "don't hang together" (XXVIII, 177). On the one hand it advocates man's cultivation of charity and confidence (I Corinthians 13) and asks him to believe that "the Lord shall be thy confidence, and shall keep thy foot from being taken" (Proverbs 3:26), while on the other hand it cautions that "the day of the Lord so cometh as a thief in the night . . . when [people] shall say, Peace and safety; then sudden destruction cometh upon them. . . . Therefore let us not sleep, as do others; but let us watch and be sober' " (I Thessalonians 5:2–6). Indeed, Christ himself forewarns his disciples that before his Second Coming "many false prophets shall rise, and shall deceive many. . . . But he that shall endure unto the end, the same shall be saved. . . . Then if any man shall say unto you, Lo, here is Christ, or there [Black Guinea's "Dar he be"?]; believe it not. For there shall arise false Christs, and false prophets, and shall shew great signs and wonders; insomuch that, if it were possible, they shall deceive the very elect" (Matthew 24:11–24).[11]

These passages elucidate much of the action which occurs in the final pages of *The Confidence-Man* by establishing a context for the mysterious man who is "awake in his sleep" (XLV, 274), the young boy who sells locks as a protection against the "fine thief" (278) who comes in the night, and the cosmopolitan who leads the old man away through the darkness. But fully to explicate the complex relationship between *The Confidence-Man* and the book it apparently destroys and replaces, one must look to still another work. As one of the epigraphs to this chapter suggests, Robert Burton's *The Anatomy of Melancholy* is an important source for many of the themes and images of the novel. And, as Elizabeth Foster points out, Melville was thinking of the *Anatomy* when he went to New York to arrange for the publication of *The*

---

[11] I am indebted here to Caroline L. Karcher's unpublished Johns Hopkins University master's thesis, "Herman Melville's *The Confidence Man: His Masquerade*: An April Fool's Day Apocalypse" (1966).

Confidence-Man.[12] An entry in Evert Duyckinck's diary dated October 1, 1856, reveals much of Melville's approach to this interesting book: "Herman Melville passed the evening with me—fresh from his mountain charged to the muzzle with his sailor metaphysics and jargon of things unknowable. But a good stirring evening—ploughing deep and bringing to the surface some rich fruits of thought and Experience-Melville instanced old Burton as atheistical—in the exquisite irony of his passages on some sacred matters."[13]

Melville, it appears, read Burton in much the way he read Bayle, interpreting Burton's practice of juxtaposing related pagan and Christian customs and contradictory Biblican passages as ironic attempts to suggest that all religions are fictions. In his discussion with Duyckinck he may have had in mind a passage similar to the following one:

We are taught in the Holy Scripture, that the devil "rangeth abroad like a roaring lion, still seeking whom he may devour"; and as in several shapes, so by several engines and devices he goeth about to seduce us; sometimes he transforms himself into an angel of light, and is so cunning that he is able, if it were possible, to deceive the very elect. . . . Sometimes by dreams, visions (as God to Moses by familiar conference), the devil in several shapes talks with them. . . .[14]

In any case, Burton's analysis of religious despair is of crucial importance to an understanding of the final chapter of *The Confidence-Man.* This despair results from the "absence of divine hope which proceeds from confidence" (*Anatomy*, 3:394) and is as capable of causing damnation as is its opposite, the false security of atheism. Many "fall into despair through fear of the last judgment" (397) brought on either by the wiles of the devil, which drive men to "distrust, fear, grief, mistake, and amplify whatsoever they preposterously

---

[12] *C-M*, 298.
[13] Cited by Foster, C-M, xxv.
[14] Burton, *The Anatomy of Melancholy*, 3:325.

conceive or falsely apprehend" (396) or to the "inconsiderate reading" and "misinterpretation" of "Scripture itself" (398). There is, as Burton says, "great danger on both sides" (399).

Overwhelmed as they are by the Biblical accounts of the Apocalypse, the victims of religious despair not only risk eternal damnation but suffer physical torments as well. "Their sleep is (if it be any) unquiet, subject to fearful dreams and terrors" (405); they think that "they hear and see visions, outcries, confer with devils, that they are tormented, possessed, and in hell-fire" (406). These are, of course, the symptoms displayed by the distrustful "dreamy man" (C-M, XLV, 275) who speaks from "one of the curtained berths" (273) in the final chapter of *The Confidence-Man*. He too is "awake in his sleep" (274), subject to "visions" (275), thinks he hears "divils" (277), and mistakes "apocrypha" for "Apocalypse." In attempting to protect himself from the false prophets and impostors by following Paul's advice to the Thessalonians, he apparently has placed himself in the hands of the devil.

It is not surprising, however, that the poor man's senses have been satanically deranged. He has neglected to take the traditional precautions against such an attack. It is customary that, "in such rooms where spirits haunt, good store of lights . . . be set up," along with "odours, perfumes, and suffumigations." These things "good spirits are well pleased with, but evil abhor them." For this reason, "old Gentiles, present Mahometans, and papists have continual lamps burning in their churches all day and all night, lights at funerals and in their graves" (*Anatomy*, 3:430). The "Fidèle" 's gentlemen's cabin, however, is filled with the odor of the contents of the commode–life-preserver and illuminated by one smelly lamp, and that one burning dimly.

Nevertheless, there is apparently no reason to despair, for Burton pronounces these traditional precautions "a mere mockage, a counterfeit charm, to no purpose, they are fopperies and fictions." To be saved man has only to abstain from "too much fasting, meditation, precise life, contemplation of God's judgments (for the devil deceives many by such means)," and "to fly to God, to call on Him, hope, pray, trust, rely on Him, to commit ourselves wholly to Him" (*Anatomy*, 3:431). He "enlighteneth darkness" (413); "His name alone is the best and only charm against all such diabolical illusions" (431).

As *The Confidence-Man* demonstrates, however, to follow this advice is to escape despair only to fall victim to the wiles of the mysterious impostor. Man, destined for either the "mad-house" or the "poor-house," finds himself in the absurd position of the old farmer who, with his money belt in hand and life-preserver under arm, places his "trust" in "Providence, as in man" (*C-M*, XLV, 285) and allows himself to be led away by the "charming" dispenser of light, the "original" cosmopolitan.

The final chapter of *The Confidence-Man* is an epitome of the entire novel, for its action destroys the Christian cosmos by demonstrating that its parts "conflict to chaos" and identifies the new one which will replace it. The novel's final sentence—"something further may follow of this Masquerade"—does not look outward toward an unknown darkness but leads circularly back to the beginning. The cosmos composed of those "barren planets," all of which now have either "gone out from exhaustion, or been extinguished," is replaced by one centered around the "revolving Drummond light" of the "original character."

It is precisely this circularity, however, which makes the literary career "unreal" and mars it with a "secret absurdity." The new fiction not only destroys the old one but carries the seed of its own desolation. Because it, too, has more than "one planet to one orbit," its parts also "conflict to chaos." And, since it is constructed from "old materials" (XXXII, 204), and is even more artificial than the one it replaces, it moves closer to that mute, white emptiness from which everything is born.

This whole process is nicely dramatized by the juvenile peddler who appears in the novel's final chapter. As Franklin observes, the boy embodies most of the important characteristics of the avatars of the confidence man and is, at the same time, one of the advocates of distrust. In addition, he is the only antagonist who seems himself intimately involved in the confidence man's game. After giving the cosmopolitan a "wink expressive of a degree of indefinite knowingness" (XLV, 279), he suggestively asks, "is the wind East, d'ye think?" (280). This ambiguous boy is, in short, a "new kind of monster" (XXX, 201), one of a "new species of characters" found by the narrator in the "man-show" at the "fair" (XLIV, 270). Indeed, the boy admits to having "kept a toystand at the fair in Cincinnati last month" (XLV, 277–78).

But although one of a new species, he is not "born in the author's imagination—it being as true in literature as in zoology, that all life is from the egg" (XLIV, 271). Like the cosmopolitan who "federates, in heart as in costume, something of the various gallantries of men under various suns" (XXIV, 151), the mysterious boy is related to at least one of the cosmic characters he replaces. He is an evolved form of the boy-god Hermes the thief.[15] This diabolical child, in addition to being in charge of the wild and domestic animal kingdoms, was the god of merchants, the god of doors and roads who protected men in their dealings with strangers. Since he was often described as the inventor of the lyre and the art of fire-making, he came to be regarded as a giver of good things, a little Prometheus.[16]

There obviously is a striking resemblance between this ambiguous figure and Melville's juvenile peddler, who sells both toys and "travelers' conveniences." He is associated with ani-

[15] R. W. B. Lewis ("The Confidence Man," *Trials of the Word* [New Haven, Conn., 1965], p. 69) associates Hermes with the confidence man but not with the juvenile peddler.
[16] See, for example, Norman O. Brown, *Hermes the Thief* (Madison, Wis., 1947).

mals through his "leopard-like teeth" (XLV, 277) and his foot, which moves like the "hoof" of a "mischievous steer in May" (280); he carries with him, among other things, "a miniature mahogany door, hinged to its frame," (277); and he is pronounced a "blessed boy" and a "public benefactor" (281) by the old man who buys his wares. Even his "ragged" appearance, his striking laughter, and sparkling eyes link him to Hermes. In the *Anatomy* Burton recalls the story told by Marlowe in "Hero and Leander" of the Destinies' punishing Hermes for rejecting their love:

> Yet as a punishment they added this,
> That he and *Pouertie* should alwaies kis;[17]

and the poet in the Homeric "Hymn to Hermes" calls attention to Hermes' laughter and in three places mentions the sparkle in his eyes.[18]

The most important aspect of the boy's association with Hermes, however, is the light which it sheds on his relationship with the cosmopolitan. If one recalls that near the conclusion of the Homeric Hymn Hermes and Apollo (brothers but antagonists as a result of the child's theft of the oxen of the sun) trade gifts and become friends, the following exchange between the peddler and the cosmopolitan assumes a special significance: " 'You seem pretty wise, my lad,' said the cosmopolitan; 'why don't you sell your wisdom, and buy a coat?' 'Faith,' said the boy, 'that's what I did to-day, and this is the coat that the price of my wisdom bought. But won't you trade?' " (278).

But the boy and the cosmopolitan are not simply Greek gods in nineteenth-century clothing. They belong to a "new species." For example, the "plumagy aspect" of the cosmopolitan,

---

[17] See 1:302, and Christopher Marlowe, "Hero and Leander," first Sestyad, ll. 69–70, in *Works*, ed. C. F. Tucker Brooke (Oxford, 1962), p. 503.
[18] See Brown, *Hermes the Thief*, p. 76.

which causes Coonskins to call him a "Toucan fowl" (XXIV, 149), serves to distinguish him from Apollo, as the sun god's description of his prophetic powers makes clear:

> Yet, truly any man shall have his will
> To reap the fruits of my prophetic skill,
> Whoever seeks it by the voice or wing
> Of birds, born truly such events to sing.
> Nor will I falsely, nor with fallacies
> Infringe the truth on which his faith relies,
> But he that truths in chattering plumes would find,
> Quite opposite to them that prompt my mind,
> And learn by natural forgers of vain lies
> The more-than-ever-certain Deities,
> That man shall sea-ways tread that have no tracts,
> And false or no guide find for all his facts.[19]

The cosmopolitan and the juvenile peddler are a new set of mythic brothers in the tradition of Hermes and Apollo, Prometheus and Epimethus, Thor and Loci, and Christ and Satan, who compromise their differences and work together to confuse their victims thoroughly. That they are obviously fictional figures, products of a self-conscious novelist, does not decrease their effectiveness. In their "paper-and-ink investiture[s]" they can act "more effectively upon mankind" than they would "in a flesh-and-blood one" (XXX, 195). Although they are more artificial than the figures they destroy and replace, they are also more "original" or "real" because they bring with them the "true light" of incandescence, which both opens eyes and corrupts morals by revealing the source of all of man's colors and roles.

The Confidence-Man presupposes a world where "all doers are actors," a place where life is an unreal masquerade which

---

[19] "A Hyme to Hermes," in *Homer's Batrachomyomachia, Hymns and Epigrams*, ed. Richard Hooper, trans. George Chapman (London, 1858), ll. 952–63. Although Melville did not receive his copy of this book until 1858, *The Confidence-Man* leaves little doubt that he had an earlier acquaintance with the Homeric Hymn.

is performed against a background of a blank, white emptiness. All contemporary human activities, all existing institutions and values, have been fashioned not out of nothing but from the vast storehouse of fictions which form man's cultural heritage. From the "superinduced superficies" (*P*, XXI, 335) of "natural earth," the "Egyptian wise men" evoked "the transcendent mass & symetry & . . . of the pyramid" and, from the "insignificant thoughts that are in all men," the "transcendent conception of God" (*JUS*, 64). And from these first tricksters in their cradle of civilization are derived all of man's values and institutions. In *Pierre* and *The Confidence-Man* Melville dramatizes a theory of history which sees human progress as the successive swallowing up of one fiction by a new and more artificial one.

Since all of man's activities and institutions are the products of self-conscious creative acts, the literary artist is himself a part of the empty masquerade. Consequently, he is not able, as Ishmael is, to escape the human and material fictions and to reveal the horrible truth which lies behind their surfaces. The self-conscious gestures of the narrators of *Pierre* and *The Confidence-Man* lift the veil of illusion only to replace it with a newer, more artificial one. Their fictions, like those which surround them, are born of self-interest and the "bill of the baker." Like the Egyptian priests, Moses, who was schooled in their arts, and Christ himself, the artist is a confidence man. Writing too is a sham; the literary cosmos is as deceitful as the Christian one. "Truth is voiceless" (*M*, XCIII, 248), and for thirty-four years after *The Confidence-Man*, so was Herman Melville.

Art

In placid hours well-pleased we dream
Of many a brave unbodied scheme.
But form to lend, pulsed life create,
What unlike things must meet and mate:
A flame to melt—a wind to freeze;
And patience—joyous energies;
Humility—yet pride and scorn;
Instinct and study; love and hate;
Audacity—reverence. These must mate,
And fuse with Jacob's mystic heart,
To wrestle with the angel—Art.

HERMAN MELVILLE

THE END OF MELVILLE's public career as a writer of fiction is marked by *The Confidence-Man*, but he left at his death an apparently unfinished manuscript which remained unpublished until 1924.[1] As Melville's last masterpiece, separated by thirty years from his other fiction, the story invites an autobiographical interpretation. And, indeed, it has become the subject of an intensive critical quarrel. Regarded on the one hand as Melville's final acceptance of the facts of reality and on the other as his most ironic portrayal of a terrestrial world where celestial ideals cannot exist,[2] *Billy Budd* is made to seem almost as ambiguous as *The Confidence-Man*.

Although the story contains within itself sufficient clues for a meaningful explication of its methods and themes, the fact that it has become the subject of such controversy and the circumstances surrounding its creation demand that it be viewed, if possible, in the context of Melville's other fiction. Since *The Confidence-Man* seems to invalidate the possibility of meaningful fiction and marks the end of the short but productive period of Melville's public career, the very fact of *Billy Budd*'s existence appears to suggest that he modified the theory of fiction dramatized in the earlier novel.

Billy Budd, however, represents no new departure for Melville, for it looks back not to *The Confidence-Man* but two years beyond it to the novelette "Benito Cereno." Published in 1855, this story is a product of the period in which Melville was seriously questioning the role of fiction in a world of lies, but it precedes the comic and ironic dismissal of the literary art found in *The Confidence-Man*. Because its narrator shares important methodological and thematic concerns with the narrator of *Billy Budd*, the earlier story not only provides an insight into the more ambiguous later one but also points to its place in the body of Melville's fiction.

"Benito Cereno," written two years before *The Confidence-Man*, shares its concern with the problems of the relationship

---

[1] For an account of the growth of the *Billy Budd* manuscript as well as a history of the text, see the Harrison Hayford and Merton M. Sealts, Jr., edition of *Billy Budd* (*BB*, 1–24).

[2] The argument is summarized by Hayford and Sealts (*BB*, 24–39).

between fiction and reality, although this theme is less explicitly dramatized in the shorter piece. While it is true that the story is filled with words which describe the actions of confidence men, they are confined, for the most part, to descriptions of Delano's mistaken vision. Cereno seems to him to act by "design," to be engaged in some kind of "pretense" (90), to be guilty of either "innocent lunacy, or wicked imposture" (76)—in short, to be a practicer of the "craft of some tricksters" (77). Delano is, however, mistaken about Cereno; although he is engaged in a masquerade, it is one into which he has been forced by the apparently innocent Negroes. Moreover, as was not the case in *The Confidence-Man*, reality seems as last to break through the disguises of appearances, and Delano's "benighted mind" is, at the end of his experience, apparently illuminated by a flash of revelation when he discovers that the masquerade has been directed by the Negroes.

The development of the story is, in fact, centered around Delano's gradual movement toward illumination. A carefully unified spatial and temporal structure, the story proper begins at sunrise with Delano's sighting of the "San Dominick" and ends at night on the same day with Delano's revelation, Cereno's rescue, and the subsequent capture of the Negroes. Reality seems to triumph over appearances as the Negroes are at last seen "with mask torn away" (119), and the meaning of the ambiguous words "Follow your leader" seems finally revealed when the canvas mask which had covered the hull is "whipped away" (119) revealing the skeleton of Aranda.

The end of the carefully structured account of Delano's deception and illumination is not, however, the end of "Benito Cereno." In addition to the main narrative there are two other sections: a series of extracts taken from "official Spanish documents" which record the investigation of a court of inquiry of the "whole affair" (123); and a short flashback, "retrospectively, or irregularly given" (138), which describes conversations between Delano and Cereno following the rescue of the latter. That these two fragments, in addition to shedding "light on the preceding narrative" (123), also serve to undercut the unities of time, place, and action is clear enough. Less clear but very important is the light which the inclusion of these fragments casts on the narrator's motives and methods. A clue is provided by an important passage written three years earlier in *Pierre*:

while the countless tribes of common novels laboriously spin veils of mystery, only to complacently clear them up at last; and while the countless tribe of common dramas do but repeat the same; yet the profounder emanations of the human mind, intended to illustrate all that can be humanly known of human life; these never unravel their own intricacies, and have no proper endings; but in imperfect, unanticipated, and disappointing sequels (as mutilated stumps), hurry to abrupt intermergings with the eternal tides of time and fate. (VII, 166)

The main narrative of "Benito Cereno" seems to operate in much the same way as those "common novels" which the narrator of *Pierre* describes. The mysteries introduced in the beginning at sunrise appear to be cleared up as darkness falls near the end: the Negroes are captured, and the "San Dominick" is towed back into the harbor. The intricacies of "Benito Cereno," however, are not unraveled this easily. The narrator's ironic query as to whether or not Delano's "undistrustful good nature" implies, "along with a benevolent heart, more than ordinary quickness and accuracy of intellectual perception" (55) suggests that the American captain is not a man gifted with profound insight. But in the narrative proper the reader is limited to Delano's point of view; he is made to experience the events on board the "San Dominick" through the eyes of the "undistrustful" captain. For this reason it is only in the last two sections of the story, when Cereno's account of his experiences is described in the official language of the court of inquiry and Delano and Cereno are seen through the eyes of the narrator, that the reader comes to see the "deeper shadows" (55) of "Benito Cereno."

While the simpleminded Delano believes that he finally understands his experience aboard the "San Dominick," the narrator and reader look for more light to be shed on the "juggling play" (104) in which Benito and Babo are the central characters. Like Delano, the reader wonders "what was the truth" (82), but unlike the good captain he does not feel that the simple act of unmasking has revealed it. As with *The Confidence-Man*, the real problem lies not so much in deciding who wears the mask as in discovering the implications of the masquerade. For this reason, the reader comes to the extracts hoping, like the narrator, that they will "shed light on the preceding narrative, as well as, in the first place, reveal the true port of departure and true history of the San Dominick's voyage" (123). The documents, however, prove to be "disappointing sequels," for while they give the factual history of the ship's voyage, they raise more questions than they answer. The factual account is as much a masquerade as were the actions of the subtle Babo. Although the narrator hopes that the documents may serve "as the key to fit into the lock of the complications which precede" (138), and thereby unlock the "San Dominick" 's hull, they prove as misleading as the key which is "suspended by a slender silken cord, from Don Benito's neck" (75).

While the extracts clear up such matters as the reason for Atufal's chains (126), the attack on the Spanish boy by the Negroes (136), and the whispered conversations between Cereno and Babo (132); identify the sparkling object which Delano sees in the hand of one of the sailors (136); and describe in detail the barbaric cruelty of the Negroes as well as the later revenge of the sailors on the Negro captives, they make no attempt to deal with the questions of meaning and motive. In fact, the naïveté and shallowness implicit in the language of the documents underscores the irony present in the fact that the Negroes, who are regarded as cargo along with "thirty cases of hardware" (124), reverse the relationship between master and slave. Similarly, by reporting, in a matter-of-fact and unemotional language, that the Negresses—one of whom Delano had regarded as an image of "naked nature," "pure tenderness and love" (87)—were not only "satisfied at the death of their master, Don Alexandro" but that "had the negroes not restrained them, they would have tortured to death, instead of simply killing, the Spaniards" (135), the documents raise important questions concerning the relationship between the Negroes and the Spaniards. These questions are only complicated by the further revelation of the behavior of the sailors toward the Negroes after they have been captured and shackled to the ring bolts of the deck.

The documents, then, instead of shedding light on the preceding narrative, cast over it additional shadows. Problems which remained beneath the surface while the events were seen through Delano's naïve eyes merely become more obvious when the events are described in the absurdly selective language of the court of inquiry. Only when the reader reaches the "retrospectively, or irregularly given" account (138) of the conversations between Cereno and Delano does he begin to see the full extent of the intricacies and shadows of Cereno's experience. Here for the first time attention is focused on the Spaniard's response to the mutiny, an issue which the preceding sections had approached only by recording the fact that he had retired to a monastery. The sensitive Cereno is unable to explain away the "malign machinations and deceptions" to which he has been exposed by accepting Delano's view that "all is owing to Providence" (139). He senses that a "shadow" has been cast over him by the Negro and feels himself blown by the winds of his experience toward his "tomb" (139).

Something of the nature of this destructive "shadow" is revealed in the narrator's description of one aspect of Cereno's experience which the Captain finds too horrible to discuss at all:

But if the Spaniard's melancholy sometimes ended in muteness upon topics like the above [the Negro], there were others upon which he never spoke at all; on which, indeed, all his old reserves were piled. Pass over the worst, and, only to elucidate, let an item or two of these be cited. The dress, so precise and costly, worn by him on the day whose events have been narrated, had not willingly been put on. And that silver-mounted sword, apparent symbol of despotic command, was not, indeed, a sword, but the ghost of one. The scabbard, artificially stiffened, was empty. (140)

As unwilling as Cereno to discuss the meaning of the masquerade of which he has been a part is Babo, who from the time of his capture to his "voiceless end," "uttered no sound" (140). It is this mutual silence, ambiguously maintaining the connection between master and slave, which points to the central concerns of "Benito Cereno." Both the Spaniard and the Negro are inextricably bound together because they have been the primary participants in a subversive masquerade which has transformed cosmos into chaos. Cereno's being forced to dress and act the part of captain while in the position of slave undermines the authenticity of a bureaucratic world where all of man's roles have an extra-human foundation.

The world represented by the "San Dominick" is a feudal one, composed of a number of planes arranged in order of dignity and connected by a net of master-servant relationships. This is a "follow your leader" world (58), a place where it is "with captains as with gods" (64), for in the captain is "lodged a dictatorship beyond which, while at sea, there was no earthly appeal" (63). And surely one effect of Cereno's association with Charles V is to connect the parallel planes of ship and nation.[3] That the order and stability implied by this hierarchical system are illusory is suggested by the narrator's description of both the ship and its captain. Although in its time "a very fine vessel," the "San Dominick" now seems like one of the "superannuated Italian palaces" which, "under a decline of masters, preserved signs of former state" (57). The apparel of the god-like captain Cereno suggests the "image of an invalid

[3] See Franklin's discussion of William Sterling's *The Cloister Life of the Emperor Charles the Fifth* as a source for "Benito Cereno" (*The Wake of the Gods*, pp. 136–50). The influence of Franklin's valuable study is obvious throughout my discussion of the story.

courtier tottering about London streets in the time of the plague" (69). To Delano he seems either "one of those paper captains . . . who has little of command but the name" (71) or a "low-born adventurer, masquerading as an oceanic grandee; . . . one playing a part above his real level" (77). Indeed, the "San Dominick" is filled with so many "strange costumes, gestures, and faces" that it seems "unreal," a "shadowy tableau just emerged from the deep, which directly must receive back what it gave" (59).

"Benito Cereno," however, is not a story which celebrates the replacing of Cereno's feudal world with the republican one of Delano, for Delano also regards Providence as the ground for universal order. His Protestant, democratic scheme merely eliminates most of the bureaucratic machinery and thereby reduces the "theatrical aspect" of life's "juggling play" (104). When the chief mate of the "Bachelor's Delight" directs the attack on the "San Dominick," he reveals the essential similarity between the worlds of the two ships by directing his men to "Follow your leader!" (122).

It is Delano's shallow vision rather than the superiority of the system he represents which protects him from the shadow of Cereno's experience. Lacking the Spaniard's insight, he regards the Negroes' revolt as a momentary disruption of natural order: " 'But the past is passed; why moralize upon it? Forget it. See, yon bright sun has forgotten it all, and the blue sea, and the blue sky; these have turned over new leaves.' 'Because they have no memory,' he dejectedly replied; 'because they are not human' " (139). It is because he has a memory that Cereno is unable to forget the withered leaves of his past experience and to accept the bright blueness of the sea and sky as any more than another mask. The shadow cast by the Negro has not merely darkened his world but has robbed it of its supporting substance and left him surrounded with "artificially stiffened" but empty forms. For Cereno the sun, sea, and sky remain as they were when the "San Dominick" first entered the harbor of St. Maria:

The morning was one peculiar to that coast. Everything was mute and calm; everything gray. The sea, though undulated into long roods of swells, seemed fixed, and was sleeked at the surface like waved lead that has cooled and set in the smelter's mould. The sky seemed a gray surtout. Flights of troubled gray fowl, kith and kin with flights of troubled gray vapors among which they were mixed, skimmed low and fitfully over the waters, as swallows over meadows before storms. Shadows present, foreshadowing deeper shadows to come. (55)

This is a world composed entirely of surfaces, with all of its parts mixed and confused. Shadows here do not lead to essential forms but to "deeper shadows." Sky and sea are almost indistinguishable and both seem equally artificial. The sea, product of a smelter's mould, is "laid out and leaded up," "soul gone, defunct" (93); and the "surtout" sky is the first of a series of sinister, artificial coverings. Like the "San Dominick," which seems a "shadowy tableau just emerged from the deep," nature also is composed of an enigmatic set of shadows and surfaces which apparently conceal some terrifying secret.

But what is the nature of the reality which lies hidden beneath the artificial surfaces of nature and the costumes and roles of Cereno and the Negroes? To the reader familiar with Melville's other fiction, a partial answer to this question is suggested by the narrator's description of the "San Dominick" as a "white-washed monastery" (57). As is the case with the "white-washed" "Fidèle," this ship, "launched, from Ezekiel's Valley of Dry Bones" (57), with a skeleton for a figurehead, is an image of the blank background against which life's unreal play is performed. And also, like the "Fidèle," the Spanish vessel is the stage for a masquerade which is ontologically subversive. Not only is the ship described as a "white-washed monastery," but Delano first thinks that he sees a "ship-load of monks" because the Negroes resemble "Black Friars pacing the cloisters" (57). Cereno's cabin is filled with objects related to monasticism, and he resembles a "hypochondriac abbot" (62), while Babo seems a "begging friar of St. Francis" (68). Moreover, when Cereno is rescued from the "San Dominick," he merely moves from a metaphoric monastery to a real one. He even maintains the services of Babo through his symbolic equal, "the monk Infelez" (137), who becomes his "special guardian and consoler, by night and by day" (123). For Benito Cereno the shadow of the Negro falls not only over the decks of the ship but over all existence, and for this reason, as he returns from sea to land, he finds only another and larger "San Dominick." That this is the meaning of his monastic retirement is implied by the fact that although Babo's "slight frame, inadequate to that which it held," is "burned to ashes," his head, "that hive of subtlety," is "fixed on a pole in the Plaza" and looks toward the church where the bones of Aranda are entombed and toward the monastery where Cereno finally dies (140). The slave-owning businessman Aranda and Captain Cereno, representatives of the world of established social forms, are introduced by Babo to the fictitiousness of their world and are brought face to face with the ambiguous but ineluctable facts of a shadow world full of hate and violence where slave is master and master slave, a world of death in life.

The social realm is not, however, the only part of the world of appearances which is invalidated by Babo. Just as his masquerade as a servant while in the position of master undermines the whole structure of a social order based on this apparently essential relationship, so his and other Negroes' ability to seem "nothing less than a ship-load of monks" inverts and invalidates a higher order which is also based on the tie between master and servant. While playing the role of monkish servant Babo assumes the powers of God the master as he forces the Spaniards to "keep faith with the blacks" (129). That he in fact possesses the ability to punish those who do not keep his commandments is evidence enough to call into doubt Delano's traditional but naïve view that "all is owing to Providence" (139).

By casting a shadow over the basic master-slave relationship, Babo destroys the ground for order in the social, political, and religious realms. He reveals the true meaning of the symbolic figures on the "San Dominick" 's "shield-like stern-piece" (58). The carving of the "dark satyr in a mask, holding his foot on the prostrate neck of a writhing figure, likewise masked" (58) is a synecdoche for the entire story; like Cereno's masquerade it is a subversive parody of the "follow your leader" world. This "relic of faded grandeur" is a "mythological device" which seems to testify that man's roles have divine authorization. Babo, however, discovers that the two figures are easily reversible and thereby puts in question the possibility of any kind of legitimate sanction for either. Near the end of the masquerade the meaning of the two masked figures is extended when the "prostrate negro," ground under Delano's foot, is discovered "snakishly writhing up from the boat's bottom," with a dagger aimed "at the heart of his master" (118).

Babo's masquerade, then, is not discredited by a discrepant reality, for the "facts" which are in conflict with it are no less unreal. The master-servant relationship is not an essential one but is another shadow concealing a skeletal reality which is best described by the images of death that permeate the story. Complete with funeral march "supplied by the chanting oakum pickers" (59) and carrying the "cadaverous" Cereno (70) as well as a skeleton figurehead, the ship, with its "sarcophagus lid" (98) doors, is a huge coffin. After having glimpsed this frightening world of darkness and death, Cereno is no longer able to return to that other brighter but illusory world of forms. So it is that after three months in the monastery, no longer cadaverous but a corpse indeed, his body is "borne on the bier" (140), an obvious replacement for the "hearse-like" ship (58).

If the theme of "Benito Cereno" is in part the fictitiousness of social, political, and religious forms, its method is a demonstration of the illusory nature of the architectonic fiction. As the limited point of view of the first part of the story suggests, the intricacies of human life can never be revealed by the carefully rounded and self-contained fiction. "Truth [has] its ragged edges" (*BB*, XXVIII, 128); and as the two sections of the story which are "retrospectively, or irregularly given" suggest through the shadows which they cast over the preceding narrative, the subversive nature of truth forces all meaningful fictions to end in "disappointing sequels."

ii

That the methods and themes of *Billy Budd* closely parallel those of "Benito Cereno" is clearly suggested by the narrator's introduction to the three short "sequels" which follow the account of Billy's life and death aboard the "Bellipotent." In way of an apology for his inclusion of the description of Vere's death, the account of Billy's crime by a naval chronicle, and the ballad "Billy in the Darbies," the narrator generalizes on the nature of form in fiction.

> The symmetry of form attainable in pure fiction cannot so readily be achieved in a narration essentially having less to do with fable than with fact. Truth uncompromisingly told will always have its ragged edges; hence the conclusion of such a narration is apt to be less finished than an architectural finial.
> How it fared with the Handsome Sailor during the year of the Great Mutiny has been faithfully given. But though properly the story ends with his life, something in way of sequel will not be amiss. Three brief chapters will suffice. (128)

In addition to suggesting that *Billy Budd*, like "Benito Cereno," will end in "disappointing sequels," this passage serves as a warning to the reader to pay close attention to the material which follows; for as the method of "Benito Cereno" demonstrates and as the narrator affirms here, truth is revealed only when formal order is destroyed. The obvious implications of the narrator's words, then, is that the meaning of *Billy Budd* is likely to be found by explicating the relationship which the sequels have to the story proper.

As the large amount of *Billy Budd* criticism makes clear,

entral ambiguity and therefore the central problem of the story grows out of what seems to be the narrator's equivocal attitude toward Captain Vere.[4] Since the narrative leaves little doubt of either Billy's prelapsarian and Christ-like innocence or of Claggart's devilish depravity, it is Vere's methods of dealing with the confrontation between these two cosmic characters which provides the central drama of the story. As the critical quarrel over Vere's motives testifies, however, the meaning of the drama is not easily understood. Is Vere the object of the narrator's pointed irony or the tragic hero of the story? This is the central problem of *Billy Budd*.

But if the narrative proper leaves the reader in doubt as to the narrator's attitude toward Vere, the sequels provide a number of fairly clear and important clues. Of crucial significance is the fact that the narrator's apology for his three "ragged edges" directly follows, and is a commentary on, a concise statement of Vere's metaphysical position: " 'With mankind.' he would say, 'forms, measured forms, are everything; and that is the import couched in the story of Orpheus with his lyre spellbinding the wild denizens of the wood.' And this he once applied to the disruption of forms going on across the Channel and the consequences thereof" (XXVII, 128). It is clear from the narrator's own comments, which associate form with the illusions of "pure fiction" that this is at least one area in which he disagrees with Vere. Captain Vere, however, like Benito Cereno, is dedicated to the preservation of an ordered world. A member of the "aristocracy" (VII, 62) and a ruler of men, he is a man whose "settled convictions were as a dike against those invading waters of novel opinion social, political, and otherwise" (62). As Vere's allusion to the French Revolution "going on across the Channel" suggests, he recognizes that with a breakdown in forms comes social

---

[4] Interesting in this connection is the observation of Hayford and Sealts that the "cumulative effect" of Melville's final revisions in the *Billy Budd* manuscript was "to throw into doubt not only the rightness of Vere's decision and the soundness of his mind but also the narrator's own position regarding him" (*BB*, 34).

and political chaos and, as the later mention of the Revolutionary ship, the "Athée," implies, religious chaos as well. And, as his use of the Orpheus myth makes clear, he regards man's artistic endeavors as an important part of the "measured forms" with which he keeps out chaos.

The narrator, however, is interested in truth, not the maintenance of illusion. Unlike Orpheus, who seems a kind of confidence man,[5] he seeks to spellbind no one. Instead of leaving the reader with the apotheosis of Billy and the formal order of Vere's martial world, he chooses to add "something in the way of sequel." By this act he throws a shadow of ambiguity over what would otherwise be a tragic account of the failure of celestial innocence to survive in a terrestrial and martial world. While the narrative proper portrays a fallen world which is incapable of dealing with child-like innocence, it also implies the possibility of a safe, ordered existence free from irrationality and violence. As long as man is obedient to martial law, a system designed for his own protection as well as that of the captain and the King, he can live his life secure in the belief that he inhabits an orderly universe. When the narrator emphasizes the breakdown in the "symmetry of form" of his fiction, however, he exposes not only a flaw in his story but a crack in the foundation of that orderly world it describes.

Vere appears last to the reader not as the self-controlled stoic who witnesses Billy's execution, but as a dying man with his reason destroyed by the effects of opium. Killed in a battle with the "Athée," Vere is a victim of the formless forces of barbarism and irrationality. The "disruption of form going on across the Channel" reaches into his well-ordered world and destroys him. Although the "Athée" is finally defeated by the "Bellipotent" and the command of the ship is passed in an orderly fashion from Vere to the senior lieutenant as martial

---

[5] The confidence man in his role as the man from the Black Rapids Coal Company is described as moving like "Orpheus in his gay descent to Tartarus" (*C-M*, 34).

order is apparently maintained, the narrator's comment that the "Athèe" is the "aptest name . . . ever given to a warship" (XXVIII, 129) suggests another possibility. That the "Athée," nominal symbol of the formless world which Vere fears and despises, is at the same time a perfect representative of the orderly martial world which Vere himself commands suggests that chaos may in fact lurk within the forms themselves. This hint is strengthened when the reader remembers the narrator's earlier discussion of the incongruity implicit in the fact that in the man-of-war world the "Prince of Peace" serves in the "host of the God of War—Mars" (XXIV, 122). The presence of this one small paradox in a world which admits no ambiguities is enough to call into doubt the validity of the entire system.

Perhaps even more damaging to Vere and the world he represents is the narrator's suggestion that, had he lived, his spirit " 'spite its philosophic austerity may yet have indulged in the most secret of all passions, ambition" (XXVIII, 129). This observation, when coupled with an earlier suggestion that the captain might have let himself "melt back into what remains primeval in our formalized humanity," implies that there lurks within him the seeds of irrational and chaotic action. The narrator's equivocal hint that Vere may have been ambitious holds open the possibility that he acted not entirely on the dictates of military necessity in his handling of Billy's case. He may have been driven by a desire to avoid the possibility of any shadow's being cast on his official reputation. It is, of course, clear enough that the reader can never be sure of Vere's secret motives; the point is, however, that the mere presence of ambiguity is enough to undermine his world of "measured forms."

While the first of the three sequels casts ambiguous shadows on Vere's motives and on the stability of the "Bellipotent" 's world, the second tends to undercut the validity of the entire system on which the man-of-war world is founded. By basing his judgment of Billy on the practical and unambiguous law of the Articles of War, Vere had thought himself able to avoid any confusing consideration of motive. The drumhead court which tries Billy has to deal in no way with problematical questions of "intent or non-intent" (172). The account of the Billy Budd-Claggart encounter which appears in an "*authorized* naval chronicle of the time" (XXIX, 130; italics mine), however, suggests that the martial world is not always singlemindedly devoted to pure fact. Not only are the facts of the experience falsified and distorted, but motives are deduced from the twisted facts. Claggart is said to have been "vindictively stabbed" (130); Billy is called depraved and Claggart judged "patriotic"; and additional irony is present in the fact that Budd, an Englishman of the "Saxon strain" (II, 51), is called an "alien," while Claggart, who has a "bit of accent in his speech" (VIII, 65), is regarded as a pure Englishman.

The point is, of course, that Vere's faith in the reliability of official forms is shown to be misplaced by the "authorized" but completely distorted report. Around the facts of the death of Claggart and the execution of Billy is constructed an official but completely fictional account of the situation. As the narrator points out, the description in the naval chronicle is the only report "that hitherto has stood in human record to attest what manner of men respectively were John Claggart and Billy Budd" (XXIX, 131). The martial world is content to let the lie remain.

It is important to notice, however, that while the official account is full of lies, it is formally complete and leaves no doubt that at last all is right in the martial world. The criminal is judged and executed and "nothing amiss is now apprehended aboard H.M.S. *Bellipotent*" (131). Like the narrator's account in the story proper, the "authorized" version ends with a statement of the triumph of "measured forms." But the narrator, by making this official version of the story one of the "ragged edges" of his own "inside narrative," destroys the illusion of order which both his own and the official versions imply. Just as Babo's disruption of the "measured forms" aboard the "San Dominick" exposes a shadow which permanently strains and calls into doubt the very foundation on which Cereno's world is built, so the drama which takes place on the "Bellipotent" puts the principles around which Vere's world is organized to a test which eventually results in their collapse.

The final "sequel" of *Billy Budd* is an account of another view of the events of the story which contrasts with the narrator's "inside" one. Knowing nothing of the "secret facts of the tragedy" (XXX, 131), the other sailors aboard the man-of-war rely on their instincts in making their evaluation of Billy Budd. The ballad "Billy in the Darbies," which is the "rude utterance" of their "general estimate of his nature" (131), is, in its own way, as much a distortion of the facts as the account in the naval chronicle. The sailors, although among the ruled rather than the rulers, are still a part of the man-of-war world; and thus it is that they accept the fact that Billy's punishment was "unavoidably inflicted from the naval point of view," although they "instinctively felt that Billy was . . . as incapable of mutiny as of wilful murder" (131).

The ballad makes no attempt to detail the facts of the situation or to defend Billy's actions, but is merely a poetic account of his response to his impending death. Like the official version, however, it is controlled by the point of view of its composer, one of the sailors from Billy's watch. Filled with nautical terms and developed around a series of plays on words, the ballad is a perfect illustration of the sailor's view of the world. The ironic reverses of fortune which he learns to face and accept are present in the observations that the moon "will die in the dawning of Billy's last day"; " 'tis me, not the sentence they'll suspend"; and "all is up; and I must up too" (132). Billy's child-like mind is incapable of even this mildly ironic perception: "to deal in double meanings . . . of any sort was quite foreign to his nature" (I, 49). Similarly, the references to

"Bristol Molly" and the "drum roll to grog" are clearly references to aspects of the sailor's life which seem alien to "Baby Budd."

Like the official account, then, the ballad illustrates the need for an "inside narrative" which records the true facts of Billy's life and death. Since the sailors do not question the law which destroys Billy, but, indeed, like Vere, seem to regard it as a tragic necessity demanded by the forms of the world in which they live, their account of his death is as fallacious as the "authorized" one.

The appalling truth of *Billy Budd* is not that innocence must be sacrificed to maintain the order of the world, but rather that innocence is destroyed by the forces of chaos and darkness masquerading as "measured forms." The "Bellipotent" is the "Athèe" hiding behind the cloak of the impostor chaplain she carries; and the Articles of War merely cover with an official mask the same irrational forces which are found undisguised "across the Channel." As Babo and the confidence man illustrate, the forces of darkness and chaos achieve their greatest success when they take on and use the forms which men create in order to convince themselves that they live in an ordered world.

The glimpse into the nature of the "measured forms" is provided by the narrator of *Billy Budd* by the deliberate destruction of his fiction's "symmetry of form." In other words, the method of his story is the meaning of its theme; and his statement that "truth uncompromisingly told will always have its ragged edges" is not merely a commentary on the nature of fiction but on the nature of reality as well. Just as the colors of the spectrum are for Ishmael masks for that "colorless all color," white, so to the narrators of "Benito Cereno" and *Billy Budd* the social, political, and religious forms of the world are but convenient disguises for that formless and chaotic force which underlies all things.

While the circumstances surrounding the writing of *Billy Budd* give a special import to John Middleton Murry's assertion that it was Melville's "last will and spiritual testament,"[6] there is little reason to suppose that E. L. Grant Watson's description of the story as Melville's "testament of acceptance"[7] can have more than a limited application. Although it is true that the very fact of the story's existence implies that Melville modified the cynical view of fiction expressed in *The Confidence-Man*, *Billy Budd* is not the product of a sentimental senility or a second childhood.

In *Billy Budd* Melville returns to a narrative mode with which he had experimented earlier in "Benito Cereno," one which differs significantly from those used in his novel-length fictions. The narrators of these stories are not merely writers of fiction; they are, in effect, critics of their own work. Gifted, as it were, with a double consciousness, they create their fictions and then explicate them through study of sources. Finding that the stories they have told conceal the truth with their "symmetry of form," they add by way of "sequel" additional facts which, since they are outside the spatial and temporal dimensions of the narrative proper, destroy its formal unity. The disruptive power of the "sequels," however, does not derive from their status as representatives of a more real reality. On the contrary, these factual additions are shown to be as unreal as the fictional world they burden. Indeed, the juxtaposition of the fictional and factual realms results in the destruction of the authenticity of each and leaves the reader face to face with a positive emptiness, an oppressive and threatening blankness. Herman Melville's vision remains apocalyptic to the end. His metaphysics of emptiness led him to a recognition of the "secret absurdity" implicit in the novelist's commitment to "Vital Truth," and his devotion to that goal left silence as his only alternative.

[6] "Herman Melville's Silence," *TLS*, No. 1173 (July 10, 1924), p. 433.
[7] "Melville's Testament of Acceptance," *NEQ*, 6 (1933):319–27.

INDEX

Adam: Tommo as, 42

Adam Bede: authorial intrusions in, 10–11

Adventure: in *T*, 39–40, 44; in *M*, 49; as rejection of actuality, 50; in *R*, 60–61; glass ship as image for, 61–62; in *M-D*, 83

Ahab: 66; as creation of Ishmael, 84, 89–90; tragic world of, 88; as tragic hero, 90, 104; confronts whiteness, 102–4; Ishmael rejects, 105; interprets Moby-Dick, 112

Aleema, 49, 51

Allen, Don Cameron, 123*n*

Alphabet: useless to man, 97; Isabel's knowledge of, 140

Ambassadors, The: Preface to, 14, 15, 16; point of view in, 14–18 *passim*; relation to Preface, 16–18

American, The: Preface to, 13–14; point of view in, 14

Anatomy of Melancholy, The, 123*n*: as source for *C-M*, 188–91, 193

Angel: as deceiver in "China Aster," 181

Animal imagery: in *C-M*, 152

Annatoo, 49

Apocalypse. *See* Bible

Apocrypha. *See* Bible

Apollo: cosmopolitan as, 185

April Fools' Day, 158

Aranda, Don Alexandro, 200, 203, 207

Architect: Ishmael as, 93; writer as, 124

"Arcturion," 47, 48, 49, 54, 58

Artufal, 202

"Athèe," 211: as a symbol of chaos, 211, 212

Autobiography: and Melville's fiction, 33

Autolycus, 171, 172

Babbalanza, 53, 56

Babo: his masquerade, 202; as friar, 206; as God, 207; as subversive, 207–8; mentioned, 214

"Bachelor's Delight," 205

Ballad, Ned, 48, 54

Barth, John, 19

Bayle, Pierre, 187

"Bellipotent," 209, 212, 214, 215

"Benito Cereno," 199–209, 215–16

Benito Cereno: Delano's view of, 200; effect of mutiny on, 203, 205–6, 208; his masquerade, 204–5; his death, 207; compared with Vere, 210, 214

Bible: as guide book, 65; Luke, 122; Exodus, 122, 185; Numbers, 123; Pierre's use of, 133–34; Revelation, 162, 184, 185, 186, 187, 190; compared with the story of the Indian-hater, 180; Genesis, 183–84; Apocrypha, 186, 187, 190; designed to confuse, 186, 188; Corinthians, 188; Matthew, 188; Proverbs, 188; Thessalonians, 188

See A Note on Texts, p. xiii, for abbreviations used in the Index.

Biblical: names in *M-D*, 86–87; analogues in *IP*, 143–46; structure in *C-M*, 162, 184

Billy Budd, 199, 209–16

Billy Budd, 21, 38: as Christ, 210; described in naval chronicle, 213; described in "Billy in the Darbies," 214–15

"Billy in the Darbies": as subversive sequel, 214–15

Bird imagery, 164

Black Guinea, 152, 176, 177

Bland, 66, 78–79

Blindness: White Jacket's, 75; in *WJ*, 77; in *M-D*, 102, 108; Ahab's, 102–3;

Bloomer, Captain, 104

Blunt, Jack, 63

Bolton, Harry: as mirror for Redburn, 66–67

"Bon Homme Richard": battle with "Serapis," 147–48

Books: in "HHM," 22–23; as foundlings, 26–27; use in *R*, 60, 62–63; *The Wealth of Nations*, 62–63; *The Bonaparte Dream Book*, 63; as truth tellers, 84; as sources of creation, 93; whales as, 94, 96–98; as material objects, 96; Queequeg as, 96–97; Ishmael as, 100; life as, 106; made from stony materials, 124–25; Pierre as, 132, 133; importance in Pierre's life, 132–38; Lucy as, 133; Isabel as, 134; as mirror of life, 134; the failure of Pierre's, 137–38; as maps, 156

—guide books: Dwight's *Travels*, 23–24; in *R*, 24, 63–65; as mirrors of reality, 63; as maps, 64; the Bible as, 65, 66; *Hamlet* as, 136; novels as, 156

Booth, Wayne, 4–5

B.R.C. man, 176

Brodtkorb, Paul, Jr., 85

Brown, Norman O, 192*n*, 193*n*

Bulkington, 21

Bunker Hill Monument: as symbol in *IP*, 142–43

Burton, Robert, 123*n*: Melville's reading of, 189

Cain, 86

Cannibalism: in *T*, 41, 43; in *M-D*, 87, 96

Caterpillar-butterfly: its metamorphosis, 155, 157; as sign of nature's masquerade, 156

Charlemont: story of, 173–74; mentioned, 175

"China Aster," 175, 180–81

Christ: Sermon on the Mount, 118, 120, 127, 133, 134; as impostor, 122, 123, 128, 130, 134, 170; lamb-like man as, 160; birth of, 162; as confidence man, 170; linked to cosmopolitan and narrator, 170; on the shade of solar lamp, 185

Church of the Apostles: named for set of impostors, 127; history of, 127–28

Claggart, 21, 66, 210, 213

Clothing: of lamb-like man, 159; of Colonel Moredock, 179; use of, in "Benito Cereno," 203–5

—coat: as disguise, 157, 158; of cosmopolitan, 157–58, 161; of P.I.O. man, 158; of harlequin, 167

—jacket: symbol in *WJ*, 71–79;

symbol in *M-D*, 72; Ishmael's, compared with White Jacket's, 73; importance of color, 74–75; as mirror of reality, 77, 78
—surtout: disguise in "BC," 206
Color: as mask, 74–75, 100–2, 107, 157–62 *passim*, 215
Colorlessness. *See* Whiteness
Confession: *R* as, 60, 67
Confidence-Man, The, 21, 58: compared with *WJ*, 79; compared with *P* and *IP*, 141; discussed, 150–95; compared with "BC" and *BB*, 199; mentioned, 202, 216
Conrad, Joseph, 7: compared with Melville, 21, 26, 100
Conventions: soliloquies as, 84, 88; stage directions as, 84, 88; names as, 87; of Shakespearean drama, 88; invocations as, 89; literary, 90, 151; phallic jokes as, 94–95; to conceal truth, 126; social, 152
Conversion: in *T*, 43
Coonskins, 157–58, 177
Cosmopolitan, the: compared with Bland, 79; as impostor, 157, 172, 182; compared with other avatars, 158; related to lamb-like man, 159, 161–63; as butterfly, 161; as role player, 167; as actor, 168, as harlequin, 170; linked with Christ and the narrator, 170; as storyteller, 173–74; compared with Shakespeare and narrator, 174; his analysis of Colonel Moredock, 179–80; learns from "China Aster," 181; as an original character,

182, 183, 185–86; as Apollo, 185; as source of light, 191; relation to juvenile peddler, 193–94; mentioned, 152
Counterfeit: world as, 130
Counterfeiting: importance in *WJ*, 78–79
Cowper, William, 35–36
Cream, William (the barber), 152, 161
Crippled cynic, 151, 153, 178

Darkness: in Conrad, 26; Conrad's, compared with Melville's whiteness, 100
Deafness: caused by sounds of nature, 108
Death imagery: in "BC," 208
Delano, Captain Amasa: movement toward illumination, 200; point of view, 200–1, 202, 203, 206; conversations with Cereno, 201, 203
Democracy in America, 18
Digressions: in *C-M*, 153–54
Disguise: in *C-M*, 161; of the confidence man, 163; in "BC," 200. *See also* Clothing; Color; Masks
"Dolly," 39, 41, 44
Domestic novel: *P* in the tradition of, 117, 129
Donjalolo, 54
Don Quixote: as anti-novel, 6
Don Quixote: as original character, 182
Dream: importance in *M*, 54–55
Dreamer: artist as, 55–56
Drummond light, 183, 185–86
Duck-billed beaver: inconsistency of, 155; identifies masquerade in nature, 156
Duyckinck, Evert, 189

Dwight, Timothy: importance in "HHM," 23–25; compared with Hawthorne, 24–25

Eden: *Typee* as, 40
Editor: narrator of *IP* as, 141–48 *passim*
Egbert: on philosophy, 169–70; as storyteller, 180–81; mentioned, 178
Egypt: birthplace of the gods, 92, 97, 195; birthplace of hieroglyphic writing, 97
Egyptian priests: as confidence men, 195
Eliot, George: use of intrusive narrator, 10–12
Enceladus, 130

Facts: collection of, 83–84; fiction based on, 155; as fiction in "BC," 208; disruptive power in "BC" and *BB*, 209, 216
Factual world: movement away from, in *M-D*, 83–84
Fall of man: in *T*, 40
Falsgrave, Reverend, 131
Feidelson, Charles, 47*n*
"Fidèle," 156: lamb-like man's effect on, 159–60; white ship, 160; mentioned, 161, 206
Fielding, Henry: creator of new kind of writing, 7–8; theory of fiction, 8–10; compared with Henry James, 9
Fire: symbol of truth, 125
First-person narrative: meaning of, for Melville, 33; use by Montaigne, 33; *T* as, 37–46 *passim*; *M* as, 47–58 *passim*;

R as, 59–67 *passim*; *WJ* as, 70–79 *passim*; *M-D* as, 83–113 *passim*; abandoned in *P*, 117, 128–29
Form: illusory, 83, 117, 209; in fiction, 209, 211; disruption of, 210; narrator's view of, 210; Vere's view of, 210–11; to conceal chaos, 212; as mask, 215; nature of, 215
Fortunate Fall myth: in *Tom Jones*, 7–8
Foster, Elizabeth, 159*n*, 188
Franklin, Benjamin: as confidence man, 146
Franklin, H. Bruce, 92*n*, 118, 152, 204
French Revolution: as subversion, 210
Friedman, Norman, 4*n*
Frye, Northrop, 67
Fussel, Edwin, 178*n*

Glass ship: symbol in *R*, 61–62
Glendinning family: feudalistic heritage of, 131
God: as human fiction, 119; as silence, 120; finger of, 122–23
Gold doubloon: as mirror, 101
Golden Inn, 112
Goneril, 176, 177
Goodman, Frank. *See* Cosmopolitan, the
Great Expectations, 59
Greylock. *See* Mountain
Guide books. *See* Books: guide books

Hall, James: as storyteller, 178–80 *passim*
Hamlet: as fiction, 136; as guide book, 136

Hamlet: as original character, 182

Hartly, David, 34

Hautia, 52–53

Hawthorne, Nathaniel, 19–20, 22: as guide in Preface to *Mosses*, 24; Melville's analysis of, 24–25; man and artist distinguished, 27; compared with Shakespeare, 27–28; man and artist compared, 28; mentioned, 37, 52

"Hawthorne and His Mosses": discussed, 21–29; mentioned, 36, 85, 112, 151

"Heart of Darkness," 105

Herb doctor, 164–65: compared with narrator, 165, 166

Hermes: juvenile peddler as, 192–93

Hieroglyph whale as, 96–98

Hieroglyphic writing, 83–84, 96–98

Hoffman, Daniel, 107*n*

Holland, Laurence, 16*n*

"Hyme to Hermes, A": as source for *C-M*, 193–94

Impostor: Christ as, 122, 123, 128, 130, 134, 170; Apostles as, 127; Moses as, 130; narrator of *P* as, 130; Isabel as, 135; confidence man as, 151; butterfly as, 157; cosmopolitan as, 157, 162, 182; Autolycus as, 171–72; narrator of *C-M* as, 174; Colonel Moredock as, 179–80; Cereno as, 200; chaplain as, 215

Indian-hater: characteristics of, 177–78

Infelez: as Babo's symbolic equal, 207

Intrusive narrator: in *Tom Jones*, 7–10; in *Adam Bede*, 10–11; in American novel, 19–20; in *C-M*, 153

Irony: in *R*, 60; in *WJ*, 68; in *IP*, 143–45

Irving, Washington, 19

Isabel: her letter, 133; as book, 134; as impostor, 135; relation to narrator, 138–41; removed from human institutions, 139

Ishmael: Redburn as, 66; in the masthead, 76; as Sub-Sub's commentator, 84; as pseudonym, 85–87; compared with Cain, Job, and Jonah, 86; as cannibal, 87; view of names, 87; as dramatist, 89–91; as whale author, 92–93; as architect, 93; as book, 100; as weaver, 106–8, 111, 125; narrative method of, 117; theory of color, 158; mentioned, 33, 36, 58, 118, 195, 215

Ishmael-ism, 86

Israel Potter, 21, 141–48

Israel Potter: as author, 143; importance of name, 143–45

Jacket. *See* Clothing: jacket

Jackson, 21, 65, 66

James, Henry: and recent criticism of novel, 3; on art of fiction, 12–13; relation of prefaces to novels, 12–18 *passim*; mentioned, 37

Job, 86

Jonah, 86

Jones, John Paul: as savage, 147

Juvenile peddler: relation to

Juvenile peddler (*cont'd*)
cosmopolitan, 192; as Hermes, 192–93

Karky, 42–43
King Lear, 28
Kitto, John, 187
Kostanza, the, 56

Lamb-like man: prepares way for other avatars, 159; compared with cosmopolitan, 159, 161–63, 182; effect on "Fidèle," 159–60; "advent" of, 160; crucifixion and resurrection of, 161; mentioned, 38, 184
Language: as usage, 126–28
Leg: Tommo's, 40–43, 44
Lewis, R. W. B., 18, 192n
Library: allows freedom, 56; use in *R*, 61; importance to Ishmael, 93; as Ishmael's home, 94; security of, 96
Lies: Ishmael's, 105
Light imagery: in *M-D*, 102–3; in *C-M*, 158, 161, 183–86 *passim*, 190–91, 194
Lima: the white city, 111
Liverpool, 62
Lombardo, 56
Loom, 106–8, 109, 111, 118, 125
"Loomings," 86
Lubbock, Percy: on Henry James, 3–4
Lukács, Georg: on the novel, 3n, 6

Madness: result of exposure to truth, 21; and memory, 35; Pip's, 104–5; avoided by narrator of *IP*, 146. *See also* "Sane madness"
Maintop: symbol in *WJ*, 72–73; 75–76; in *M-D*, 76
Manco Capac, 159, 184
"Man of Questionable Morality, A": discussed, 177–80; mentioned, 175
Man with the weed: as actor, 168–69
Map: guide books as, 64; books as, 156; novels as, 164
Mardi: as response to critics of *T*, 46; discussed, 46–58; mentioned, 37, 59, 71, 123, 128
Marlow: as liar, 105
Marlowe, Christopher, 193
Marvel, Bill, 48, 54
Masks: names as, 87; social usages as, 90; canvas, 200; in nature, 205
Masquerade: life as, 21, 137; writer as participant in, 126, 130, 195; narrator of *IP* removed from, 147; in nature, 156; Cereno's enforced, 200, 204, 205, 208; documents as, in "BC," 202; ontologically subversive, in "BC," 204, 206; Babo's, 207; on "San Dominick"'s stern-piece, 208; in *BB*, 215
Masthead. *See* Maintop
Materiality: whale as, 91; unknowable, 94; Moby-Dick as, 104; stink of, 109; mountain as, 118–23; conceals truth, 126
Material objects: as hieroglyphs, 83–84; books as, 96; as walls of silence, 98; Ishmael's retreat from, 98–99; Ahab's desire to know and control, 104; as mirrors, 104
Media, 53, 56
Memory: importance for Mel-

ville, 34–37; in *M*, 47, 53–54; gives radical freedom, 55; in *R*, 60, 67; man with the weed's analysis of, 177

Metamorphosis: of the caterpillar, 157; of Charles Arnold Noble, 172, 174

Middlemarch: narrator of, 11–12

Millennium: in *WJ*, 69

Miller, J. Hillis, 6, 7

Milton, John, 89, 126

Mining metaphor, 119–25, 131

Mirror: in *Adam Bede*, 10; guide books as, 63; Harry Bolton as, 66; jacket as, 77; art as, 85; whale as, 99; gold doubloon as, 101; material objects as, 104; sea as, 105; books as, 134, 156

Miser, 164, 176

Moa Artua, 38

Moby-Dick: 21, 24, 28, 37, 67, 117, 128: as gloss for *WJ*, 72–73, 74–75; discussed, 83–113; compared with *P*, 118

Mohi, 53

Monastic imagery, 179–80, 206–7

Montaigne, Michael de, 33

Moredock, John: story of, 177–80; as impostor, 179–80

Moses: as impostor, 122–23, 130; obtains water from stone, 123, 130–31; horned altar of, 185; as confidence man, 195

Mosses from an Old Manse: Preface to, 22, 24

Mountain: Sinai, 118; Delectable, 118, 120; sermon on, 118, 120, 127, 133, 134; Greylock, 118, 142; image of materiality, 118–23; of Titans, 120; narrator inspired by, 130

Murray, Henry, 128

Murry, John Middleton, 216

Names: as fiction, 27; importance in *M-D*, 85–87; as mask, 87; meaning of Ishmael's, 87; artificiality of, 126–28; importance in *IP*, 144

Narcissus, 85

Narrator: Melvilleian, 35–37; as anthropologist, 38; as miner, 121; as impostor, 130; as editor, 141–48. *See also* First-person narrative

"Neversink," 68, 69

New England: as metaphor in "HHM," 22–25 *passim*

Noble, Charles Arnold, 170: as storyteller, 178

Novel: form of, 3–18 *passim*; in America, 18–21; as mimetic form, 153, 154–65 *passim*; as autonomous form, 153, 165–74 *passim*

Omoo, 46, 47, 128

Oroolia, 51

Orpheus: as spellbinder, 210; as confidence man, 211

Ortega y Gasset, José, 3n, 6, 7n

Osiris, 92

Paradise Lost, 7, 10, 89n

"Parki," 49

Paulson, Ronald, 4

Pedro, Don, 111

"Pequod": as stage, 84, 88, 90; mentioned, 105, 110, 111

Perspectivism, 7

Phallic jokes, 94–95

Picaresque structure: in *R*, 59

Picture of Liverpool, The, 64–65

Pierre, 117–41: compared with *IP*, 142, 147; mentioned, 21, 58, 148, 195, 201

Pierre, 21, 117–41 *passim*

P.I.O. man, 157–58, 165, 177

Pip, 21, 104–5, 107

"Pleasures of Memory, The," 35

Plinlimmon, Plotinus, 38, 70: compared with narrator of *P*, 130, 141

Point of view: importance, 3; defined by Booth, 4–5; as thematic concern, 7; in James's fiction, 12–18 *passim*; in *The Floating Opera*, 19; in *The Sketch Book*, 19; importance for Melville, 33–37. *See also* Melville's novels by title

Polonius, 152, 171

Polynesian culture, 38, 44–46

Pottery metaphor, 176–77

Pseudonymity: in "HHM," 22–23; in *M-D*, 85–87

Pyramid: as symbol in *P*, 119–20

Queequeg: as book, 96–97; mentioned, 106

Realism: problem of the novel, 3, 6; in *WJ*, 69; in *C-M*, 155–57

Redburn, 24, 33, 37: Melville on, 58–59; discussed, 59–67; mentioned, 71

Reid, Thomas, 34–35

Religion: as fable, 83, 92, 97; and fiction, 166–67

Revelation, 162, 184, 185, 186, 187, 190

Riddel, Joseph, 33*n*

Riga, Captain, 61

Ringman, John, 168–69

Roberts, Henry: his representation, 154–55; mentioned, 177

Rodgers, Samuel, 35

Romance: and Hawthorne and Melville, 19–20; Melville accused of writing, 46; *Mardi* as realm of, 52

Romanticism: and Hawthorne, 21

Rousset, Jean, 6

Saddle Meadows: as world of appearances, 131–32, 137

"Samuel Enderby," 104

"San Dominick," 200, 201, 202: as representative of feudal world, 204–5; compared with "Bachelor's Delight," 205; compared with "Fidèle," 206; as image of reality, 206; as monastery, 206–7; symbolic stern-piece of, 208; mentioned, 214

"Sane madness," 26, 28, 108. *See also* Madness

Satan (of Milton): as original character, 182

Scarlet Letter, The: Introduction to, 19–20

Schorer, Mark, 4*n*

Science: as fiction, 83, 97

"Serapis": battle with "Bon Homme Richard," 147–48

Shakespeare, William: discussed in "HHM," 25–26, 27–28; compared with Ishmael, 88; as impostor, 171; compared with cosmopolitan, 174

Shenly, 69

Silence: as creative source, 57; and whales, 98; as voice of God, 121; Isabel committed

to, 139; narrator of *P* attracted to, 141; of lamb-like man, 159; of Babo and Cereno, 203–4
Smith, Adam, 62
Social reform: in *WJ*, 68
Soliloquies, 84, 88
Somoa, 49
Souvage, Jacques, 4*n*
Stage: "Pequod" as, 89; world as, 125, 126, 148, 151, 163
Stage directions, 84, 88
Starbuck, 90
Starobinski, Jean, 87*n*
Stavrou, C. N., 90*n*
Steelkilt, 112
Stern, Milton R., 40*n*, 118*n*, 132*n*
Stone: imagery in *P*, 118–25; tables, 122
Stubb, 96
Sub-Sub, 83–84
Subjectivism: as novelistic problem, 5, 10; in *Adam Bede*, 10; in *Middlemarch*, 11, 12; in James's fiction, 12–13; in nineteenth-century American novels, 18–21; in *WJ*, 68

Taji, 33: relation to Yillah, 50–52, 54; as dreamer, 53; quest of, 53; as image of narrator's dream, 55; as image of man's subjection to time, 57; Pierre compared with, 137
Tartan, Lucy: as book, 133
Tattooing: in *T*, 43
Thompson, Lawrence, 68, 78*n*
Thoreau, Henry David, 18, 19
Toby, 39
Tocqueville, Alexis de, 18
Tom Jones: authorial intrusions in, 7–10

Tommo, 33, 38: swollen leg of, 40–43, 44; as Adam, 42
"Town-Ho's Story, The," 110–13
Tragic dramatist: Ishmael as, 90
Tragic hero: Ahab as, 90, 104
Travels in New England and New York, 23–25
Typee, 37–46: mentioned, 49, 71, 128

Usages: as masks, 90; as prisons for the writer, 126, 128; language as, 126–28; domestic relations as, 137; as limitations on actors, 169

Vere, Starry: compared with Cereno, 210; narrator's view of, 210; death of, 211; position undermined, 212
Vishnoo: as whaleman, 92
Vivia, 138

Walden, 19
Wasserman, Earl R., 102*n*
Water imagery: in *P*, 130–31
Watson, E. L. Grant, 216
Wealth of Nations, The, 62–63
Weaving metaphor, 106–8, 109, 111, 118, 125
Whale: as book, 84, 94, 96–98; as image of materiality, 91; as hieroglyph, 91, 96–98; as absence, 98; as mirror, 99
White Jacket, 33, 37: Melville on, 59; discussed, 67–79
White light: source of all colors, 102–3, 158; as light of the original character, 185–86
Whiteness: dangers of confronting, 21; in *WJ*, 74–76, 77–79; in *M-D*, 75, 100–4; asso-

Whiteness (*cont'd*)
　　ciated with lamb-like man,
　　159, 160; color of "Fidèle,"
　　159–60; in "BC," 206
"Whiteness of the Whale, The":
　　as gloss for *WJ*, 74–75
Willamilla, 54
Winsome, Mark, 169, 170, 178

Woodcock, Squire, 144
"World of lies," 24, 26, 57, 85,
　　125, 129, 131, 199

Yamaya, Saburo, 118*n*
Yillah, 49, 50–52 *passim*, 53, 54,
　　58
Yoomy, 53

THE JOHNS HOPKINS PRESS

*Designed and illustrated
by Arlene J. Sheer*

*Composed in Janson text and Weiss display
by The Colonial Press Inc.*

*Printed on 60-lb. Warren's Olde Style
by The Colonial Press Inc.*

*Bound in Columbia Milbank Vellum and Holliston Sailcloth
by The Colonial Press Inc.*